FORUM SHOPPING

OTHER TITLES IN THIS SERIES:

Shipbuilding Contracts
SECOND EDITION
by Malcolm A. Clarke
1992

Time-Barred Actions
SECOND EDITION
Edited by Francesco Berlingieri
1993

Liability for Damage to the Marine Environment
Edited by Colin de la Rue
1993

The York–Antwerp Rules
SECOND EDITION
by N. Geoffrey Hudson
1996

Bill of Lading: A Document of Title to Goods
by Michael Bools
1997

Shipbrokers and the Law
by Andrew Jamieson
1997

Ship Arrest Handbook
Edited by Paul Smith
1997

Douglas & Geen on The Law of Harbours, Coasts and Pilotage
FIFTH EDITION
by Richard Douglas OBE, Peter Lane and Monica Peto
1997

Liability for Oil Pollution and Collisions
by Oya Özçayır
1998

Commencement of Laytime
THIRD EDITION
by Donald Davies
1998

Bills of Lading and Bankers' Documentary Credits
THIRD EDITION
by Paul Todd
1998

FORUM SHOPPING

EDITED BY

CARE L J.H. BARON VAN LYNDEN, LL.M.

Attorney, Rotterdam Bar

LLP

LONDON HONG KONG

1998

LLP Reference Publishing
69–77 Paul Street
London EC2A 4LQ
Great Britain

EAST ASIA
LLP Asia
Sixth Floor, Hollywood Centre
233 Hollywood Road
Hong Kong

First published 1998

British Library Cataloguing in Publication Data
A catalogue record for this book
is available from the
British Library

ISBN 1–85978–193–4

Typeset in 10/12 Plantin
by Mendip Communications Ltd, Frome, Somerset
Printed in Great Britain by
WBC Limited,
Bridgend, Mid-Glamorgan

PREFACE

Trade is an international business. This complicates matters, as different jurisdictions and therefore different laws may be involved. On the other hand however, it creates chances: chances to choose the jurisdictions where one's interests are best protected. This choice of jurisdiction is often referred to as: Forum Shopping.

The phrase "Forum Shopping" sometimes has an unpleasant edge to it. In our opinion it is unjustified. The world is bigger than one country, and chances should be explored when they are there.

Particularly the above applies in shipping. A ship will call on many different countries, cargoes will be loaded and discharged in such countries, and freight will be payable in loading or discharging ports in such countries. Thus, many jurisdictions may qualify for conservatory measures or the instituting of proceedings.

But how to choose? One cannot know each and every system. And more than one kind of question must be answered: is there jurisdiction in a specific country, and if so, what are the advantages of going to such country?

In the context of this book, the first kind of question is being addressed: what are the rules for jurisdiction in the various countries. In this first issue Western Europe and a number of countries bordering the Mediterranean are being dealt with. Contributors in these countries have been asked to answer a questionnaire with a number of questions concerning the possibilities of jurisdiction and conservatory measures in their country.

This book may therefore be helpful in deciding where possible measures or proceedings could be started.

May 1998 CAREL J.H. BARON VAN LYNDEN

CONTENTS

THE QUESTIONNAIRE

1. ***Jurisdiction***

What are the general grounds on which courts will accept jurisdiction? (defendant and/or plaintiff)

(a) Domicile
(b) Has a place of business/residence/office
(c) Assets located within the jurisdiction
(d) Act complained of within the jurisdiction
(e) Contract governed by local law
(f) Conventions
(g) Clause attributing jurisdiction
(h) Other (e.g. instruction)
(i) Counterclaim/third party proceedings

2. ***Maritime claims***

(a) Is there special jurisdiction for maritime claims based on arrest of a vessel in the jurisdiction?
(b) Specific? e.g. place of loading/discharge, collision, salvage
(c) What are the grounds for arrest?
(d) Need the arrested vessel be connected with the claim or can other vessels in the same legal (or beneficial) ownership also be arrested?
(e) What procedural differences apply to special maritime jurisdiction?
(f) What juridictional rules are there as to limitation of liability?

3. ***Service of proceedings***

What rules apply to service of proceedings outside the jurisdiction?

4. *Costs*

What are the costs implications of starting proceedings?

(a) Court fees
(b) Lawyers' fees (standard scale or by agreement or contingency fees)
(c) Recovery of costs from unsuccessful party
(d) Security for costs

5. *Interim arrest*

(a) Are interim arrest/freezing of assets/other provisional measures permitted to provide security for domestic proceedings and/or proceedings in another jurisdiction?
(b) What criteria apply to this?
(c) Is there a limit on jurisdictions whose proceedings are recognised for this purpose?
(d) Is there a requirement for counter-security?
(e) Can applications be made *ex parte*?
(f) How quickly can an order be made?
(g) Will the order bind third parties?
(h) What are the consequences of breach of an order?
(i) Is there a limit to types of asset, e.g. physical asset/account balances?
(j) What if third parties are affected, e.g. airliner?
(k) What other provisional measures may be ordered, e.g. appointment of surveyor or receiver, security?

6. *Recognition of judgments/awards*

(a) What treaties/conventions apply (i) to enable judgments to be enforced abroad and (ii) to enable enforcement of foreign judgments domestically?
(b) What procedure is followed to enforce a foreign judgment (i) governed by a treaty/convention and (ii) not governed by a treaty/convention?
(c) What about foreign arbitration awards?
(d) Will proceeds of a judgment be freely exportable?

7. *Other remarks*

CHAPTER 1

AUSTRIA

Dr Susanne Fruhstorfer and Dr Felix Klement
Weiss - Tessbach Rechtsanwälte - OEG, Rotenturmstraße 13, A–1010 Wien, Austria

1. GENERAL GROUNDS ON WHICH COURTS WILL ACCEPT JURISDICTION

Introduction: international jurisdiction

Until 1 January 1998 it was comparatively difficult to determine if Austrian international jurisdiction could be approved. There were relatively few statutes granting Austrian courts international jurisdiction and these statutes related only to matrimonial, paternity, property matters and the law concerning persons. In the absence of explicit statutes jurisdiction had to be accepted if Austria was bound to give jurisdiction under international law (e.g. under the Lugano Convention) or if the case brought before the court had "sufficient connection to the Austrian territory" (*ausreichende Nahebeziehung zum Inland*). In relation to sufficient domestic connection, the Austrian Supreme Court had developed an entire doctrine (*Indikationentheorie*), which was, however, rather vaguely worded and as a result the court decisions were hard to predict. With an amending law to the Austrian Act on Court Jurisdiction (*Jurisdiktionsnorm* (JN)) which entered into force on 1 January 1998 this situation changed completely.

The Austrian legislature ruled that in each case in which local jurisdiction is applicable by law, Austrian international jurisdiction has to be approved (section 27a JN). Cases in which international law differs from these rules are the only exclusions. In practice that means that jurisdiction is always given if one of the places of jurisdiction mentioned below (items (a) to (i)) exists. In addition, the Supreme Court has to grant jurisdiction (section 28 JN) (even if there is no court of local jurisdiction) if:

(a) Austria is bound to give jurisdiction on the basis of a Convention under international law;
(b) the plaintiff is an Austrian citizen, domiciled in Austria, has his/her usual residence or place of business in Austria and the enforcement of rights abroad is impossible or cannot reasonably be acceptable;
(c) Austrian international jurisdiction, but not the jurisdiction of any specific Austrian court, was stipulated and is evidenced by documents (see below 1(g)).

If International jurisdiction is missing, courts have to dismiss the claim no matter at what stage proceedings are and declare the foregoing proceedings null and void. According to section 42 para. 2 JN even a final and conclusive judgment can be cancelled by the Supreme Court upon application by the highest administrative authorities if it turns out that Austrian courts did not have jurisdiction.

(a) Domicile

The place of general jurisdiction is determined by the domicile of the defendant (section 66 JN). Domicile ("Wohnsitz") is the place where a person settles down with the intention to choose it as his/her permanent residence. The general jurisdiction of a physical person is also established by his/her usual residence, which is determined simply by the fact of a continuing residence at a certain place. If a person has his/her domicile and usual residence in the districts of different courts, the plaintiff is free to choose the court at which an action is filed.

Persons who have no domicile or usual residence in Austria or anywhere else in the world may be sued at the court competent for their current place of residence.

Persons who have no current residence in Austria or of whom such current residence is unknown may be sued before the court competent for their last place of domicile or residence in Austria in connection with any liabilities which arose during their stay in Austria or are to be fulfilled in Austria (section 67 JN).

(b) Place of business/office

The general place of jurisdiction of legal entities (limited liability companies, stock corporations, associations, etc.) or other legal personalities which are not legal entities, such as limited partnerships, is determined by their principal place of business (section 75 JN). In case of doubt, the principal place of business is deemed to be the place of administration of the legal entity/legal personality.

Physical persons and legal entities (legal personalities) which entertain a business establishment at a place other than their principal place of business may also be sued at the court competent for the place of the business establishment if the dispute concerns business activities of the branch office (section 87 JN—elective venue).

(c) Assets located within the jurisdiction

Actions based on a property claim against physical persons or legal entities/ personalities without a general place of jurisdiction in Austria (domicile, permanent residence, principal place of business, compare items 1(a) and 1(b) above) can be brought before the court of the district in which assets of the defendant or the object in dispute are located (section 99 JN).

If the assets in question are claims, the domicile or the usual place of residence of the defendant's debtor is considered the place at which the assets are located.

The value of the assets must not be disproportionately smaller than the amount in dispute. The Supreme Court ruled that assets equalling one third of the amount in dispute may give reason for jurisdiction—assets in the amount of one sixth may not.

It is also to be noted that the jurisdiction of the assets' location does not apply *vis-à-vis* persons domiciled in a Contracting State of the Lugano Convention (see item 1(f) below) as such venue is deemed an "exorbitant" venue.

(d) Forum actus in tort cases

Action concerning damages caused by homicide, injury to persons, deprivation of liberty or damage to physical objects can be brought before the court of the place where the event causing the damage occurred (*forum actus* in tort cases, section 92a JN).

(e) Contract governed by local law

The fact that a contract is subject to Austrian law—whether on the basis of an agreement by the parties on the choice of law or pursuant to the provisions of Austrian Conflict Rules (Internationales Privatrecht)—does not automatically provide for Austrian courts to have jurisdiction. Austrian courts are competent for claims arising out of contracts governed by Austrian law only if also other facts give rise to the applicability of such jurisdiction.

The place of performance of a contractual obligation is basically irrelevant for the question of jurisdiction; only if the parties involved explicitly agree on such place of performance and if documentary evidence can be produced to prove this agreement, may actions relating to the existence or non-existence of a contract, to the fulfilment or rescission of a contract and to compensation claims owing to non-fulfilment be filed with the court competent for the place of performance (section 88 I. JN).

Among persons/entities who conduct a commercial enterprise, the competence of a certain court is also determined by accepting an invoice transmitted together with or even before the respective goods if such invoice states that payment is to be effected at a certain place and that actions may be brought before the competent court of that very place. If such reference or the invoice in general is rejected as not being in compliance with the agreement or if the invoice is returned without comment or the delivery to which the invoice relates is refused as not having been ordered, no "jurisdiction of the place of invoice" is constituted (section 88 II. JN). Such jurisdiction will in any case only apply to claims arising in connection with the delivery of movable goods; it is not applicable for claims in connection with a contract for work done and materials supplied.

(f) Conventions

The Convention on Jurisdiction and Enforcement of Judgments in Civil and Commercial Matters concluded at Lugano on 16 September 1988 (Lugano Convention) entered into force in Austria on 1 September 1996. Apart from this multilateral convention (which will be addressed in more detail below), Austria has ratified the following multilateral conventions relating to the jurisdiction of the contracting parties:

- Convention on the Contract for the International Carriage of Goods by Road (CMR);
- Convention for International Railroad Traffic (COTIF);
- Convention for the Unification of certain rules relating to International Carriage by Air (WA);

In addition, Austria has concluded bilateral treaties on acknowledgment and enforcement, which partly also relate to international jurisdiction, with the following states: Belgium, Germany, Finland, France, United Kingdom of Great Britain and Northern Ireland, Israel, Italy, Liechtenstein, Luxembourg, Netherlands, Norway, Sweden, Switzerland, Spain, Tunisia, Turkey.

In the relationship with Contracting States of the Lugano Convention, these treaties are replaced by the Lugano Convention in the areas covered by it (civil and commercial matters).

Lugano Convention

The provisions on jurisdiction stipulated by the Lugano Convention prevail over the respective Austrian provisions if the defendant has his/her domicile within the territory of a Contracting State.

As already mentioned in item 1(c) above, the "jurisdiction of the place where the assets are located" (section 99 JN) does not apply *vis-à-vis* persons who are domiciled within the territory of a Contracting State of the Lugano Convention.

In the following, only the main differences between the provisions on jurisdiction as stipulated by the Lugano Convention on the one hand and by Austrian law on the other will be discussed.

Pursuant to Article 5(1) of the Lugano Convention, persons having their domicile within the territory of a Contracting State may be sued in Austria if the place of performance of a contract is located in Austria, irrespective of the place of performance being explicitly agreed in the contract or not or determined by the rules of the law applicable to the contract. Pursuant to section 88 JN (cf.

item 1(e)) an action may be filed with the competent court of the place of performance only if the parties to the respective contract have agreed on such place of performance in writing and if documentary evidence can be produced. The place of performance determined merely by the law applicable to the contract does not constitute jurisdiction.

Whereas section 92a JN stipulates that in matters relating to tort only such courts have jurisdiction which are competent for the place where the act causing the damage was committed, Article 5(3) of the Lugano Convention provides that an action may also be brought before the court competent for the place where the actual damage occurred.

The Austrian legal provisions on jurisdiction are extended by the provisions of the Lugano Convention relating to insurance and consumer contracts (sections 3 and 4), which stipulate that insurers or entrepreneurs may be sued by policy-holders and consumers respectively also before the court competent for the domicile of the latter. Sections 3 and 4 of the Lugano Convention thereby introduced the almost unknown concept of the "jurisdiction of the plaintiff's domicile" into Austrian law.

The exclusive jurisdictions contained in Article 16 of the Lugano Convention more or less correspond to those stipulated in the JN (cf. item 1(h)).

The Lugano Convention allows the prorogation of jurisdiction to settle any disputes which have arisen or may arise in connection with a particular legal relationship, provided one of the parties is domiciled in a Contracting State. The agreement has to be either in writing or evidenced in writing, or in a form which is in accordance with the established practices of the parties or any other form according with a usage of trade (Article 17). According to section 104 JN, however, a prorogation always has to be in writing or evidenced in writing (cf. below item 1(g)).

(g) Clause attributing jurisdiction

Parties can agree that one or more courts of first instance competent for certain places as indicated in such agreement are to have jurisdiction to settle any dispute which has arisen or which may arise in connection with a particular legal relationship. Such agreement must be evidenced by document (section 104 JN). As far as complaints against consumers (based on a consumer contract) are concerned, only a prorogation in favour of the court of the place of domicile, permanent residence or employment of the consumer is valid (section 14 of the Austrian Consumer Protection Act). In addition, any agreement which excludes any legally applicable jurisdiction for complaints filed by the consumer against the entrepreneur is not legally valid *vis-à-vis* the consumer.

International jurisdiction may also arise if the defendant gives a statement before an Austrian court without claiming lack of competence of such court; this does, however, only apply if the defendant was represented by an attorney at law or a notary or if the judge cautioned the defendant about the statement giving rise to jurisdiction. This rule does not apply to mandatory venues, to disputes relating to immovable property (see item (h)), and to the exclusive jurisdictions set out in Article 16 of the Lugano Convention (see item (f) above).

(h) Other exclusive and elective venues

For certain types of disputes, the provisions of the JN stipulate exclusive venues and mandatory venues. A venue is "mandatory" if the jurisdiction of a certain court as prescribed by law cannot be altered even by agreement of the parties.

The JN stipulates *mandatory venues* for instance for the following matters:

- certain disputes in connection with shareholders' relationships (for instance to contest resolutions of the general meeting); the court competent for the registered seat of the company will have jurisdiction (section 83b JN);
- disputes arising out of partial obligations ("Teilschuldverhältnisse"), provided claims have to be enforced against a common administrator (section 83a JN);
- claims under the Atomhaftpflichtgesetz (Act on Liability for Nuclear Damages) (section 42 Atomhaftpflichtgesetz);
- actions requesting the determination of claims in bankruptcy proceedings contested by the receiver (section 111 Bankruptcy Code).

We speak of an exclusive venue in cases in which the general jurisdiction (pursuant to domicile, usual residence, principal place of business, cf. 1(a) and 1(b) above) or elective venues (cf. below) are excluded, but agreements by the parties on other competent courts are admissible.

Exclusive venues are stipulated for the following matters:

- disputes among spouses (sections 76, 76a JN);
- paternity suits (sections 76b, 76c JN);
- probate proceedings (section 77 JN);
- suits by and against judges (section 79 JN);
- disputes relating to immovable property (sections 81 to 83 JN): actions claiming the existence or non-existence of a right *in rem* in immovable property have to be brought before the court competent for the district where the property is located; such court is also competent for disputes relating to leases over such property;
- disputes on intellectual property rights and copyright; as a matter of principle the competent court for the registered seat of the defendant has jurisdiction;
- infringements of patent rights; the Vienna Commercial Court has exclusive jurisdiction for all complaints and injunctions (section 162 Patent Act).

Elective venues

The provisions of the JN stipulate 19 elective venues; other Austrian laws also set forth certain elective venues. The most important elective venues are:

- venue of the place of performance (see above item 1(e));
- venue of the "place of invoice" (see above item 1(e));
- *forum actus* in tort cases (see above item 1(d));
- venue of the place where the assets are located (see above item 1(c));
- venue of the place of business (see above item 1(b));
- venue of the "place of payment" of a bill of exchange or a cheque (section 89 JN); persons liable under a bill of exchange or a cheque may be sued before the court competent for the place of payment by the owner of the bill of exchange or cheque;
- venue of the counterclaim, of the main court proceedings and of the joinder of parties (see item 1(i) below).

Disputes between employers and employees are subject to special regulations; irrespective of whether the employer or the employee files the action, the plaintiff may choose at its discretion that such court will have jurisdiction which is competent for the district where:

- the employee has his/her domicile or his/her usual residence during the time the employment relationship existed or at the time the employment was terminated;
- the employer's company has its registered seat;
- the employee had to render his/her services; or
- the consideration had to be paid.

(i) Counterclaim/third-party proceedings

Section 96 JN stipulates that a counterclaim may be filed with the court where the respective complaint was filed if the claim enforced by the counterclaim is connected to the claim enforced by the complaint or would be suitable for a set-off, or if the counterclaim requests the determination of a legal relationship or right disputed in the course of court proceedings.

Several persons which, in view of the dispute, are in legal community or are entitled or obliged jointly or on the same grounds, may be sued jointly (joinder of parties) before every Austrian court having general jurisdiction for one of the parties or, if there are principal defendants and co-defendants, for one of the principal defendants (section 93 JN). This rule does not apply if the respective dispute is subject to an exclusive joint venue (for instance in lease matters) or if the venue agreed by the parties is not applicable (for instance in case of consumers).

Complaints for the enforcement of a claim to any asset or right subject to a dispute between other persons (*Hauptintervention*) may be filed with the same court until the first dispute is finally decided (section 94 JN).

2. MARITIME CLAIMS

There is no special jurisdiction for maritime claims based on an arrest of a vessel in Austria. Vessels of domestic navigation according to the Protocol no. 2 concerning the arrest and seizure of vessels of domestic navigation may only be arrested or seized if the vessel is on Austrian territory. As the sovereign territory of Austria is landlocked, arrests of ocean-going vessels are not possible. Rules governing maritime claims are very rare and of no practical relevance.

The only two statutes worth considering are section 90 JN and section 6 of the Austrian Navigation Act.

According to section 90 JN, proceedings concerning the hire of an ocean-going vessel, maritime contracts on affreightments or passenger carriage may be brought before the court competent

(i) for the place where the defendant is resident;
(ii) for the place where the goods are to be delivered to;
(iii) for the final destination of the passenger's journey; or
(iv) for the place where the journey is interrupted.

According to section 6 of the Austrian Navigation Act 1981 claims against owners or skippers of Austrian vessels concerning the acquisition or the operation of a vessel may be brought before an Austrian court even if the defendant is not resident in Austria.

3. SERVICE OF PROCEEDINGS

Two scenarios are to be considered, namely service of proceedings within and service of proceedings outside Austrian territory.

3.1 Service of proceedings outside Austrian territory

According to section 11 of the Zustellgesetz (Bundesgesetz vom 1. April 1982 über die Zustellung behördlicher Schriftstücke) (Act on Service of Proceedings), existing treaties between states have to be applied. The most important treaty to consider is the convention relating to civil procedure concluded in The Hague in 1954. According to this treaty a request for service shall be addressed by the Austrian consul to the competent court of the country where the documents are to be served. The fact that such a request for service does not have to be addressed to the competent ambassador makes the service of writs easier.

In addition to the multilateral treaty of The Hague, Austria has concluded bilateral treaties concerning the service of writs with Belgium, Denmark, Germany, France, Great Britain, Italy, Luxembourg, Netherlands, Switzerland, Turkey, Spain, Finland, Norway, Sweden and Israel. These bilateral treaties further facilitate the service of writs by Austrian courts. In particular, the Austrian court may ask the courts of the Contracting States to serve the proceedings themselves. If there are no such treaties in force, an Austrian civil court may serve a writ by mail accompanied by an internationally acknowledged confirmation of receipt (return slip). This might be the case if writs are to be served, for instance, in Argentina, Australia, Bahamas, Barbados, Belgium, Bolivia, Botswana, Brazil, Canada, Chile, Colombia, Costa Rica, Cuba, Cyprus, Dominican Republic, Ecuador, Egypt, El Salvador, Fiji, Finland, France, Gambia, Ghana, Grenada, Guatemala, Guyana, Haiti, the Holy See, Honduras, Iceland, India, Israel, Italy, Jamaica, Japan, Jordan, Kampuchea, Kenya, Laos, Lebanon, Lesotho, Libya, Luxembourg, Malawai, Malaysia, Malta, Mexico, Morocco, Nauru, New Zealand, Netherlands, Nicaragua, Nigeria, Norway, Pakistan, Panama, Paraguay, Peru, Portugal, Saint Christopher–Nevis–Anguilla, St Lucia, Saint Vincent, Sierra Leone, Singapore, Sri Lanka, Suriname, Swaziland, Sweden, Switzerland, Tanzania, Thailand, Tonga, Trinidad and Tobago, Uganda, Uruguay, UK, USA, Venezuela, West Samoa, Zambia.

If service cannot be effected within a reasonable period of time (which according to the Austrian jurisdiction is approximately eight months) the prosecuting party may, according to section 121 of the Austrian Code of Civil Procedure, apply for service by public announcement or substituted service upon a person appointed by the court.

3.2 Service of proceedings within Austria by foreign courts

If there is a treaty between Austria and the state requiring service, according to section 12 of the Austrian Zustellgesetz the rules of the treaty, i.e. the above-mentioned rules and regulations, are applicable. In most cases the foreign consul or the court of the state from which the proceedings emanate are required to request service by the Austrian court. The Austrian courts will then effect service.

If there is no international treaty in force courts may effect service of foreign writs according to the rules of the Zustellgesetz (i.e. mainly by registered mail). A request for a special service not foreseen in the law on services may only be granted if such a service does not contravene Austrian *ordre publique*.

According to section 12 para. 2 of the Zustellgesetz, the delivery of a foreign writ in a foreign language may be refused if there is no certified German translation of the writ enclosed.

4. COSTS

(a) Court fees

Court fees will be incurred upon the issue of proceedings of each instance. The fees arise upon the petition being submitted to the court and have to be paid at the commencement of the proceedings. In proportion of the overall costs the court fees are relatively small and not of major economic concern. According to the Court Fee Act 1984 as amended in 1997, for instance, an amount in dispute of between ATS 500,000 and ATS 1,000,000 triggers a fee of ATS 13,520 for the proceedings of the first instance; of ATS 19,880 for the proceedings of the second instance; and of ATS 26,510 for the proceedings of the third instance. If the amount in dispute is between ATS 1,000,000 and ATS 2,000,000, the court fees for the first instance amount to ATS 27,040; for the second instance to ATS 39,770; and for the third instance (Supreme Court) to ATS 53,030.

(b) Lawyers' fees

If no other fees are agreed between the client and the attorney, the attorney's fee has to be calculated on the basis of the Austrian Act on Attorney's Tariffs. The calculation of fees depends upon the amount in dispute and the type of services rendered. In addition to the basic tariffs set forth in the Act, the so-called "Einheitssatz" may be added, i.e. an additional fee of 60% and 50% respectively (if the amount in dispute exceeds ATS 100,000) by which additional services (such as letters to the client, telephone calls, etc.) are deemed to be reimbursed.

Pacta de quota litis, contingency fees and reductions not justified by the merits are basically not admissible.

(c) Recovery of costs from unsuccessful party

The unsuccessful party has to bear the costs arising as a result of the proceedings. In the event of a partial victory, the parties have to pay their proportional share of the entire cost incurred. The unsuccessful or partly unsuccessful party, however, only has to bear the fees of the other party's lawyer calculated in accordance with the Austrian Attorney's Tariffs scheme (see above 4(b)) and is not bound by other agreements between his opponent and its lawyer.

(d) Security for costs

According to section 57 of the Austrian Code on Civil Procedure, foreign plaintiffs have to provide security for costs, if the defendant applies for it. There are certain exceptions for this regulation, such as if the plaintiff has his habitual residence in Austria or if a judgment binding the plaintiff to pay the costs of the proceedings would be enforceable in the state of the habitual residence of the plaintiff (like under the Lugano Convention or other multi- or bilateral treaties, see item 6 below). There is no duty to provide security for costs if the plaintiff has sufficient immovable property in Austria.

5. INTERIM ARREST

(a) General

Basically, Austrian courts may upon application issue provisional injunctions either prior to the initiation of court proceedings or in the course of the proceedings in order to secure the rights of one of the parties involved. Injunctions mainly serve to secure the creditor's rights in respect of any future enforcement proceedings and are issued to maintain the status quo in order to prevent the debtor from doing any act which might render the future satisfaction of the creditor's claims more difficult or impossible.

The court competent for provisional injunctions to be issued prior to the initiation of court proceedings is the district court having general jurisdiction for the defendant (cf. items 1(a), 1(b) above) or, if no such general jurisdiction applies, the district court competent for the place where the respective asset which is to be subjected to the injunction is located or where the third-party debtor has its domicile, residence or registered seat.

A provisional injunction may only be issued if it can be executed in Austria. According to the prevailing jurisdiction of the Supreme Court Austrian courts have jurisdiction for the issuance of an injunction to be executed abroad only if an international treaty provides for the acknowledgment and execution of the injunction abroad.

(b) Which criteria apply to this?

The issuance of an injunction to secure a monetary claim is subject *evidence* being produced on the *claim* of the applicant and the *actual danger* of such claim becoming uncollectable; such actual danger is also deemed to exist if the judgment would have to be enforced in states which are not parties to the Lugano Convention or the Brussels Convention.

If an injunction is issued prior to the initiation of court proceedings, the court is obliged to stipulate an adequate delay during which the complaint has to be filed; if the delay expires without a complaint having been filed, the injunction is to be revoked.

(c) Limit on jurisdiction whose proceedings are recognised

An injunction to secure claims subject to court proceedings already pending or threatened abroad may be issued in Austria only if court judgments issued by such foreign jurisdiction are acknowledged and enforceable in Austria, i.e. if a treaty on the acknowledgment and enforcement of court judgments exists between Austria and such other state or if such other state is a Contracting State of the Lugano Convention (cf. item 6(a) below).

(d) Requirement for counter-security

The court may at its discretion request that the applicant for an injunction deposits adequate security if the jeopardised claim cannot be sufficiently evidenced and if any damage possibly caused to the other party can be reimbursed by a monetary consideration, of if the court—on the basis of the respective circumstances—considers the provision of such security to be necessary despite sufficient evidence of the jeopardised claim having been produced.

(e) Can applications be made ex parte?

In particularly urgent cases, the court may issue an injunction *ex parte*. In such case the party subjected to the injunction may raise objections within 14 days from receipt of the injunction; such objections do not, however, suspend the enforcement of the injunction already issued.

(f) How quickly can an order be made?

A provisional injunction is issued by way of summary proceedings. It is difficult to make a generally applicable assessment as to how much time will elapse between the application being filed and the injunction being issued as this will depend on the specific circumstances of each case; it is, however, possible to obtain a provisional injunction within two or three days.

(g) Will the order bind third parties?

A provisional injunction might affect a third party insofar as an injunction prohibiting the sale or pledge of movable physical property renders the acquisition of such property or the acquisition of a contractual pledge by a third party null and void if such third party was aware or should have been aware of the prohibition. Third parties, who are debtors of the opponent party, can also be affected, as the order may prohibit them from effecting payment to the opponent party (so-called "Drittverbot", cf. item 5(i) below). There are a number of remedies available to third parties whose rights are affected by the enforcement of a provisional injunction.

(h) What are the consequences of breach of an order?

The impediment of enforcement proceedings and interim injunction in connection with (future) enforcement proceedings may be prosecuted under criminal law.

(i) Limit to types of assets

If monetary claims are to be secured, the court may issue only the following orders:

- — to keep and administrate movable physical property of the opponent party, including the order to deposit money;
- — to prohibit the sale or pledge of movable physical property;
- — to prohibit a debtor of the opponent party to effect payments to such opponent party (so-called "Drittverbot").

This means that monetary claims may be secured exclusively by movable property and claims of the opponent party; not, however, by immovable property. The situation is different in the case of non-monetary claims to performance, sufferance or omission.

(j) Other provisional measures

The so-called "Exekution zur Sicherstellung" is not an injunction within the strict meaning of the word but is an execution granted within a judgment by an Austrian court which is not final and conclusive in securing outstanding monies.

Such "Exekution zur Sicherstellung" plays a role in practice if a judgment by default has been issued and the debtor filed an objection.

The court may seize movable property or the right to a claim against a third party. A mortgage might be registered with the land register or real estate might be sequestered.

6. RECOGNITION OF JUDGMENTS/AWARDS

(a) Treaties/conventions applying (i) to enable judgments to be enforced abroad and (ii) to enable enforcement of foreign judgments domestically

Foreign judgments are only recognised and enforced in Austria, if the judgment would be enforceable in the state from which it originates and if reciprocity is secured by a bilateral or multilateral treaty between the states.

As mentioned above under item 1(f), Austria is a Contracting State of the Lugano Convention. This treaty renders the enforcement of judgments of the

Austrian courts possible in all Contracting States and—likewise—the judgments of courts of Contracting States are enforceable in Austria. The judgment of Contracting States are recognised in all Contracting States *ipso iure*.

In addition Austria has entered into bilateral recognition and enforcement treaties with Belgium, Finland, France, Germany, Great Britain and Northern Ireland, Israel, Italy, Liechtenstein, Luxembourg, Netherlands, Norway, Spain, Sweden, Switzerland, Tunisia and Turkey. In the relationship with Contracting States of the Lugano Convention those treaties are displaced by the Lugano Convention in the areas covered by it (civil and commercial matters).

(b) Procedure to be followed to enforce a foreign judgment

As mentioned above, only foreign judgments governed by a treaty or convention are enforceable in Austria. A judgment of a Contracting State of the Lugano Convention can be enforced in Austria if the creditor applies for a so-called "Vollstreckbarkeitserklärung". A Vollstreckbarkeitserklärung is a ruling of the court confirming that the judgment in question is enforceable. In order to obtain such ruling the creditor has to enclose several documents listed in Articles 46 and 47 of the Convention. Normally, a copy of the judgment and a document establishing that the judgment is enforceable under the law of the state of origin and has been effectively served will be sufficient.

The bilateral treaties mentioned above under 6(a) basically follow the same system. As under the Lugano Convention, there is no specific procedure for the recognition of the judgment. The procedure of the enforcement is similar to the above-described procedure for judgments falling under the terms of the Lugano Convention.

Decisions which violate Austria's *ordre publique* or arise from a procedure which violates the defendant's right of due process of law (full hearing) cannot be enforced in Austria. This is also true if legal proceedings concerning the same matters have been commenced in Austria prior to the proceedings being initiated in the state where the judgment in question originates. As a rule a foreign judgment cannot be enforced in Austria if the state where the judgment comes from did not have jurisdiction under the applicable bilateral treaty.

(c) Foreign arbitration awards

Austria is a Contracting State of the Convention on the Recognition and Enforcement of Foreign Arbitral Awards concluded in New York in 1958. According to the Convention, to which more than 100 states are members, Austria is required to recognise and enforce practically any other arbitral awards. In addition Austria entered into the Convention on international commercial arbitration. Combined these conventions allow a refusal of a recognition or an enforcement of arbitral award in very limited circumstances. The procedure to enforce foreign arbitral awards is similar to that for the enforcement of decisions of state courts. The creditor has to apply for a "Vollstreckbarkeitserklärung".

(d) Proceeds of a judgment

Proceeds of a judgment are exportable like any other assets—no special rules apply.

CHAPTER 2

BELGIUM

Paul Verguts, Marc van Looveren, Olivier Gossieaux
Dieryck, van Looveren & Co, Korte Lozanastraat 20-26, B-2018 Antwerpen, Belgium

1. GENERAL RULES OF JURISDICTION

The rules of jurisdiction are laid down in multiple articles. They can be found in the Belgian Code of Civil Procedure, BCCP, conventions or treaties, construed by case law and doctrine. The Belgian courts generally have or will have some jurisdiction in the following cases.

(a)(i) Defendant based in Belgium

Under Belgian law, one of the four decisive elements conferring territorial jurisdiction is the domicile of the defendant. Accordingly, if a plaintiff brings suit in Belgium against a defendant based in Belgium, the courts will generally assume jurisdiction.

This *actor sequitur forum rei* rule, laid down in Article 624, 1 BCCP, is one of the basic principles on jurisdiction. The same idea can be found in a number of international conventions, e.g. The 1968 Brussels Convention on Jurisdiction and Judgments.

Article 36 BCCP defines "domicile" as the place where the person is entered into the civil register and has his main residence. Under Belgian law all persons residing in Belgium have to be entered into the register—however, this does not necessarily imply that they actually can be found at the entered address. The Code of Civil Procedure makes a distinction between domicile and place of residence. The latter consists in "every establishment, such as the place where a person has an office or conducts business".

The same distinction applies to legal persons. A legal person can be summoned in the place where, according to the memorandum of association, its seat is located. But this place does not always coincide with its actual seat or principal place of business. The latter is the place where the legal person has its central administration.

The rule contained in Article 624, 1 BCCP applies as soon as one of the defending parties has been summoned before the judge of his domicile. In other words, it is sufficient that one of the defending parties has his domicile or his seat in Belgium to declare the Belgian judge "*ratione loci*" competent. However, the rule cannot be applied when parties agree to a valid jurisdiction clause, insofar permitted by applicable national or international legislation.

(a)(ii) Plaintiff based in Belgium

Article 638 BCCP stipulates that if jurisdiction of the Belgian Courts cannot be established on the basis of any of the specific grounds of Article 635 and 636 BCCP, a plaintiff based in Belgium can bring the case before the court of his domicile or his residence. This rule, however, is subject to many limitations. First, this rule does not apply where a convention stipulates otherwise. Secondly, it will not apply when parties have agreed on a different jurisdiction (without prejudice to certain rules of mandatory application). Finally, in the absence of convention or agreement, the application of Article 638 will be subject to the restrictions contained in Article 636 of the BCCP: a foreigner sued under Article 638 before a Belgian court by a plaintiff based in Belgium will be allowed to decline the jurisdiction of the Belgian courts if he can establish that before the courts of his country of origin the Belgian defendant would be allowed the same (principle of reciprocity).

(b) Place of business/residence

The Code of Civil Procedure makes a distinction between domicile and place of residence. The latter consists in "every other establishment, such as the place where a person has an office or conducts business".

The same distinction applies to legal persons. A legal person can be summoned in the place where, according to the memorandum of association, its seat is located. But this place does not always coincide with its actual seat or principal place of business. The latter is the place where the legal person has its central administration.

(c) Assets located within the jurisdiction

If the 1968 Brussels Convention applies, the courts of the place where the immovables are situated will have jurisdiction (Art. 16(1)).

(d) Act complained of within the jurisdiction

If the 1968 Brussels Convention applies, the courts of the place where the tortious act complained of has taken place, will have jurisdiction (Art. 5(3)). If the Convention does not apply, Article 635, 3 BCCP, ruling the same, can be applied.

(e) Contract governed by local law

A distinction has to be made between the applicable law and the competent court. The fact that Belgian law would be applicable to a contract, does not necessarily imply that the Belgian courts will have jurisdiction. One will have to consult the rules provided in the BCCP, as well as the treaties and conventions.

(f) Conventions

In the hierarchy of sources of law, international conventions prevail. Consequently, when a convention to which Belgium is a contracting party confers jurisdiction on the Belgian courts, they will assume jurisdiction, even when, according to Belgian law, they would not have jurisdiction.

The most important convention dealing with jurisdiction is the 1968 Brussels Convention. In Article 2(1) of the Convention, the adage "*actor sequitur forum rei*" has been provided: notwithstanding the stipulations of the Convention, those having their domicile on the territory of a Contracting State, regardless of their nationality, will be called before the courts of that state.

To decide whether a party has his domicile on the territory of a Contracting State, the judge applies his internal legislation (Art. 52(1) of the Convention).

When the defendant has his domicile on the territory of a Contracting State, he can only be sued before the judge of another Contracting State on the basis of the special rules on jurisdiction, as mentioned in sections 2 and 6 of Title II (Jurisdiction)—see Article 3(1) of the Convention.

Article 57 of the Convention, however, stipulates that the rules of the Convention will not apply if the jurisdiction issue has been dealt with in other specific conventions (e.g. the 1952 Arrest Convention, the 1952 Collision Convention).

(g) Clause attributing jurisdiction

Without prejudice to rules of mandatory application, parties are free to agree upon a specific jurisdiction, and the Belgian courts will respect such agreements.

As far as the jurisdiction clause is concerned, one has to distinguish material jurisdiction from territorial jurisdiction. Since "material" jurisdiction rules are of public order, parties cannot make agreements to that extent and, for example, make an agreement to bring a case which should be brought before the Labour Court, before the Commercial Court. Territorial jurisdiction rules, however, are not of mandatory application.

Principally, a jurisdiction agreement is a contract, so that the general principles of contract law will have to be applied. The question of acceptance will often give rise to discussion. An agreement on jurisdiction being a consensual agreement, a written document is not required—although such would of course establish evidence and avoid discussion.

Very often, merchants will enter a jurisdiction clause into the contract and it can often be found in standard conditions printed on order notes, delivery notes and invoices.

Between merchants, an accepted invoice is considered proof of the agreement. Consequently, when a merchant wishes to contest the opposability of the general conditions, more specifically the jurisdiction clause, he will have to protest the invoice within a short period of time.

It is needless to say that in international trade also a jurisdiction clause is generally accepted. Indeed, in the (amended) Article 17 of the 1968 Brussels Convention it is explicitly stipulated that forum clauses have to be made either by written agreement, or by a written confirmation of an oral agreement, or "in international trade or commerce, in a form which accords with the practices in that trade or commerce of which the parties are or ought to have been aware".

However, the jurisdiction clause has no absolute scope of application. Article 634 BCCP stipulates that the rules concerning counterclaims and claims for third party intervention, and rules applicable to *lis pendens*, commencement of actions and related actions are applicable to territorial jurisdiction. This stipulation, however, is not of public order, so that case law and doctrine can be found where it is said that one can depart from those principles by agreement. It is, however, generally accepted that in the case of a claim in third party intervention, a jurisdiction agreement will have no binding force. The same goes for related actions.

(h) Other (e.g. instruction)

Insofar as no convention or agreement stipulates otherwise, one is allowed under Belgian law to transfer the title to sue. The result would be that someone else could start the proceedings in his own name. Since the court of the plaintiff, in some limited situations, may assume jurisdiction, such a transfer of title to sue can work to create jurisdiction.

(i) Counterclaim/third-party proceedings

In Articles 563–566 BCCP, a number of rules have been elaborated regarding counterclaims and claims for third party intervention. Those rules are applicable to the territorial jurisdiction (Art. 634 BCCP). The latter article is, however, not concerned with international jurisdiction of the Belgian courts in relation to foreigners, governed by Articles 635–638 BCCP. Article 635, 6° stipulates that the judge also has jurisdiction in respect of foreigners, when the matter is connected to a case already pending before the Belgian court. The same has been provided in Articles 21 and 22 of the 1968 Convention.

Moreover, the Belgian judge will have jurisdiction over claims for third party intervention, when the main proceedings are pending before a Belgian court (Art. 635, 9° BCCP). When the leading claim has been declared inadmissible, the judge will remain competent to deal with the counterclaim.

2. MARITIME CLAIMS

(a) Is there special jurisdiction for maritime claims based on arrest of a vessel in the jurisdiction?

The provision provided for in Article 633 BCCP, i.e. that claims relating to interim arrest (*saisie conservatoire*) and enforcement can exclusively be brought before the place of the arrest, unless provided otherwise, is of public order.

In a number of situations an interim arrest can create jurisdiction and this will for instance be the case for the interim arrest of seagoing vessels (see the 1952 Arrest Convention).

Under Article 1467, 1 BCCP, the judge can allow arrest of seagoing vessels located in the district, if the conditions as provided for in article 1468 BCCP are fulfilled (the conditions are literally taken from the 1952 Arrest Convention—see below).

(b) Specific? e.g. place of loading/discharge, collision, salvage

(i) Place of loading/discharge

For many years now, the court of the place of loading or discharging of the cargo as mentioned in the bill of lading is considered, without exception, as the competent forum.

One hereby applies the idea that a transport contract is performed not only in the place of discharge, but already commences at the place of loading. Consequently the Belgian courts will also have jurisdiction when the goods have been discharged in a foreign port, but loaded in a Belgian port. One exception could be that the bill of lading does not mention a Belgian loading or discharging port, but that the goods have been loaded or discharged in Belgium only due to an act of God.

Finally, the rule that the courts of the place of loading or discharging have jurisdiction, is only true insofar as it concerns the relation between the third holder of the bill of lading and the carrier. When the shipper is the claiming party or when the bill of lading has not been negotiated, then the forum clause will have to be examined.

(ii) Collision

Belgium enacted the International Convention on certain rules concerning civil jurisdiction in matters of Collision (Brussels 1952) on 24 March 1961, so that the rules on jurisdiction provided for in this Convention can be found in Article 637 BCCP.

A claim for collision between seagoing vessels or between a seagoing vessel and a river-vessel can exclusively be brought before the following courts:

— Before the court of the normal residence of the defendant or one of the seats of the company;
— Before the court of the place where the vessel of the defendant, or another vessel belonging to the same defendant, was arrested, provided that this arrest was legitimate, or before the court of the place where the arrest could have been made but instead the defendant provided security;
— Before the court of the place of the collision, when the collision occurred in ports and roads that are in inland waterways.

(iii) Salvage

The last stipulation of Article 635 BCCP is that dealing with salvage in high seas or in foreign waters. When the vessel, against which claims are brought at the time of the service of the writ, is located in Belgian waterways, the Belgian judge will also have jurisdiction in respect of foreigners (Art. 635, 11, BCCP).

(c) What are the grounds for arrest?

The arrest of a seagoing vessel can only be allowed to guarantee one of the maritime claims enumerated in Article 1468 BCCP, and the underlying cause should be one of the cases provided for in this article. The 17 possible causes have been taken from Article 1, a–q of the 1952 Arrest Convention. For instance, a plaintiff will have a maritime claim in the case of damage caused by a vessel (e.g. by collision); salvage; charterparties; contracts of carriage of goods by a vessel, evidenced by charterparty or bill of lading; delivery of goods or material to a vessel for the management or the maintenance of it, etc.

(d) Need the arrested vessel be connected with the claim or can other vessels in the same legal (or beneficial) ownership also be arrested?

Either the vessel to which the claim is related can be arrested (e.g. vessel X will be arrested in order to obtain security for the wages of the Master of vessel X), or any other vessel in the ownership of the debtor of the maritime claim can be arrested (e.g. arrest of a vessel X or Y belonging to the debtor).

In *The Omala* (1976) and *The Heinrich J* (1993) judgments, the Supreme Court ruled that the ship in connection with which the claim arose can be arrested even if the owner of that vessel is not personally liable for that claim. Consequently, the arrest of that ship can be allowed for charterers' debts.

(e) What procedural differences apply to special maritime jurisdiction?

Maritime claims in general will be governed by the rules laid down in the BCCP.

With respect to arrest of a seagoing vessel, the procedure is slightly different. As set out above the plaintiff will have to dispose of a maritime claim as provided for in Article 1468 BCCP. Furthermore, the urgency will be presumed (which will not be the case under the normal rules of arrest) and the maritime claim as such will not have to be evidenced. According to established case law and doctrine, an allegation is sufficient. Finally, arrest is rather cheap and very quick: a unilateral request will be presented and the magistrate who has jurisdiction to grant leave to arrest has to be accessible 24 hours a day.

(f) What rules are there as to limitation of liability?

As far as limitation of liability of the shipowner is concerned, the Belgium Sea Act contains one article (Art. 47), incorporating the 1976 LLMC Convention. Save for Article 2, 6 1, litt. d and e, the said Convention will have full application. Proceedings as to the establishment and distribution of the fund are laid down in Article 48 and following of the Sea Act.

3. SERVICE OF PROCEEDINGS OUTSIDE THE JURISDICTION

The method of service outside the jurisdiction will depend on the plaintiff's knowledge of the prospective defendant's domicile or residence. A first distinction has thus to be made between cases where the domicile or residence of the defendant has been identified and cases where they are unknown or unidentified.

Where the defendant has an identified or known domicile abroad, the service of the writ outside the jurisdiction must be made by a bailiff through registered mail. Service will then be deemed to have been effected by the remittance of the envelope to the post office in Belgium against the receipt (Art. 40 BCCP). If the defendant is not domiciled in one of the neighbouring states, the writ must be sent by air mail. If however the prospective defendant is domiciled in a state which is party to an international convention regulating service of the writ, the rules of the particular convention or treaty must apply. It is worthwhile mentioning the existence of the different Hague Service Conventions.[1] Apart from these general conventions Belgium has entered into various agreements or bilateral treaties regulating the service of judicial documents in that particular country.[2]

1. The Treaty of The Hague of 1 March 1954, ratified by Belgium through the Act of 28 March 1954 and the Treaty of The Hague of 15 November 1965 concerning the service and the notification of judicial documents in civil and commercial matters, ratified by Belgium through the Act of 24 January 1970.

2. E.g. the agreement signed in Brussels on 25 April 1959 between the Belgian government and the government of the Federal Republic of Germany, the Convention of 1 March 1956 between Belgium and France concerning mutual legal aid in civil and commercial matters, the Agreement of 30 December 1937 between Belgium and The Netherlands, the agreements between Belgium and Luxembourg of 11 and 19 March 1974.

If the defendant's domicile or residence is unknown to the plaintiff, service can be effected through the Public Prosecutor's office. The bailiff will then hand over the original of the writ to the "Procureur du Roi". It is then his responsibility to take the necessary steps to bring the writ to the attention of the prospective defendant. Such method of service is considered the ultimate remedy and can only be accepted if the plaintiff has exercised all efforts to determine the domicile or residence of the defendant.

4. COSTS OF PROCEEDINGS

Cost implication of proceedings

Apart from lawyer's fees, the costs directly relating to the proceedings are the costs of service of writ amounting to 10.000 BEF in usual circumstances (costs vary according to place and time of service) and the court fees (which are generally very low).

(a) Court fees

See above.

(b) Lawyers' fees

A lawyer is in principle free to determine his fees or negotiate his fees with his clients. In general the intervention of a lawyer will be charged on a time sheet basis for advice and small litigation. In larger litigation cases, the lawyer can calculate his fees on the basis of the amounts claimed.

(c) Recovery of costs from the unsuccessful party

A party's costs (*frais et dépens*) will be itemised in his pleadings. Recoverable costs will include various court fees, the bailiff's fees, judicial expert's fees, witness expenses and certain expenses incurred by the successful party. They do not include the fees of the successful party's counsel for the preparation and conduct of the case, other than a nominal amount fixed by scale. These so-called procedural indemnities (*indemnités de procédure*) are normally much lower than the fees actually payable by a party to his counsel.

Decisions as to costs are in the discretion of the court. Normally the losing party will be ordered to pay the successful party's costs, but partial success in an action may result in obtaining an order for only part of the costs, e.g. in case costs have been made by mere negligence or have been proven to be useless.

(d) Security for costs

According to Article 851 of the Judicial Code, proceedings can be suspended until the foreign plaintiff has put up security for payment of procedural costs. Various bilateral or multilateral conventions derogate from the above provisions in favour of the nationals of the Contracting States, e.g. The Hague Convention on civil procedure of 1 March 1954 and the CMR Convention of 19 May 1956.

5. INTERIM ARREST

(a) Are interim arrest/freezing of assets/other provisional measures permitted to provide security in other jurisdictions?

Apart from the possibility of obtaining protective measures through summary proceedings (*référés*) such as the appointment of an expert or a sequestrator (cf. (k)), there are various forms of arrest available as interim relief pending trial or enforcement of a judgment.

Provisional and protective measures can be available in aid of proceedings in a foreign country, but the arrest of assets situated outside Belgium is not permitted by Belgian law. On the other hand, a Belgian judge can order measures to be performed outside Belgium if other jurisdictional grounds exist. It can therefore be envisaged to obtain the appointment of a court surveyor for a survey to be held in, for example, Manila.

There are different types of interim arrest (*saisie conservatoire*), depending on the type of assets to be attached. The arrest of tangible and movable goods is called *saisie mobiliere* (Arts. 1422–1428 BCCP) and the arrest of the defendant's assets held by a third party, such as a debt (notably a bank account), is called *saisie-arrêt conservatoire* (Arts. 1445–1460 BCCP). Other forms of provisional arrest are *saisie immobiliere conservatoire*, arrest of real property (Arts. 1429–1444 BCCP), *saisie-revendication*, arrest of property which is the subject of an action for a claim and is in the possession of a third party (Arts. 1462–1466 BCCP), *saisie conservatoire sur navires*, arrest of seagoing vessels and arrest of inland navigation ships (Arts. 1560–1626 BCCP—cf. above), *saisie en mature de contrefaçon*, arrest of counterfeited goods or goods manufactured as a result of a patent infringement (Arts. 1481–1488 BCCP).

(b) What criteria apply to this?

Three conditions must be fulfilled before leave to arrest movables can be granted by the Judge of Arrests. For that purpose the application must contain a detailed description of the nature of the claim and must show that the arrestor has a good *prima facie* case. The arrestor's claim itself must meet three different criteria. First, the claim must be liquidated, i.e. quantified or at least capable of provisional quantification. Secondly, the claim must be due, thus not affected by a stipulation as to time or condition; and thirdly the claim must be certain, not subject to serious arguments.

As proceedings relating to arrest are summary proceedings, the general condition of urgency must equally be met. The arrestor must show that there is an urgent risk that unless the arrest is effected, he may be deprived of the benefits of any judgment. The granting of the leave to arrest is in the complete discretion of the judge.

For specific forms of arrest, the burden of proof might be different or even alleviated, for example in the case of ship arrest the arrestor must only allege the existence of a maritime claim and the urgency is presumed.

(c) Is there a limit on jurisdictions whose proceedings are recognised for this purpose?

There can be no limit on jurisdictions as long as the goods to be arrested are situated within Belgium. Arrest or other provisional measures can also be used as aid or interim relief for arbitration proceedings or proceedings in foreign jurisdictions.

(d) Is there a requirement for counter-security?

In general, there is no requirement for counter-security. Although the granting of leave to arrest and the conditions relating to the leave to arrest are within the sole discretion of the judge, the latter cannot impose any conditions which burdens the position of the arrestor. Therefore, counter-security cannot be imposed except where permitted by law. There are two notable exceptions to the rule that counter-security cannot be imposed: arrest of a ship (Art. 1467 BCCP) and arrest of counterfeited goods (Art. 1483 BCCP).

If the arrest is effected notwithstanding the fact that security has not yet been granted, arrest will be declared null and void.

Provisional measures will generally be granted without the imposition of counter-security, but, in order to safeguard the financial interest of the party against whom the measure is granted, the plaintiff will be ordered to pay the provisional sums and retainers demanded by the experts, or sequestrators.

(e) Can applications be made ex parte?

All applications relating to arrest are made *ex parte* to the Judge of Arrest. In some circumstances, an arrestor may also instruct a bailiff to carry out an interim arrest without the intervention of a judge on the basis of a formal document of private nature such as a bill of exchange, a cheque, a lease, an insurance policy or a will. Similarly, the leave of the Judge of Arrests is not required for the provisional arrest of assets in aid of execution of a judgment, even if the judgment has not been declared provisionally enforceable and is not yet *res judicata*.

The manner in which other provisional measures can be obtained can differ. In extremely urgent cases, provisional measures such as the appointment of an expert or sequestrator can be obtained through an *ex parte* application to the President of the Commercial Court or Court of First Instance. Such procedure can only be allowed in cases where, in the terms of Article 584 BCCP, the existence of an "absolute necessity" can be proven. If the measure is granted by the President, it will in most cases oblige the applicant to initiate summary proceedings to have the measure confirmed or quashed after an opposition.

On the other hand if the President refuses to grant the measure sought, there will be no other alternative than to initiate summary proceedings and request the measure sought.

(f) How quickly can an order be made?

As applications for leave to arrest are generally dealt with on an *ex parte* basis, the order for the arrest can be obtained very quickly: if the application for leave to arrest is presented to and granted by the judge in the morning, the court order for the arrest can be obtained from the registry in the afternoon. In some of the larger jurisdictions, e.g. Antwerp, one can even present the application for leave to arrest at the judge's home after office hours.

Applications for provisional measures not relating to arrest, e.g. appointment of surveyor or sequestrator, must either be brought by summons, whereby the obligatory lapse of time between the time of service and the hearing is a minimum of two days, or by way of *ex parte* application to the president of the court. As indicated above the second alternative is limited to situations where the existence of absolute necessity can be shown.

One must also consider that in shipping matters the judicial code allows the summoning of the defendant from hour to hour. Theoretically, the writ, summoning the defendant to appear in court in the afternoon, can thus be served on the same day. In other matters, one can also apply to the president of the court for a shortening of the lapse of time between service of the writ and the hearing.

(g) Will the order bind third parties?

The principal effect of interim arrest is to freeze the asset arrested within the patrimony of the debtor. It equally implies that in the circumstances the arrested goods cannot be moved.

This could therefore affect the rights of third parties, e.g. rights of cargo owners after arrest of a vessel, or rights of the carrier after arrest of cargo.

(h) What are the consequences of breach of an order?

The non-compliance with an order for the arrest of certain goods could constitute a tortious act. In some circumstances, breach of an order of arrest will be considered a criminal offence. Article 507 of the Criminal Code specifies that the withholding, destruction or damaging of arrested goods can be punished by a criminal court.

(i) Is there a limit to types of asset, e.g. physical asset/account balances?

If the debtor is a physical person, as opposed to a company, certain goods cannot be arrested and there is a limit on the amounts that can be arrested. Article 1408 and following BCCP enumerate those goods and amounts, e.g. household linen, assets necessary for the exercise of the debtor's profession, books necessary for study.

Apart from rules pertaining to state immunity, some specific legislation can also provide for limits in the type of assets to be arrested, e.g. works of literature or music as long as they have not been published or finished.

(j) What if third parties are affected, e.g. airliner?

As indicated above, third parties affected by the arrest, e.g. owners of cargo in an arrested vessel, charterers or owners of a vessel carrying cargo which has been arrested in an interim port, normally have no alternative but to abide by the court order authorising arrest of the goods. Since the order for the arrest will generally have been obtained *ex parte*, they have the possibility to initiate third party opposition proceedings against the order for the arrest. Similarly, a third party whose rights are affected by the order may apply to the court for it to be discharged or varied.

(k) What other provisional measures may be ordered, e.g. appointment of surveyor or receiver, security?

Apart from arrest, other provisional measures may be ordered by the President of the Court. There is in principle no limit as regards the kind of measure to be ordered as long as the measure is provisional and does not affect the merits of the case. One can therefore easily envisage the appointment of a court surveyor, or a sequestrator to hold goods that are the subject matter of a dispute between parties, e.g. the accounts of a company or arrested and discharged cargoes which would allow the carrying vessel to sail.

6. RECOGNITION OF JUDGMENTS AND AWARDS

(a) What treaties/conventions apply?

(i) To enable judgments to be enforced abroad

Whether a judgment can be enforced abroad will depend upon the legislation of the country where enforcement is sought.

(ii) To enable enforcement of foreign judgments domestically

A great number of treaties are available for the enforcement of foreign judgments. The main distinction must in our opinion be made between the European Convention on Jurisdiction and Enforcement of Judgments of 27 September 1968 and other treaties or conventions.

Amongst these other treaties one finds conventions or treaties regulating enforcement on specific matters and bilateral treaties concerning legal aid.

Note the existence of the following treaties, to which Belgium is a party:

- Treaty of Lake Success of 6 April 1950 on the death of missing persons;
- Treaty of The Hague of 1 March 1954 on the civil procedure;
- European Convention of 13 December 1955 (Article 9) on the *cautio judicatum solvi* and enforcement of judgments condemning to procedural costs;
- CMR Treaty of 19 May 1956 on international carriage of goods by road;
- Convention of The Hague of 15 April 1958 on judgments with respect to alimony for children;
- The CIM and CIV Conventions of Bern of 7 February 1970 and the Additional Agreement to the CIV Convention;
- European Convention on recognition and enforcement of judgments relating to parenthood of Luxembourg of 20 May 1980;
- Lugano Convention of 16 September 1988 on recognition and enforcement of judgments.

(b) What procedure is followed to enforce a judgment?

(i) Governed by a treaty/convention

Foreign judgments are enforceable in Belgium by all the appropriate means available in respect of Belgian judgments, once their enforcement has been authorised by the endorsement of an executory formula. Whether or not a Belgian judgment or award can be enforced abroad will depend upon the legislation of the country where enforcement is sought.

For judgments falling within the scope of application of the 1968 Convention, the procedure requires an application for enforcement to the Court of First Instance (Art. 32 of the Convention), regardless of the amount mentioned in the judgment. The application must be accompanied by an authenticated copy of the foreign judgment together with a translation into the language of the court (cf. Arts. 46–48). Although the judgment may not be reviewed as to its substance (Art. 40), the application may be refused on the grounds enumerated in the Convention (Art. 34 referring to Arts. 27 and 28). The order for enforcement is in the form of a judgment of the Belgian court. The judgment debtor is not heard on this initial application. If an order for enforcement is granted by the court, the debtor against whom the order has been made may appeal against the order before the same court (Art. 37). If, on the other hand, the order is refused, the applicant may appeal to the Court of Appeal (Art. 40). A further appeal may only be lodged by way of cassation (Arts. 37 and 40).

Apart from the 1968 Convention, various other multilateral conventions or bilateral treaties regulate the enforcement and recognition of foreign judgments on specific matters, e.g. The Hague Convention of 15 April 1958 regarding decision on alimony to children, the European Convention of 20 May 1980 on decisions relating to the custody of children.

(ii) Not governed by a treaty/convention

If none of the conventions can be applied, a Belgian court may still authorise the enforcement of the foreign judgment. The order for enforcement can be obtained by filing an application to the Court of First Instance. The court will need to be satisfied that the judgment does not offend Belgian public policy, that the rights of defence have been respected, and that the judgment is final and conclusive and in proper form according to the law of the state in which it has been rendered (Art. 570 BCCP). It will also re-examine the merits of the case and refuse enforcement if the trial judge appears to have made any error of fact or law.

(c) What about foreign arbitration awards?

As regards arbitration awards reference must be made to the New York Convention of 10 June 1958 and the Geneva Convention of 26 September 1927. Both have been ratified by Belgium. Some bilateral treaties have been entered into with France, the Netherlands, Germany, Switzerland and Austria. The terms of these conventions will have to be observed for the obtainment of the enforcement order. If no convention can be applied, an application accompanied with the original or authenticated copy of the award for an enforcement order must be filed with the President of the Court of First Instance and the procedure to be followed is described in Articles 1719 to 1723 BCCP. The application can be dismissed if the award is not final or not provisionally enforceable, if the award is contrary to public policy rules or if there are grounds for dismissal of the award.

(d) Can proceeds of a judgment be freely exported?

Yes, proceeds of a judgment can be freely exported.

CHAPTER 3

CYPRUS

Andreas Haviaras
L. Papaphilippou & Co, 1 Costakis Pantelides Avenue, P.O. Box 2313, Nicosia, Cyprus

1. JURISDICTION

The general grounds on which Cyprus courts would accept civil jurisdiction are the following:

(a) Domicile

Relief can be sought against any person domiciled in Cyprus; or where the action is for the administration of the movable property of any deceased person who at the time of his death was domiciled in Cyprus.

(b) Place of business/residence/office

Relief can be sought against a person ordinarily resident in Cyprus or, being a company, having its registered office in Cyprus.

(c) Assets located within the jurisdiction

Jurisdiction will be accepted where the whole subject matter of the action is immovable property of any kind situated in Cyprus; or where any act, deed, will, contract, obligation or liability affecting immovable property of any kind situated in Cyprus, is sought to be construed, rectified, set aside or enforced in the action; or for the execution (as to property situated in Cyprus) of the trusts of any written instrument, of which the person to be served is a trustee, which ought to be executed according to the law of Cyprus; or the action is an admiralty action *in rem* against a ship being within the territorial waters of Cyprus at the time of filing the action.

(d) Act complained of within the jurisdiction

The action must be founded on a civil wrong committed in Cyprus.

(e) Contract governed by local law

The fact that a contract is made to be governed by Cyprus law does not by itself confer civil jurisdiction upon Cyprus courts. The court would however assume jurisdiction if the action is one brought to enforce, rescind, dissolve, annul or otherwise affect a contract or to recover damages or other relief for or in respect of the breach of a contract—

(i) made in Cyprus; or
(ii) made by or through an agent trading or residing in Cyprus on behalf of a principal trading or residing out of Cyprus, or is one brought in respect of a breach committed in Cyprus of a contract wherever made, even though such breach was preceded or accompanied by a breach out of Cyprus which rendered impossible the performance of the part of the contract which ought to have been performed in Cyprus.

(f) Conventions

Jurisdiction will be accepted where there is a claim for civil liability for oil pollution under the International Convention on Civil liability for Oil Pollution Damage made in Brussels on 29 November 1969.

(g) Clause attributing jurisdiction

The inclusion in any contract of a jurisdiction clause may confer civil jurisdiction on Cyprus courts, which, however, may refuse to entertain the action if Cyprus appears to be *forum non conveniens.*

(h) Other

Jurisdiction will be accepted where any injunction is sought as to anything to be done in Cyprus, or any nuisance in Cyprus is sought to be prevented or removed, whether damages are or are not also sought in respect thereof.

(i) Counterclaim/third-party proceedings

The courts will accept jurisdiction where the counterclaim of the defendant is a counterclaim which the court has the power to deal with, although if it was brought as a separate action the court would not resume civil jurisdiction to deal with it. Further the court may give leave under proper circumstances for a person or entity to be invited as third parties in proceedings pending before it against another person duly served in Cyprus although such third person or entity is not domiciled or resident in Cyprus.

2. MARITIME CLAIMS

(a) Is there special jurisdiction for maritime claims based on arrest of a vessel in the jurisdiction?

The admiralty jurisdiction in Cyprus is exercised by the Supreme Court and in doing so it has the same powers and jurisdiction as those vested in and exercised by the High Court of Justice in England in its admiralty jurisdiction on the day immediately preceding 16 August 1960.

The Admiralty Court of Cyprus, when entertaining an action *in rem* against a ship which is within the territorial waters of Cyprus, has the jurisdiction to issue a warrant of arrest of such ship.

(b) Specific

The jurisdiction of the Supreme Court may be invoked by an action *in rem* and lead to a warrant of arrest of a ship when:

(i) the claim in question is for a maritime lien. The maritime liens recognised by the laws of Cyprus are:
  - — damage done by a ship
  - — salvage
  - — seamen's and master's wages
  - — master's disbursements
  - — bottomry

(ii) the claim is a statutory lien, i.e.
  - (a) a claim to the possession or ownership of a ship or to the ownership of any share therein;
  - (b) any question arising between the co-owners of a ship as to possession, employment or earnings of that ship;
  - (c) a claim in respect of a mortgage of or charge on a ship or any share therein;
  - (d) a claim for damage done by a ship;
  - (e) a claim for damage received by a ship;
  - (f) a claim for loss of life or personal injury sustained in consequence of any defect in a ship or in her apparel or equipment or of the wrongful act, neglect or default of the owners, charterers or persons in possession or control of a ship or of the master or crew thereof or of any other person for whose wrongful acts, neglects or defaults the owners, charterers or persons in possession or control of a ship are responsible, being an act, neglect or default in the navigation or management of the ship, in the loading, carriage or discharge of goods on, in or from the ship or in the embarkation, carriage or disembarkation of persons on, in or from the ship;

(g) a claim for loss of or damage to goods carried in a ship;
(h) a claim arising out of any agreement relating to the carriage of goods in a ship or to the use or hire of a ship;
(j) a claim in the nature of salvage;
(k) a claim in the nature of towage in respect of a ship or an aircraft;
(l) a claim in the nature of pilotage in respect of a ship or an aircraft;
(m) a claim in respect of goods or materials supplied to a ship for her operation or maintenance;
(n) a claim in respect of the construction, repair or equipment of a ship or dock charges or dues;
(o) a claim by a master or member of the crew of a ship for wages and any claim by or in respect of a master or member of the crew of a ship for any money or property which, under any of the provisions of the Merchant Shipping Acts, is recoverable as wages;
(p) a claim by a master, shipper, charterer or agent in respect of disbursements made on account of a ship;
(q) a claim arising out of an act which is or is claimed to be a general average act;
(r) a claim arising out of bottomry;
(s) a claim for the forfeiture or condemnation of a ship or of goods which are being or have been carried, or have been attempted to be carried, in a ship, or for the restoration of a ship or any such goods after seizure, or for droits of Admiralty.

(c) What are the grounds for arrest?

The Cyprus Admiralty Jurisdiction Order 1893 provides that an application for a warrant of arrest of a ship may be brought only in an action *in rem*. Such application must be in writing and be accompanied by an affidavit. The affidavit must state the nature and extent of the claim and the fact that such claim is not satisfied. It must also frankly disclose all matters which are relevant to the case.

(d) Need the arrested vessel be connected with the claim or can other vessels in the same legal (or beneficial) ownership also be arrested?

The ship to be arrested must be connected with the claim except in the case of claims under para. 2(b)(ii)(d) to (r) above when the action *in rem* may also be brought against another ship which at the time the action is brought is in the same legal or beneficial ownership.

The English Administration of Justice Act 1956 is applicable in Cyprus and therefore the provisions of section 3 of the said Act for arrest and sister ship arrest apply. The interpretation of section 3(4)(a)(b) of the Act given in *The Evpo Epnic* [1988] 3 All ER at p. 810 is also applicable in Cyprus.

(e) What procedural differences apply to special maritime jurisdiction?

The rules applicable for maritime claims are those laid down by the Cyprus Admiralty Jurisdiction Order 1893. Under these rules an admiralty action may be an action *in rem* or an action *in personam*. Where the said Order makes no provision about any matter, then, by virtue of rule 237, the practice of the Admiralty Division of the High Court of Justice of England so far as it shall appear to be applicable shall be followed.

The main procedure differences applicable to maritime jurisdiction are:

(i) The Civil Procedure Rules applicable to civil proceedings other than admiralty provide that when the defendant is residing abroad the plaintiff must, before filing the action, apply and obtain leave to file and issue a writ of summons. The Admiralty Jurisdiction order 1893, however, does not make any such provision for the actions *in personam* and therefore the writ of summons in an admiralty action *in personam* is filed and issued without such leave. In any event the plaintiff must apply and obtain leave to serve such writ outside the jurisdiction.

(ii) Under the Admiralty Rules any party may apply for a review of an order of the court within seven days of its issue (apart from the right of appeal) whereas such a procedure is not available in the Civil Procedure Rules.

(iii) A person interested in the *res* in an action *in rem* may, without becoming a party to the action, file a caveat against the release or against the arrest of the ship or against the payment out of the proceeds of sale without first being notified. Such a procedure is not available in the Civil Procedure Rules.

(iv) Any party to an action *in rem* or any interested person in the ship who has obtained leave to intervene in the proceedings under which the ship is arrested may apply for the sale of the ship *pendente lite*.

(f) What jurisdictional rules are there as to limitation of liability?

A shipowner may limit his liability either under the Carriage of Goods by Sea Law Cap. 263 which incorporates the Hague Rules or under sections 502 and 503 of the English Merchant Shipping Act 1894. It must be noted that there is debate as to whether the English Merchant Shipping Act 1958 is applicable in Cyprus. There is no case decided on the point although there is one pending. It is action no. 168/96 *P. T. Dharma Niaga Ltd* v. *Earnest Navigation Company Limited* and its outcome will solve this uncertainty. In both cases the limitation of liability may (where the claimants are numerous) be invoked either by a limitation action by which the shipowner is seeking to create the limitation fund or by way of counterclaim if the claimant would be only one.

3. SERVICE OF PROCEEDINGS

Both in civil and in admiralty proceedings service of process outside the jurisdiction needs the prior leave of the court. The leave is sought by an *ex parte* application accompanied by an affidavit.

The affidavit must satisfy the court that:

(i) The cause of action is one for which the court would assume civil or admiralty jurisdiction as the case may be; and
(ii) The plaintiff has *prima facie* a good cause of action.

The order allowing the service outside the jurisdiction will limit the time after the service within which the defendant must file an appearance and it shall also contain a direction that if the defendant does not so file an appearance the notice of any application in the action may be given by posting a copy on the court notice board.

Cyprus has ratified the Convention of the Service Abroad of Judicial and Extra Judicial Documents in Civil or Commercial Matters made in The Hague on 15 November 1965 by Law No. 40/82 and therefore its provisions are applicable in Cyprus.

Further, Cyprus has entered into an agreement with Greece for legal co-operation on matters of civil, family, commercial and criminal law which has been ratified by Law No. 55/84. Section 1 of the said law extends the application of the Agreement to matters of admiralty law as well. The Agreement provides a method of service of process from the one country to the other to citizens of the two countries alone.

4. COSTS

The costs involved in starting proceedings in Cyprus are as follows.

(a) Court fees

Stamp fees are to be affixed on the writ of summons, the applications, affidavits, etc, and depend on the value of the subject matter of the action.

(b) Lawyers' fees

Lawyers' fees are payable for court work. These are determined either by the court scale which depends on the value of the subject matter or by agreement. Contingency fees are not permitted by the Rules of Etiquette of the Cyprus Bar Association. Lawyers are also entitled to extrajudicial lawyers' fees. These are fees which are not covered as court fees and are regulated by the rules of the Cyprus Bar Association.

(c) Recovery of costs from unsuccessful party

The successful litigant almost invariably is awarded the costs of the proceedings. This relates only to (a) and (b) above. Therefore the extrajudicial fees are not covered by the order for costs.

(d) Security for costs

A defendant in an action brought by a non-resident plaintiff may apply by summons for security for costs. The security ordered relates to the costs under (a) and (b) above only.

5. INTERIM ARREST

(a) Are interim arrest/freezing of assets/other provisional measures permitted to provide security for domestic proceedings and/or proceedings in another jurisdiction?

Cyprus courts during the pendency of any action and in the exercise of their civil jurisdiction under several laws have the power to issue interim orders or injunctions to freeze assets.

The said provisions are:

(i) Section 4(1) of the Civil Procedure Law Cap. 6 whereby the court has power to issue an interim order for the sequestration, preservation, custody, sale, detention or inspection of any property being the subject matter of the action pending a final judgment or pending execution of a judgment.

(ii) Under section 5 of the Civil Procedure Law Cap. 6 whereby the court in actions for debts or for damages has the power to issue interim orders or injunctions in relation to immovable property registered in the name of the defendant or in relation to immovable property for which the defendant is entitled to become the registered owner.

(iii) Section 32 of the Courts of Justice Law No. 14/60 whereby the court may grant an injunction (interlocutory, perpetual or mandatory) or appoint a receiver in all cases in which it appears to the court just or convenient so to do notwithstanding that no compensation or other relief is claimed or granted together therewith.

Under this section Cyprus courts are vested with power to issue Mareva injunctions.

A Mareva injunction under Cyprus law is granted in a case where a plaintiff has brought an action in Cyprus against a foreign or Cypriot defendant and the defendant has money or chattels within the jurisdiction which if he were not prevented from doing so he would be free to remove out of the jurisdiction, before the plaintiff could bring his action to trial and if successful obtain and enforce a judgment against him. A Cyprus Mareva injunction is not extended to property outside the jurisdiction. See *Botteghi* v. *Bolt Head Navigation* [1985] 1 CLR 114 and *Pasteila Maritime Co Ltd* v. *National Iranian Tanker Co Ltd* [1987] 1 CLR 583. There is District Court case law that a Mareva injunction is issued not only to prevent the transfer of the assets outside the jurisdiction but also to prevent the waste of assets within the jurisdiction. See Action No. 190/82 *M. Stavrou* v. *L. Georgiou* (D.C. Limassol).

(iv) Section 30 of the Merchant Shipping (Registration of Ships, Sales and Mortgages) Law No. 45/63 whereby the Supreme Court of Cyprus may if it thinks fit (without prejudice to the exercise of any other power of the court), on the application of any interested person, make an order prohibiting for a time specified any dealing with a ship or any share therein and the court may make the order on any terms or conditions the court may think just.

(v) Sections 2(b)(i) and 9 of the International Commercial Arbitration Law No. 101/87 whereby a District Court of Cyprus may, on an *ex parte* application, order conservatory measures either before or during the pendency of an international arbitration. An arbitration is considered as International if (a) at the time of making the agreement the place of business of the parties is in different States or (b) the place where the arbitration will take place or the place of execution of significant part of the obligations under the commercial relation that is the subject matter of the arbitration is outside the State where the parties have their place of business. This is the only case where a Cyprus court may issue "conservatory measures" for proceedings in another jurisdiction.

(vi) Section 9 of the Charging Orders Law No. 31(1)/92 whereby the court may issue a provisional injunction charging government bonds, bonds issued by a Cypriot company or bonds issued by a foreign company but registered in a Registry kept in Cyprus, Unit Trust units and funds in court belonging to the defendant and which may extend to dividends or other income therefrom.

(b) What criteria apply to this?

The criteria which need to be satisfied for each one of the above interim orders and injunctions are very similar. That is to say:

(i) An order applied for under section 4(1) of the Civil Procedure Law Cap. 6 is issued only if the subject matter of the order is the same as the subject matter of the action. See *Compania Portuguesa de Transportes Maritime of Lisbon* v. *Sponsalia Shipping Co Ltd* [1987] 1 CLR 11.

(ii) The requirements which need to be satisfied for an order under section 5 of the Civil Procedure Law Cap. 6 are (a) that the plaintiff has a good cause of action and (b) that by the sale or transfer of the immovable property to any third person it is probable that the plaintiff may be hindered in obtaining satisfaction of the judgment if given in his favour.

(iii) An application for an injunction under section 32 of the Courts of Justice Law No. 14/60 must satisfy the court before the issue of such an injunction (a) that there is a serious question to be tried at the hearing; (b) that there is probability that the plaintiff is entitled to relief; and (c) that unless the order is issued it shall be difficult or impossible to do complete justice at a later stage. See *Odysseos* v. *Pieris Estates* [1982] 1 CLR 557.

(iv) The order made under section 30 of Law No. 45/63 is issued by the Supreme Court and not the District Court and the applicant must be interested in the ship herself. Under Cyprus case law suppliers of a ship are not interested in the ship herself whereas a mortgagee is. See *Pastella Marine Co Ltd* v. *National Iranian Tanker Co Ltd* [1987] 1 CLR 583 and *K. Yerasakis* v. *Waft Shipping Company Ltd* [1989] 1 CLR 395. Further it is not necessary to have an action pending. It is an autonomous procedure.

(v) An application for an order under section 2(b)(i) and 9 of Law No. 101/87 should satisfy the same requirements as those provided for under section 32 of Law No. 14/60.

(vi) An application for an order under section 9 of Law No. 31(1)/92 will be considered by the court in the light of the personal financial situation of the defendant and the possibility of causing damage to other creditors. The court must be satisfied that the plaintiff has *prima facie* a good cause of action and that unless the order prohibiting the transfer is issued a judgment in favour of the applicant may remain unsatisfied.

(c) Is there a limit on jurisdictions whose proceedings are recognised for this purpose?

Not applicable.

(d) Is there a requirement for counter-security?

The court almost invariably orders the applicant to file security, to be used if it is shown to the court that there was no probable ground for the bringing of the plaintiff's action, for the reasonable compensation of the defendant for expense and injury which may be occasioned to him by the execution of the injunction.

(e) Can applications be made ex parte?

All applications for the issue of the interim orders and injunctions described above are made *ex parte* by the plaintiff(s) alone. A defendant who has a counterclaim cannot apply for an interim order or injunction. See *Symeou* v. *Michael* (1983) 1 JSC 262.

(f) How quickly can an order be made?

Ex parte applications for injunctions are usually dealt with by the court either the same day they are filed or in the next one or two days.

(g) Will the order bind third parties?

The aforesaid orders, with the exception of that based on section 30 of the Merchant Shipping (Registration of Ships, Sales and Mortgages) Law No. 45/63, are not binding on third parties, whereas that order is binding upon the Registrar of Ships as well although it is a third party. However, a third person who has knowledge of the order and who acts or abets the defendant in disobeying the injunction may be liable to contempt of court proceedings.

(h) What are the consequences of breach of an order?

The persons to whom the injunction is addressed if they fail to comply are liable to contempt of court proceedings. If they are found guilty they are liable to a fine or imprisonment or both. The same applies to any person aiding or abetting the defendant to disobey an injunction.

(i) Is there a limit to types of asset?

The types of assets which may be frozen are:

(i) under section 4(1) of the Civil Procedure Law Cap. 6 the subject matter of the action only;
(ii) under section 5 of the Civil Procedure Law Cap. 6 immovable property registered in the name of the defendant or of which he is entitled to be registered as owner;
(iii) under section 32 of Law No. 14/60, the assets may be money, bank account balances or chattels;
(iv) under section 30 of the Law No. 45/63 the asset must be a Cyprus ship or any share therein;
(v) under section 9 of Law No. 32(1)/92, the assets may be government bonds, bonds of a Cypriot company, bonds of a foreign company which are registered in a Registry within Cyprus, Unit Trust units and funds in court.

(j) What if third parties are affected?

A third person affected by such an injunction cannot directly file an opposition or apply to set aside the order. The third person must first apply and obtain leave to become a party to the action. See Appeal No. 7368 *Heli Air (Egypt) J.S.C.* v. *Reinchard Dreschner and others.*

(k) What other provisional measures may be ordered?

The courts have also the power to appoint a receiver under section 32 of the Courts of Justice Law No. 14/60. In winding-up proceedings of a limited liability company, and by virtue of the provisions of section 227 of the Companies Law Cap. 113, the court may appoint a provisional liquidator.

6. RECOGNITION OF JUDGMENTS/AWARDS

(a) What treaties/conventions apply (i) to enable judgments to be enforced abroad and (ii) to enable enforcement of foreign judgments domestically?

Cyprus has ratified two treaties/conventions which regulate the registration of foreign judgments in Cyprus and of Cypriot judgments abroad for execution. The first one is the Convention on the Recognition and Enforcement of Foreign Judgments in Civil and Commercial Matters and Supplementary Protocol thereto ratified by Law No. 11/76 and the other is an Agreement for legal co-operation between the Republic of Cyprus and the Republic of Greece in matters of Civil, Family, Commercial and Criminal Law ratified by Law No. 55/84.

(b) What procedure is followed to enforce a foreign judgment (i) governed by treaty/convention and (ii) not governed by treaty/convention?

(i) Foreign judgment governed by treaty/convention

The procedure for the registration of a foreign judgment under the Convention ratified by Law No. 11/76 is provided for by Articles 13 and 14 of the same Convention. According to the said articles an application needs to be filed and be accompanied by:

(a) a complete and authenticated copy of the foreign decision together with a true translation in Greek duly certified as such by a diplomatic or consular agent or by a sworn translator or by any other person so authorised in either State;

(b) documentary evidence that the judgment is not subject to review and is enforceable in the State of origin.

The same procedure applies for the registration of judgments under the Agreement ratified by Law No. 55/84.

(ii) Foreign judgment not governed by treaty/convention

If a foreign judgment is not governed by the above treaties/conventions then the judgment creditor shall proceed either:

(a) by registering it under the provisions of the Foreign Judgments (Reciprocal Enforcement) Law Cap. 10; or
(b) by bringing in Cyprus a common law action before the appropriate court, using as cause of action the foreign judgment. See Civil Appeal 8578 *Achilleas Constantinou* v. *Publishing Company Demokritos Ltd.*

The procedure which needs to be followed for the registration of a foreign judgment under the provisions of the Foreign Judgments (Reciprocal Enforcement) Law Cap. 10 is that of rule 3 of the Foreign Judgments (Reciprocal Enforcement) Rules.

The applicant/judgment creditor files an *ex parte* application in the appropriate District Court accompanied by an affidavit:

(a) exhibiting a certified copy of the foreign judgment and a translation of it in Greek authenticated by affidavit,
(b) stating that:
    (i) the applicant is entitled to enforce the judgment;
    (ii) the judgment is not satisfied or stating the extent to which it was satisfied;
    (iii) on the date of the application the judgment is still enforceable in the country of the original court; and
    (iv) if the judgment is registered it will not be liable to be set aside for one or more of the reasons set forth in rule 6 of the said Rules.

(c) What about foreign arbitration awards?

International arbitration awards may be registered under the provisions of the International Commercial Arbitrations Law No. 101/87. Section 35(2) of the Law provides that the party seeking execution may apply to the court and accompany his application with the original or a duly authenticated copy of the award and of the agreement to submit to arbitration both duly translated in Greek.

Foreign arbitration awards are recognised and enforced under the provisions of Law No. 84/79 which ratified the Convention on the Recognition and Enforcement of Foreign Arbitral Awards done at New York on 10 June 1958.

Under this Convention the application for such recognition and enforcement must be accompanied by (a) the duly authenticated original award or a duly certified copy thereof, (b) the original agreement or certified copy thereof and, if the above are not in the Greek language, then with a duly certified Greek translation of the above certified by an official or sworn translator or by a diplomatic or consular agent.

See Appl. No. 74/95 *Beogradska Banka* reported in the decisions of the Courts of Cyprus (1995) Vol. 7.

(d) Will proceeds of a judgment be freely exportable?

Proceeds of judgment are exported through a bank operating in Cyprus, which will secure a formal approval of the Central Bank by presenting a copy of the judgment.

CHAPTER 4

DENMARK

Lars Rosenberg Overby and Bent Nielsen
Reumert & Partners, DK–1021, Bredgade 26, Copenhagen K, Denmark

1. JURISDICTION

The general grounds on which courts will accept jurisdiction are as follows.

(a) Domicile

The Danish courts are competent to decide disputes involving a defendant who is domiciled in Denmark: cf. the Administration of Justice Act ("AJA") section 235(1). Individuals are domiciled at the place of their residence (AJA section 235(2)) whereas companies with limited liability, partnerships and associations are domiciled at their principal place of business (AJA section 238(1)).

(b) Place of business/residence/office

Legal proceedings may be commenced against individuals and legal entities that conduct business in Denmark at the place where the activities are conducted from (AJA section 237).

(c) Assets located within the jurisdiction

Unless the defendant is domiciled within the EU/EFTA area the presence of assets in Denmark owned by the defendant will give the Danish courts jurisdiction (AJA section 246(3)).

(d) Act complained of within the jurisdiction

Denmark recognises the doctrine of *forum delicti commisi* and therefore the Danish courts would have jurisdiction in the event that the claim arose from a tortious act committed in Denmark.

(e) Contract governed by local law

The fact that a contract is governed by Danish law is not a ground on which the courts will accept jurisdiction.

(f) Conventions

AJA section 247(1) provides that the jurisdiction of the Danish courts is to be determined by the 1968 Brussels Convention and the Lugano Convention if the subject matter falls within the scope of these conventions. However, jurisdiction may be created by way of arrest of a vessel. In that case the court issuing the arrest order would have jurisdiction to decide the dispute regardless of the conventions (AJA section 246a).

Further, Denmark is party to other conventions which may create or exclude jurisdiction in Denmark namely:

- The 1956 CMR Convention.
- The 1969 CLC Convention (and Protocol of 1992).
- The 1955 Warsaw Convention.
- The 1980 COTIF/CIM Convention.

(g) Clause attributing jurisdiction

Jurisdiction clauses are generally valid in Denmark (AJA section 245) although there are certain requirements as to clarity, and where the 1968 Brussels Convention and the Lugano Convention applies the requirements therein must be fulfilled. However, specific rules of a convention may render a jurisdiction clause invalid.

(h) Other

(i) Arrest

If the defendant has prevented arrest of an asset by giving security, then such security replaces, for the purpose of jurisdiction, the asset—provided always that the presence of the asset would have given ground for jurisdiction; cf. the remarks above (AJA section 246(3)).

(ii) Real estate

AJA section 241 provides that the courts of Denmark have jurisdiction when the dispute concerns the right to real estate in Denmark.

(iii) Contractual claims

If the issue concerns a contractual claim an action may be brought against the defendant provided the dispute does not concern the payment of money (unless the claim arose whilst the debtor was present in the jurisdiction and payment was due prior to his departure); cf. AJA section 242.

(iv) Consent

The defendant may submit to the jurisdiction of the Danish courts by consent.

(i) Counterclaim/third party proceedings

(i) Counterclaim

A counterclaim may always be raised provided that it can be dealt with by the same procedural rules as the plaintiff's claim. However, an independently enforceable judgment regarding the counterclaim can only be given if the courts would otherwise have jurisdiction to hear the claim or if the claim originates from the same legal relationship (cf. Art. 6(3) of the 1968 Brussels Convention).

(ii) Third-party proceedings

Either party may join third parties in the proceedings provided that the court would otherwise have jurisdiction; the claim may be dealt with under the same procedural rules as the main action and the claims are related.

(iii) Appointment of court surveyor

On application a surveyor may be appointed by the court where the object in question is situated (AJA section 343).

(iv) Maritime enquiry

A maritime enquiry can be held on application from the master, owner of the vessel or the authorities of the flag state.

2. MARITIME CLAIMS

(a) Is there special jurisdiction for maritime claims based on arrest of a vessel in the jurisdiction?

Denmark has ratified the 1952 International Convention relating to the arrest of seagoing ships ("the Arrest Convention") and by virtue of AJA section 246a the Danish courts have jurisdiction based on the arrest of a vessel. If arrest is avoided by the provision of security, then the court where the vessel would have been arrested has jurisdiction.

(b) Specific maritime jurisdiction

(i) Place of receipt or delivery of cargo

Section 310 of the Danish Merchant Shipping Act contains jurisdiction provisions for claims arising from the carriage of general cargo. Under section 310 the Danish courts have jurisdiction notwithstanding agreements to the contrary if the agreed or actual place of receipt or delivery is within Denmark. To the extent that the matter falls within the scope of the 1968 Brussels Convention or the Lugano Convention section 310 does not apply. Otherwise the defendant may be sued before the Danish courts:

— if the defendant's principal place of business is located in Denmark;
— if the contract was made in Denmark provided that the defendant has an office, sub-office or agency there through whose mediation the contract was made; or
— if the agreed place of receipt or place of delivery is situated in Denmark.

(ii) Passengers

Subject to the 1968 Brussels Convention and the Lugano Convention disputes regarding carriage of passengers and luggage can only be commenced at the place where the defendant is domiciled or has his principal place of business or at the place of departure or destination provided for in the contract (section 429 of the Merchant Shipping Act).

(c) What are the grounds for arrest?

The grounds for arrest are that the claim is a maritime claim as defined in Article 1 of the Arrest Convention and that the *prima facie* validity of the claim can be established.

(d) Need the arrested vessel be connected with the claim or can other vessels in the same legal (or beneficial) ownership also be arrested?

The arrested vessel need, in principle, only be connected with the claim in the event that the claim falls under the categories (o), (p) or (q) in Article 1(1) of the Arrest Convention. An important exception is that the vessel must be owned by the party liable for the claim.

(e) What procedural differences apply to special maritime jurisdiction?

None.

(f) What jurisdictional rules are there as to limitation of liability?

Denmark has ratified the 1976 Convention on Limitation of Liability for Maritime Claims and the 1969 Convention on Civil Liability for Oil Pollution Damage (also the 1992 Protocol) to which we refer.

3. SERVICE OF PROCEEDINGS

What rules apply to service of proceedings outside the jurisdiction?

A distinction is made between forced service and service effected by consent.

(i) Forced service

There are no specific rules in the AJA regarding service of proceedings outside the jurisdiction. Denmark has however acceded to the 1965 Hague Convention. Further, a convention has been concluded amongst the Nordic countries about mutual legal aid. A bilateral agreement has been made with Austria in 1979 about service. Outside the scope of these conventions forced service must be effected in accordance with the practice that applies to the individual country where the defendant is domiciled. As a rule, service can be effected via the local Danish embassy or consulate.

(ii) Service effected by consent

In the event that the defendant is prepared to accept service, the documents only require endorsement by the defendant or his agent that service has taken place.

4. COSTS

The costs implications of starting proceedings are as follows.

(a) Court fees

The court fees amount to a basic fee of DKK 500 plus 1% of the part of the claim that exceeds DKK 6,000. When the hearing date is fixed an additional court fee of one-fifth of the initial fee is payable (it is repaid in the event that the proceedings have been discontinued no later than six weeks before the hearing date).

(b) Lawyers' fees

Lawyers' fees are normally calculated on the prevailing hourly rate. The fee can be agreed between the client and the lawyer; however, Danish lawyers are not allowed to take instructions on a contingency basis.

(c) Recovery of costs from the unsuccessful party

Under the AJA section 312(1) the unsuccessful party is obliged to pay the successful party's reasonable costs. The court will decide on the amount of recoverable costs and it is within its discretion not to award costs at all. Normally the costs awarded by the court will not fully cover the actual costs.

(d) Security for costs

Where the plaintiff is a non-domiciliary, security for costs must be given if the defendant so requests, under section 323 of the AJA. The rule does not, however, apply to defendants domiciled in countries where Danish domiciliaries would not be required to provide security for costs, e.g. under the 1954 Hague Convention.

5. INTERIM ARREST

(a) Are interim arrest/freezing of assets/other provisional measures permitted to provide security for domestic proceedings and/or proceedings in another jurisdiction?

Under section 627 of the AJA arrest of assets can be made, provided that:

(a) the applicant's claim cannot be enforced yet; and
(b) it can be established that there is a real risk that the applicant will not obtain payment unless an arrest of the particular asset is effected. If the subject of the arrest is a vessel then the second requirement does not apply.

(b) What criteria apply to this?

The rules regarding arrest are inapplicable if an enforceable judgment or award has been obtained. As regards the risk of not obtaining payment the applicant must establish that the defendant will (probably) leave the jurisdiction, dispose of his assets or otherwise make enforcement complicated or impossible.

(c) Is there a limit on jurisdictions whose proceedings are recognised for this purpose?

There is no limit except that a judgment or award in respect of the claim must be enforceable eventually under any convention or treaty.

(d) Is there a requirement for counter-security?

Under section 629 of the AJA the court may decide that the applicant shall provide adequate security before the arrest is made. If the arrest concerns a vessel, then the amount of security is normally limited to five days of hire for the vessel under section 94(1) of the Merchant Shipping Act.

(e) Can applications be made ex parte?

The main rule is that the defendant will be notified about the hearing by the court. However, the court may in its discretion decide not to notify the defendant (AJA sections 631(2) and 493(1) and (2)).

(f) How quickly can an order be made?

That depends on the circumstances of the case and the individual court. The time and place of the hearing is entirely in the court's discretion (AJA section 491). Normally an arrest order can be obtained at very short notice if the applicant can show that time is of the essence.

(g) Will the order bind third parties?

Yes, provided that the third party is notified about the order.

(h) What are the consequences of breach of an order?

Criminal proceedings may be initiated against the person breaching an order. Further, the person may incur personal liability for the losses which the claimant suffers because of the breach.

(i) Is there a limit to types of assets, e.g. physical asset/account balances?

Any asset of monetary value may be arrested.

(j) What if third parties are affected, e.g. airliner?

An airliner cannot be the subject of an arrest (AJA section 628(2)). Otherwise third parties may intervene at the hearing only if the arrest would infringe their rights (AJA sections 631(2) and 499). The fact that an arrest causes inconvenience or even a loss to a third party does not entitle such party to intervene.

(k) What other provisional measures may be ordered, e.g. appointment of surveyor or receiver, security?

The court may order that a surveyor/expert be appointed for the purpose of assessing the value of the asset to be arrested.

The claimant must within a week after the arrest is made, commence justification proceedings. To the extent that the parties to the dispute have made an agreement as to jurisdiction then the justification proceedings should be initiated in accordance with such agreement within the said time limit.

6. RECOGNITION OF JUDGMENTS/AWARDS

(a) What treaties/conventions apply (i) to enable judgments to be enforced abroad and (ii) to enable enforcement of foreign judgments domestically?

(i) Judgments to be enforced abroad

There are no provisions in Danish law regarding the enforcement of Danish judgments abroad. Whether or not such judgment can be enforced depends entirely on the legislation in the country where the claimant seeks to enforce the judgment. In this respect Denmark is party to a number of conventions which contain provisions as to recognition and enforceability (cf. below).

(ii) Enforcement of foreign judgments domestically

The enforceability of a foreign judgment depends on whether Denmark by virtue of a treaty or convention has undertaken to recognise and enforce such judgments. In the absence of such obligations a foreign judgment, at the outset, only serves as evidence and separate proceedings would have to be commenced against the defendant here.

A foreign judgment may be enforced in Denmark pursuant to:

(a) the 1968 Brussels Convention and Lugano Convention;
(b) the treaty amongst the Nordic countries as to recognition and enforceability of judgments;
(c) the 1956 CMR Convention;
(d) the 1969 CLC Convention (and protocol of 1992);
(e) the 1980 COTIF Convention.

(b) What procedure is followed to enforce a foreign judgment (i) governed by a treaty/convention and (ii) not governed by a treaty/convention?

(i) Foreign judgment governed by treaty/convention

An application to the local competent court must be made accompanied by a true transcript of the judgment, evidence that it has been served and in the case of judgment in default, evidence that the writ of summons or similar document has been served on the defaulting party. The court may require a true translation of the documents to be submitted. The court will then consider the application and if it is allowed effect service of the decision upon the defendant.

(ii) Foreign judgment not governed by treaty/convention

Legal proceedings will have to be commenced in the ordinary manner, i.e. by issuance of a writ of summons, exchange of pleadings and ultimately a hearing. The foreign judgment will only serve as evidence although it may carry considerable weight.

(c) What about foreign arbitration awards?

Denmark has ratified the 1958 New York Convention on the recognition and enforcement of Foreign Arbitral Awards and the 1961 European Convention on International Commercial Arbitration. Arbitration awards falling within the scope of the 1958 New York Convention can be enforced on application, although the court will normally require a true translation of the award and the arbitration agreement (cf. section 2 of Order 117/1973 to the Arbitration Act).

Arbitration awards falling outside the scope of the above-mentioned convention can not be enforced in Denmark. They are, however, recognised provided they concern a matter which under Danish law can be decided by way of arbitration, and recognition would not be against *ordre public* (cf. section 1 of Order 117/1973 to the Arbitration Act). Separate legal proceedings must in this situation be commenced; cf. above under 6(a)(ii).

(d) Will proceeds of a judgment be freely exportable?

Yes.

CHAPTER 5

EGYPT

Hisham Eldib
Eldib Advocates, 2 Lumumba Street, Alexandria (21131), Egypt

1. JURISDICTION

Under the Egyptian Code of Procedure (Act 13 of 1968 as amended), Egyptian courts will accept jurisdiction in the following instances:

(a) Domicile

(i) The lawsuit is against an Egyptian national even if he has no domicile in Egypt.
(ii) The lawsuit is against a foreign subject domiciled in Egypt.
(iii) The lawsuit is directed against a non-domiciled foreign subject if he has an elected domicile in Egypt.
(iv) If one of the defendants has a domicile or residence in Egypt.

(b) Place of business

Jurisdiction is accepted if the lawsuit concerns a defendant having a place of business in Egypt.

(c) Assets located within the jurisdiction

If the claim involves an asset existing in Egypt or an obligation arising/carried out or enforceable in Egypt or bankruptcy declared therein, the courts will accept jurisdiction.

(d) Act complained of within the jurisdiction

If the subject incident (e.g. collision/salvage/general average/unlawful competition etc.) occurred in Egypt, Egypt will accept jurisdiction.

(e) Contract governed by local law

If the contract is governed by Egyptian law, Egyptian courts have jurisdiction.

(f) Conventions

There are no conventions attributing jurisdiction to Egyptian courts.

(g) Clause attributing jurisdiction

Jurisdiction will be accepted pursuant to a clause attributing jurisdiction and if the party in litigation accepts expressly or impliedly Egyptian jurisdiction.

(h) Other

Provisional or conservatory measures are available although the Egyptian court has no jurisdiction on the initial claim.

(i) Counterclaim/third-party proceedings

These will be heard if they are related to the initial claim within jurisdiction.

2. MARITIME CLAIMS

(a) Jurisdiction through arrest of a ship

There is no special jurisdiction for maritime claims based on arrest of a vessel in the jurisdiction.

(b) Specific maritime jurisdiction

Arrest of vessels is governed by the Egyptian Maritime Code promulgated by Act No. 8 of 1990 and is grounded on the claimant's right to obtain adequate security for his maritime claim.

(c) The grounds for arrest

An order (injunction) of arrest will be granted to the claimant whose claim in the face of supporting documents appears to be a good claim. It is given *in absentia* at the sole discretion of the judge and should be placed physically on the vessel, forbidding her from sailing out of the Egyptian port where she is anchored. The conservatory arrest of a vessel is given without counter-security to be put up by the claimant.

The arrested vessel is usually connected with the claim, but other vessels in the same legal or beneficial ownership can also be arrested for the subject maritime claim.

3. SERVICE OF PROCEEDINGS

Rules applying to the service of proceedings outside the jurisdiction

The Egyptian Code of Procedure as amended by Act 23 of 1992 provides for service of proceedings outside the jurisdiction which can be effected by serving the writ on the "Parquet" office (Public Prosecutor's office) to be conveyed abroad to the party concerned through diplomatic channels apart from written notice sent by registered mail with receipt.

Where the shipowner has a branch or shipping agency in Egypt, the service/notification of the writ/notice may be served on such branch or agency.

4. COSTS

(a) Court fees

The court fees for starting proceedings in respect of maritime claims are small (100 Egyptian Pounds). This will be adjusted once the claim has been decided on the merits, at the rate of 7.5% of the amount awarded, as per the judgment rendered and will be charged against the party losing the case.

(b) Lawyer's fees

Lawyers' fees are fixed in advance or after finalising of the subject matter and are borne by each party in litigation as mutually agreed.

(c) Recovery of costs from unsuccessful party

There is no recovery of costs (lawyers' fees and legal expenses) from the unsuccessful party in litigation.

(d) Security for costs

There is no security for costs either in the first instance or on appeal.

5. INTERIM ARREST

(a) For domestic proceedings or proceedings in another jurisdiction

Interim arrest, the freezing of assets and other provisional measures (e.g. sequestration/survey) are available under the Egyptian Code of Procedure to provide or establish security for domestic proceedings or claims, but not for proceedings in another jurisdiction.

(b) Criteria applying

The criteria applicable are a good subject claim and claimant's reasonable fear of losing security for the claim.

(c) Limit on jurisdictions whose proceedings are recognised for the purpose of arrests

There is no limit on jurisdictions.

(d) Counter-security

When applying for interim measures, there is no requirement for counter-security to be provided by the claimant.

(e) Can application be made ex parte?

The application is always examined *ex parte*.

(f) How quickly can an order be made?

A court order can be made within 24 hours from the time of the application.

(g) Will the order bind third parties?

The order will bind third parties who hold assets that are subject to the interim arrest/freezing order.

(h) The consequences of breach of an order

If an order is breached, the third party concerned becomes directly liable towards the claimant.

(i) Limit to types of assets

There is no limit to type of asset.

(j) What if third parties are affected?

Interim arrest is directed against the assets of the defendant/debtor and does not affect third parties as such.

(k) Other provisional measures to be ordered

Provisional measures by way of appointing surveyors may be ordered.

6. RECOGNITION OF JUDGMENTS/AWARDS

(a) Treaty/convention

There are no conventions applicable to the enforcement of judgments abroad or enforcing foreign judgments domestically.

(b) Procedures

The procedure to enforce a foreign judgment in Egypt, pursuant to Articles 296–301 of the Egyptian Code of Procedure is to obtain an *exequatur* order from the competent court through normal lawsuit proceedings, subject to the principle of reciprocity and provided that:

1. Egyptian courts had no jurisdiction of the matter and the foreign court which issued the judgment was competent according to its international rules of jurisdiction.
2. The parties of the case were validly summoned and duly represented.
3. The judgment has acquired *res judicata.*
4. The judgment does not contradict a judgment or order previously given by Egyptian courts, and does not contravene "public order".

(c) Foreign arbitral awards

The same applies to foreign arbitration awards together with the New York Convention of 10 June 1958 relating to the enforcement of foreign arbitration awards, which was adopted by Egypt in April 1959.

(d) Free exportability of proceeds

Money judgments rendered by Egyptian courts are expressed in the national currency. The equivalent amounts in foreign currency can thereafter be transferred abroad to the beneficiary through banks registered in Egypt.

CHAPTER 6

ENGLAND

David Gardner
Curtis Davis Garrard, Lancaster House, Northumberland Close, Heathrow Airport TW19 7LN

1. JURISDICTION

Introduction

England, Wales, and Berwick on Tweed (collectively "England and Wales") constitute the territorial boundaries of the English court (the Isle of Man and the Channel Islands are separate legal jurisdictions). England and Wales are party to the Brussels and Lugano Conventions (the "Jurisdiction Convention") enacted into English law by the Civil Jurisdiction and Judgments Act 1982 (the "1982 Act"). The rules allocating jurisdiction under the 1982 Act differ from those applicable at common law and reference will be made below to both.

The Jurisdiction Convention applies to civil and commercial matters; typically one party at least will be domiciled in the EU. The most significant exclusions from its ambit are insolvency proceedings, matrimonial matters, revenue, customs and administrative matters and insolvency. The common law will apply to non-EU claims.

The general grounds on which the English courts will accept jurisdiction

(a) Domicile

The 1982 Act provides, subject to the competing grounds of jurisdiction detailed below, that a defendant domiciled in a Contracting State shall, whatever his nationality, be sued in the courts of the country of his domicile. At common law if the defendant is domiciled within the jurisdiction this will usually be sufficient to give jurisdiction to the English court.

Domicile is determined as follows. An individual who (i) resides in England and (ii) the nature and circumstances of whose residence indicate he has substantial connection with England is domiciled in England. If the defendant has been resident for the last three months or more, condition (ii) is satisfied unless the contrary is proven.

A corporation has its seat in the United Kingdom if it was incorporated or formed under the law of part of the United Kingdom, and has its registered office or some other official address in the United Kingdom, or its central management or control is exercised in the United Kingdom.

(b) Place of business/residence/office

If the individual is genuinely resident in the jurisdiction this will usually be his place of domicile. A company with a place of business or office in the jurisdiction will frequently be domiciled here. In addition if the dispute arises out of the operations of a branch office this will usually be sufficient to give jurisdiction to the English courts.

(c) Assets located within the jurisdiction

The presence of assets within England and Wales does not of itself (with the exception of the special maritime jurisdiction referred to below) give jurisdiction to the English courts over substantive proceedings.

The court does have the power to grant an interim injunction (if the criteria described below are satisfied) freezing any assets within the jurisdiction, in aid of foreign proceedings.

The English court also has jurisdiction to enforce a foreign judgment against assets within England and Wales.

(d) Act complained of within the jurisdiction

Under the 1982 Act the English courts have jurisdiction in matters relating to tort, delict or quasi delict, if the harmful event occurred within England and Wales. At common law, if the claim is founded on a tort and the damage was sustained within, or resulted from an act committed within, England and Wales, the English court has jurisdiction.

(e) Contract governed by local law

Under the 1982 Act the English court has jurisdiction in matters relating to contract where England or Wales is the place of performance of the obligation in question.

At common law, the fact that the contract is governed, either expressly or by implication, by English law, will usually be sufficient to give jurisdiction to the English court.

(f) Conventions

The principal relevant convention is the Jurisdiction Convention.

(g) Clause attributing jurisdiction

Agreement of the parties made or evidenced in writing attributing jurisdiction to the English courts, gives jurisdiction to the English court under the 1982 Act. A choice of jurisdiction, either express or implied, will also usually suffice at common law.

Where the parties have agreed that the English court should have exclusive jurisdiction, the court may grant an injunction restraining proceedings brought in a foreign court in breach of that agreement.

(h) Other

The English court also has jurisdiction under the 1982 Act (insurance and certain consumer contracts are subject to special rules) over the following proceedings:

- (i) where it is seised of criminal proceedings, it has jurisdiction to hear any civil claim in damages or restitution arising from the same act;
- (ii) to hear claims against a settlor, trustee or beneficiary of a trust domiciled in England or Wales;
- (iii) in matters relating to maintenance if the maintenance creditor is domiciled here;
- (iv) in matters relating to contract, if the action can be combined with an action against the same defendant relating to rights *in rem* in immovable property, if the immovable property is situated here.

The English court will also have exclusive jurisdiction, under the 1982 Act over the following proceedings:

- (i) concerning rights *in rem* in immovable property if the property is situated here;
- (ii) proceedings whose object is the validity, nulity or dissolution of companies, legal persons or associations, if that company, person or association has its seat here;
- (iii) in proceedings which have as their object the validity of entries in public registers kept here;
- (iv) proceeding concerning certain intellectual property rights if the registration has been applied for or taken place here; and
- (v) proceedings concerned with the enforcement of an English judgment.

At common law the English courts can assume jurisdiction over the following claims:

- (i) proceedings for an injunction requiring the defendant to do or refrain from doing anything within the jurisdiction;
- (ii) proceedings where the whole subject-matter of the action is land within the jurisdiction;

(iii) proceedings in respect of debts secured on immovable property within the jurisdiction,

(iv) proceedings to execute (or for any other relief or remedy) the trusts of a written instrument which ought to be executed according to English law, and of which the person to be served with the writ is a trustee;

(v) proceedings for the administration of the estate of a person who died domiciled in England or Wales; and

(vi) probate, certain revenue claims, and proceedings under specific statutes.

(i) Counterclaim/Third-party proceedings

The English court has jurisdiction over any counterclaim arising from the same facts as those on which the original claim was based.

Under the 1982 Act, the English court, where it is seised of the main proceedings, has jurisdiction over third party proceedings unless these were instituted with the object of removing the defendant from the jurisdiction of the court which would otherwise be competent. The English court also has jurisdiction over co-defendants provided at least one of them in domiciled in England and Wales.

At common law, the English court has jurisdiction over any third party, or second or further defendant, who is a necessary and property party to proceedings in England and Wales duly served.

(j) Generally

Under the Jurisdiction Convention jurisdiction is frequently allocated on a first come first served basis. The court seised second of proceedings is required to stay its proceedings until the court seised first has declined jurisdiction.

At common law even if the plaintiff is able to establish that the proceedings fall within one of the categories in respect of which the English court can take jurisdiction, the defendant is still entitled to ask the court to decline jurisdiction on the grounds that England is not the convenient forum in which to try the case most suitably in the interest of all parties and the ends of justice.

2. MARITIME CLAIMS

(a) Jurisdiction through the arrest of a vessel

England and Wales are not party to the 1952 Arrest Convention. However many of its provisions are reflected in the Supreme Court Act 1981, which does provide a special jurisdiction to arrest ships, aircraft, and certain other categories of property both to obtain security for a claim that will be heard in another jurisdiction, and to found jurisdiction in England and Wales.

(b) Specific jurisdiction

(i) Collision actions

The provisions of the International Convention on Certain Rules concerning Civil Jurisdiction in matters of Collision are given effect by section 22 of the Supreme Court Act 1981. This restricts the exercise by the English court of jurisdiction in an action *in personam*.

(ii) Salvage

Under the 1982 Act, the English court has jurisdiction over a dispute in respect of the salvage of a cargo or freight, where the cargo or freight has been arrested in England and Wales to secure such payment or where security has been provided to avoid such an arrest.

At common law, the English court has jurisdiction to hear any claim in the nature of salvage (including any claim arising by virtue of the application, by or under section 87 of the Civil Aviation Act 1982, of the law relating to salvage of aircraft and their apparel and cargo.

(c) The grounds of arrest

These are set out in section 20(2) of the Supreme Court Act 1981.

(d) The connection between the claim and the arrested vessel

For the following claims, the right of arrest is limited to the ship, aircraft or property connected with the claim in question: (i) possession or ownership of the vessel, (ii) between co-owners as to possession, employment or earnings of that ship, (iii) a mortgage or charge on the ship and (iv) forfeiture or condemnation of a ship or of goods which are being carried or have been carried in a ship or for the restoration of a ship or any such goods after seizure or for droits of Admiralty.

The above claims, together with claims for (i) damage done by the ship, (ii) salvage, (iii) Master's and seaman's wages, (iv) Master's disbursements ("the maritime liens") permit an action to be brought against the property in question irrespective of a change in ownership.

For the remaining claims listed in section 20(2) an arrest is available against the vessel concerned and any other vessel of which the person liable *in personam* at the time the writ was issued is the beneficial owner or demise charterer. The person liable *in personam* is the owner, charterer or person in possession or control of the vessel.

An arrest can therefore be brought against a sister ship in the same legal ownership. An arrest is not however available, in the absence of fraud, against a vessel in the same beneficial ownership. The English courts will uphold the corporate veil, unless the relationship between the corporate owner and the vessel is clearly a sham or amounts to fraud or unless some other legal person can be said to be the beneficial owner.

(e) What procedural differences apply to special maritime jurisdiction?

There are a number of procedural differences between maritime and other claims. Most importantly English law draws a distinction between an action *in rem* against the vessel itself and an action *in personam* against the person liable on the claim. Generally maritime claims will be heard in the Admiralty court.

(f) What rules are there as to limitation of liability?

Under the Jurisdiction Convention, a party who will be a defendant in a maritime claim may commence proceedings for limitation of his liability in any court which would have jurisdiction over him as a defendant.

England and Wales are party to the Convention on Limitation of Liability for Maritime Claims 1976, enacted into English law by the Merchant Shipping Act 1979. Any right to limit liability may be relied upon as a defence to proceedings before the English court.

A party can also initiate its own proceedings to obtain a limitation decree, but will only be able to serve such proceedings on the defendant outside of the jurisdiction if (i) the defendant has his habitual residence or place of business in England or Wales, (ii) the cause of action arose within the inland waters of England and Wales, or within the limits of a port of England and Wales, (iii) an action arising out of the same incident or series of incidents is proceeding in the High Court or has been heard or determined there, or (iv) the defendant has submitted or agreed to submit to the jurisdiction of the High Court.

3. SERVICE OF PROCEEDINGS

If the defendant is domiciled in another Jurisdiction Convention territory, it is not necessary to obtain the leave of the English court to serve him in that country. Service must be effected in accordance with local law.

If jurisdiction is asserted under the common law, it is necessary to obtain the leave of the English court to serve him outside of the jurisdiction. Service must be effected in accordance with local law, or an applicable Convention, or through diplomatic or judicial channels.

4. COSTS

Cost implications of starting proceedings

(a) Court fees

The fees to issue a writ in the High Court (which includes the Admiralty Court) are at present £500 (for claims over £100,000). To obtain execution by the Admiralty Marshal of a warrant of arrest it is necessary to give an undertaking to meet the fees and expenses of the Admiralty Marshal; these are charged on the basis of the time and work involved.

(b) Lawyers' fees

There is no standard scale for lawyers' fees which are a matter for agreement with the client. Fees are usually calculated on an hourly basis and vary considerably. Partners in City firms generally charge £200 to £400 per hour. Contingency (no win no fee) arrangements are only permitted in very limited circumstances, principally personal injury and insolvency proceedings.

(c) Recovery of costs from the unsuccessful party

The successful party will usually be awarded his costs to be taxed if not agreed. As a guide the successful party will usually recover 60–80% of the costs he has incurred on such taxation.

(d) Security for costs

A plaintiff ordinarily resident outside the EU will commonly be required to provide security for the legal costs the defendant will incur in defending the proceedings.

Within the EU, where the plaintiff is a limited company who it appears will be unable to pay the costs of a successful defendant, he is likely to be ordered to provide security for the defendant's costs. Such security is usually provided by bank guarantee, bond or payment into court. Poverty or insolvency is not a ground for ordering an individual plaintiff to provide security for costs.

A defendant will not be ordered to provide security for costs. In deciding whether to order security for costs, the court will treat a defendant who counterclaims as a plaintiff for the purpose of the counterclaim alone.

A separate regime applies in respect of arbitration proceedings.

5. INTERIM ARREST

(a) Are interim arrest/freezing of assets/other provisional measures permitted to provide security for domestic proceedings and/or proceedings in another jurisdiction?

Strictly speaking it is not possible to arrest or freeze a defendant's assets (other than by arresting a ship or aircraft as set out above) simply in order to obtain security for a claim. The orders discussed below do not give the plaintiff any priority right to the assets frozen. They are intended to ensure the defendant has assets available to meet judgment, obtained in either domestic or foreign proceedings.

(b) What criteria apply?

An injunction freezing the defendant's assets (a "*Mareva* injunction") is available where (i) it is likely that the plaintiff will succeed in its action, (ii) it appears that the defendant has assets within the jurisdiction and (iii) it appears that the defendant may transfer or conceal the assets to defeat judgment.

(c) Is there a limit on jurisdictions whose proceedings are recognised for this purpose?

No. It is possible to bring proceedings in England and Wales to obtain a *Mareva* injunction in aid of proceedings in any foreign jurisdiction (both in and outside the EU) both before and after judgment.

(d) Is there a requirement for counter-security?

The plaintiff will usually be required to give an undertaking to meet any damages the defendant may suffer from the operation of the injunction (assuming the plaintiff is ultimately unsuccessful in his action) and an undertaking to pay any expenses an innocent third party may reasonably incur.

(e) Can applications be made ex parte?

Such applications are usually made *ex parte* and often at short notice. In urgent cases applications can be made outside of normal court hours (including evenings and weekends).

(f) How quickly can an order be made?

The order will usually be made immediately. In urgent cases the application can be prepared very quickly, even the same day on which instructions are received. The plaintiff should then serve the order on all third parties holding the defendant's assets.

(g) Will the order bind third parties?

The order binds all third parties with notice of it.

(h) What are the consequences of breach of an order?

It is a contempt of court knowingly to breach the terms of the order. Contempt is punishable by a fine or even imprisonment. A third party, with notice of the order, who assists in the disposal of the defendant's assets may also be liable to the plaintiff.

(i) Is there a limit to the types of assets affected?

No. All types of assets can be frozen including, cars, jewellery, works of art, and bank accounts. Generally the assets must be within England and Wales; exceptionally a *Mareva* injunction is available against assets worldwide.

(j) What if third parties are affected – e.g. airlines?

The court is unlikely to grant an injunction which substantially interferes with the business rights of an innocent third party. The third party can if necessary apply to the court to the vary the order.

(k) What other provisional measures may be ordered – appointment of surveyor or receiver?

The range of ancillary orders available in aid of a *Mareva* include an order requiring the defendant to disclose the extent of his assets or to attend court for examination as to his assets, orders for the discovery of documents relevant to such assets or for the administration of interrogatories designed to ascertain the whereabouts of assets, an order for the delivery up of assets belonging to the defendant, and even an order requiring the defendant to remain within the jurisdiction or to surrender his passport. The court also has jurisdiction to make an order against a third party for the disclosure of information about the defendant's assets.

A range of other interim measures, some of which can be sought in conjunction with the application for a *Mareva* injunction, are also available including:

(a) the appointment of a receiver (even prior to judgment) over the defendant's assets;
(b) an order permitting the plaintiff's representative to enter the defendant's premises and to search for documents and/or property belonging to the defendant and to preserve the same to trial (an *Anton Piller* order). This order is available *ex parte* where the plaintiff can show an extremely strong *prima facie* case that the damage, actual or potential, will be very serious, that the defendant has incriminating documents (or other things) and that there is a real possibility the defendant will destroy such documents before an order can be made *inter partes*;
(c) an order for the preservation, inspection or delivery up of property which is the subject-matter of the action, for example the delivery up of a vessel to the jurisdiction of the English courts; the court also has a discretion to order the taking of samples or the making of an experiment upon property which is the subject-matter of an action;
(d) an order for the appointment of a surveyor to inspect a vessel;
(e) an injunction requiring the defendant to do or refrain from doing any specific act; examples would include an injunction requiring the defendant to refrain from committing a particular breach of contract or tort;
(f) where the court is satisfied that if the action proceeded to trial the plaintiff would recover substantial damages from the defendant it has power to order the defendant to make an interim payment to the plaintiff.

6. RECOGNITION OF JUDGMENTS/AWARDS

(a) What treaties/conventions apply (i) to enable judgments to be enforced abroad and (ii) to enable enforcement of foreign judgments domestically?

The enforcement abroad of English court judgments will be governed by the law of the country where enforcement is sought. The enforcement of judgments within the EU is governed by the Jurisdiction Convention and the procedures will be similar to those set out below. An application to obtain the necessary certified copy of an English judgment for the purposes of such enforcement is made *ex parte* on affidavit to the High Court.

In England three principal statutory regimes govern the enforcement of foreign judgments. The 1982 Act governs the enforcement of judgments from EU countries. In addition the Administration of Justice Act 1920 (the "1920 Act") and the Foreign Judgments (Reciprocal Enforcement) Act 1933 (the "1933 Act") govern the enforcement of judgments obtained in the listed countries. The 1920 Act applies principally to judgments obtained from

Commonwealth and former Commonwealth countries, and the 1933 Act to countries such as Israel, Australia, Canada, India and Pakistan.

(b)(i) What procedure is to be followed to enforce a foreign judgment governed by a treaty/convention?

There are two aspects to the enforcement of an EU judgment (i) recognition and (ii) registration. Recognition of a judgment, within the scope of the Jurisdiction Convention, from an EU country will only be denied on the following very limited grounds (i) that recognition would be contrary to public policy, (ii) in the case of a default judgment where the defendant was not duly served in sufficient time to enable him to arrange his defence, (iii) where the judgment leads to incompatible consequences with an English judgment, (iv) where the judgment is irreconcilable with a prior non-EU judgment, and (v) where as a matter of English law the subject-matter of the judgment is not within Article 1(1).

To register the plaintiff must apply *ex parte*, such application accompanied by a copy of the EU judgment and order (together with certified translations) and evidence that the judgment has been served and is enforceable in the country of adjudication. Once registration is authorised the plaintiff is entitled to protective measures against the defendant's assets pending execution.

Enforcement under the 1920 Act and the 1933 Act is also by registration. The criteria to be satisfied to secure registration and the defences are similar to the position where no treaty is applicable set out below.

(b)(ii) What procedure is followed to enforce a foreign judgment not governed by a treaty/convention?

For a judgment to be enforceable at common law, it must be a final and conclusive judgment on the merits, for a definite sum of money, given by a competent court. The only defences are that (i) the judgment was obtained by fraud, (ii) the judgment was obtained in breach of an arbitration or choice of court clause, (iii) the judgment is contrary to natural justice, (iv) recognition would be contrary to public policy or (v) the judgment is inconsistent with a prior English judgment.

The procedure for enforcement is to sue on the debt created by the foreign judgment. It is frequently possible to obtain summary judgment on such proceedings.

(c) Foreign arbitration awards

The Arbitration Act 1996 enables any arbitration award obtained pursuant to the New York Convention to be enforced in England, by leave of the court, in the same manner as a judgment or order of the English court to the same effect.

The original duly authenticated award and arbitration agreement (or certified copies thereof) together with certified translations if necessary are required.

(d) Will the proceeds of a judgment be freely exportable?

With very minor exceptions there are no limitations on the exporting of the proceeds of judgment.

CHAPTER 7

FINLAND

Anna-Karin Mickwitz
Bützow & Co, P.O. Box 121, Pohjoisesplanadi 21A, 001 01 Helsinki, Finland

1. JURISDICTION

The general rules on jurisdiction are to be found in Chapter 10 of the Procedural Code. With a few exceptions, the rules of the Procedural Code aim at regulating the competence of the courts on a national level and not at deciding when a Finnish court can accept jurisdiction in a dispute with an international dimension. However, the most important rules on jurisdiction (e.g. domicile), which at the same time are the most general of their nature, are clearly considered to apply also in international disputes. Also many of the other provisions on jurisdiction in the Procedural Code provide guidelines for jurisdiction in an international dispute. It can be said that where a dispute has such a close connection to a certain court district that the court in question would be competent on a national level, it is likely that there is such a general connection to Finland that a Finnish court should have international jurisdiction as well. The provisions which are more particular of their nature will, however, not be treated hereunder.

(a) Domicile

The general rule on jurisdiction, which is to be found in Article 1 of Chapter 10 of the Procedural Code, is that the court of the place where the defendant is domiciled is competent.

(b) Registered place of business

Even though Article 1 of Chapter 10 of the Procedural Code explicitly applies only to persons the same principle applies to legal bodies. In regard to companies, associations and foundations (as defendant in the proceedings) the competent court is the court at the place where the body has its registered place of business.

(c) Assets located within the jurisdiction

When the defendant is not domiciled in Finland, Article 1 of Chapter 10 of the Procedural Code contains a rule which explicitly takes into account that the proceedings might have connections abroad. In regard to defendants, either persons or legal bodies, who are not domiciled or which do not have their registered place of business in Finland, the court of the place where the person or body has assets is competent. Jurisdiction based on the place where the defendant's assets are located has been considered possible in matters regarding claims and in matters regarding the law of property in relation to those assets.

It should be mentioned that jurisdiction cannot be based on the above-mentioned rule in a situation where the Convention on Jurisdiction and the Enforcement of Judgments in Civil and Commercial Matters done at Lugano on 16 September 1988 (the Lugano Convention) is applicable (see Article 3 of the Convention).

If the dispute concerns the right of ownership, or the use etc. of real estate, only the court of the place where the real estate is located is competent (*forum rei sitae*).

(d) Act complained of within the jurisdiction

In general, jurisdiction is not conferred to a court on the basis of the act complained of. However, if the act complained of relates to real estate, e.g. damage to or illegal use of real estate, the rule of *forum rei sitae* applies. Otherwise jurisdiction of the court at the place where the act complained of took place is as a main rule relevant only in regard to criminal matters.

(e) Contract governed by local law

According to Finnish law jurisdiction cannot be based purely on the fact that the contract which is the basis of the claim is governed by Finnish law.

(f) Conventions

Finland ratified the Convention on Jurisdiction and the Enforcement of Judgments in Civil and Commercial Matters done at Lugano on 16 September 1988, the so-called Lugano Convention, in April 1993, and it entered into force in Finland on 1 July 1993.

The Convention applies in civil and commercial matters whatever the nature of the court or tribunal. A requirement for the applicability of the Convention is naturally also that the matter before the court has some kind of connection to another Contracting State. Since the Convention covers almost all civil actions it has a great impact.

The general rule is that a person domiciled in a Contracting State shall, whatever his nationality, be sued in the courts of that state. The Convention does, however, provide for a number of alternative and additional fora in, for instance, matters related to contract, tort, insurance, consumer contracts, etc.

The Convention also contains a provision on jurisdiction clauses. The provision in the Convention is applicable if one of the parties to the agreement is domiciled in a Contracting State. The prorogation cannot, however, waive the mandatory provisions on jurisdiction of the Convention (e.g. in matters relating to insurance and to consumer contracts).

(g) Clause attributing jurisdiction

According to Article 11 of Chapter 10 of the Procedural Code it is possible to make an agreement deciding which court shall have jurisdiction. The agreement shall be made in writing and the court and the matter shall be stated clearly. As mentioned above the provisions of the Procedural Code are intended for national situations. It is, however, established that agreements attributing jurisdiction can be used also in international situations. In an international matter it is also possible to give jurisdiction to Finnish courts in general without mentioning a specific court.

It is, however, not possible to agree to avoid jurisdiction of a court which according to the rules on international exclusive jurisdiction is competent (e.g. *forum rei sitae*). Neither is it possible to grant jurisdiction to a court which according to the rules on exclusive jurisdiction would not be competent. In the literature the view has been expressed that an agreement on jurisdiction only can be made regarding disputes of a dispositive nature (i.e. disputes where a settlement is allowed).

An agreement on jurisdiction can be made either in regard to a future dispute arising from a particular legal relationship (e.g. as a jurisdiction clause in a contract) or after the specific dispute has arisen. In the literature it has been written that an additional requirement for, jurisdiction based on a jurisdiction clause is that the dispute should have at least some connection to Finland.

If a claim is brought to a Finnish court despite an agreement attributing the jurisdiction to a foreign court, the Finnish court will not dismiss the case of its own motion. The agreement must be invoked by the defendant. It should, however, be mentioned that there are cases where an agreement conferring jurisdiction to a foreign court has been declared unfair when the agreement has denied the weaker party of the contract (an employee or a consumer) the right which he would otherwise have had to instigate proceedings in a Finnish court.

It should be mentioned that the Lugano Convention contains its own rules on jurisdiction clauses.

(h) Other

One of the rules in Article 1 of Chapter 10 of the Procedural Code which explicitly applies in an international situation has not been mentioned above. In regard to a defendant which is not domiciled in Finland, the court at the place where he is found is competent. The rule is, however, most likely of minor practical importance.

(i) Counterclaim/third-party proceedings

The proper court for a counterclaim is the court of the original claim. The situation is the same in third-party proceedings, i.e. when a third party who is not an original party to the proceedings wishes to intervene in the dispute or when one of the parties wishes to involve a third party in the proceedings in order to secure his right of redress or right to damages the court seised with the original dispute is competent.

2. MARITIME CLAIMS

(a), (b) Special jurisdiction for maritime claims

The Maritime Act of 1994 contains a number of provisions on jurisdiction for maritime claims. The competent courts for maritime claims are the maritime courts.

The jurisdiction for maritime claims differs according to the types of claims. The main rule is that for claims where the Maritime Act is applicable, jurisdiction rests with the maritime court of the district where the defendant is domiciled or where he is permanently engaged in business or where the vessel is. If security is given to the authorities in order to prevent an arrest or other security measures in regard to the vessel, the maritime court of the place where the security is given is also competent. It should be noted that the provision cannot be relied upon in its entirety in a situation where the Lugano Convention is applicable.

When a claim concerns liability based on a contract of transportation of general cargo the competence lies only with the maritime court of the place:

- where the defendant has his main office or his habitual residence;
- where the transport contract was entered into, provided that the defendant has a place of business, a branch or a representative who arranged the conclusion of the contract at that place;
- where the contracted port of loading or the contracted or actual port of discharge is; or
- stated in the contract.

If the vessel which transported the cargo is arrested or is subjected to other security measures the maritime court of the place where such measures took place is also competent. If a security is given to the authorities to prevent such measures the maritime court of the place where the security is given is competent, too. The court last mentioned is competent even if the security is released.

Caution is required also in regard to this provision if the Lugano Convention is applicable. The provision is based on the so-called Hamburg Rules, even if those rules have not been ratified by Finland. This means that the provision of the Maritime Act, to the extent that it is not based on a binding international convention, will be overruled by the Lugano Convention.

There is also a special provision on jurisdiction for claims regarding contracts on transport of passengers and on jurisdiction in maritime criminal matters. These will, however, not be treated here.

Jurisdiction clauses are in principle allowed in maritime matters. However, when the claim is based on a contract on the transportation of general cargo or of passengers some restrictions as to the freedom to choose the competent court apply. Should one of the parties to the contract be domiciled in a state where the Lugano Convention applies, the Convention's provisions regarding prorogation of jurisdiction would apply and set aside the restrictions of the Maritime Act.

Of interest too is the fact that according to the Maritime Act maritime insurance claims fall under the jurisdiction of the General Adjuster. In Finland the General Adjuster has legal status, and there is only one General Adjuster appointed. The General Adjuster is also the only competent authority when average adjustment takes place in Finland.

When a maritime declaration is to be given the maritime court for the district where the incident took place or where the vessel or the master first arrived is competent.

(c) Grounds for arrest

The Finnish legislation on the arrest of vessels is based on the International Convention for the Unification of Certain Rules relating to the Arrest of Seagoing Ships of 1952, which entered into force in Finland in June 1996. The rules of the Convention have been implemented into Chapter 4 of the Maritime Act. The provisions of the Maritime Act are complemented by the general rules on security measures in the Procedural Code and the Execution Act. It could be of interest to mention that the Agreement with the Soviet Union Regarding the Avoidance of the Arrest of Vessels of 1985 was abolished at the beginning of June 1997.

The provisions on arrest in Chapter 4 of the Maritime Act do not apply to purely domestic situations, i.e. when the vessel is Finnish and the creditor is domiciled or has his principal place of business in Finland. The reason for this is that the provisions in Chapter 4 of the Maritime Act are somewhat more restricted than the Finnish general rules on security measures, wherefore it is considered that these restrictions should not apply in a purely national situation. Chapter 4 does not restrict the right of the authorities to arrest or detain a vessel for unpaid taxes or official charges. The provisions of Chapter 4 are also applicable only to the arrest of a vessel, and not, for example, to the arrest of cargo.

The general conditions for an arrest or other security measures are to be found in Chapter 7 of the Procedural Code. According to Article 1 of the said Chapter the applicant shall show that:

1. it is probable (*prima facie* evidence) that he has a claim which the defendant can be ordered to pay by a court decision or arbitral award enforceable in Finland or that he has a better right to the vessel than the defendant which right can be established by such a decision; and
2. there is a risk that the defendant will hide, destroy or dispose of his property or take any other measures which endanger the applicant's claim or right.

As for the first requirement, reference is made to item 6 hereunder in regard to judgments enforceable in Finland.

The applicant does not have to give any proof of the second requirement if his claim is secured by a so-called maritime lien in the vessel. Chapter 3 of the Maritime Act sets out the claims that enjoy a maritime lien (see under 2(d)). However, there is in general no difficulty to fulfil the second requirement when the arrest concerns a vessel.

The defendant has a right to file an answer to the applicant's application. According to Article 5 of Chapter 7 of the Procedural Code, however, the applicant can apply for a direct so-called interim arrest (*ex parte*), if the aim of the arrest is endangered when the defendant is heard.

The specific requirements for the arrest of a vessel are set out in Articles 3 and 4 of Chapter 4 of the Maritime Act. In addition to the requirements mentioned above, it is required that the claim for which the arrest is applied is a so-called maritime claim. The maritime claims are exhaustively listed in Article 4 which corresponds to Article 1 of the Arrest Convention.

When the applicant has obtained the arrest order he shall have it enforced by the bailiff. The applicant must provide counter-security for any loss or damage which the defendant may suffer as a result of the arrest of the vessel. The counter-security is given to the bailiff who enforces the arrest. The amount and form of the security is decided by the bailiff. In general the bailiff will require a bank guarantee issued by a Finnish bank combined with an unlimited security by a Finnish individual or company.

In order to keep the arrest in force the applicant must institute legal proceedings against the defendant within one month from the date of the arrest order.

It should be mentioned that the establishment of a limitation fund can prevent an arrest.

(d) Connection between claim and vessel or claim and owner

The arrest can be obtained and enforced against the particular vessel in respect of which the maritime claim arose. The arrest can also be enforced against any other vessel which is owned by the person who was, at the time when the claim arose, the owner of the particular ship (sister ships). The "same ownership", however, requires that the ownership of the vessel is to all parts vested with the same person or entity.

If someone other than the owner of the vessel is liable in respect of a maritime claim relating to a particular vessel, the arrest can be enforced either against the particular vessel or against any other vessel owned by the liable party. This rule is, however, very much restricted as described in the last paragraph hereunder.

It is evident that an arrest to secure the right of ownership or possession of a vessel can be enforced only against the vessel in respect of which the claim arose.

In order to secure national principles in relation to security measures Article 5 of Chapter 4 of the Maritime Act contains a provision according to which an arrest can be obtained and enforced only when measures of enforcement can be used against the vessel in Finland. Since the rule under Finnish law is that only property of the defendant can be used to secure a claim against the defendant, an arrest against a vessel in a situation where the party liable for the maritime claim is somebody other than the owner of the vessel is actually enforceable only if the maritime claim also gives the right to a so-called maritime lien. According to Article 2 of Chapter 3 of the Maritime Act the claims giving the right to a maritime lien are:

- unpaid salary or other emoluments to the master or other persons employed on board;
- port-, canal- and other waterway charges or pilotage charges;
- compensation for personal injury directly connected to the use of the vessel;
- compensation for material damage directly connected to the use of the vessel provided that the claim is not based on contract;
- salvage, compensation for wreck removal and general average contributions.

(e) Procedural differences in regard to maritime jurisdiction

According to Chapter 21 of the Maritime Act a more extensive exchange of written submissions before the actual hearing than in ordinary proceedings shall take place. In maritime matters two experts in navigation and shipping assist the court.

As mentioned in item 2(a) and (b) above marine insurance claims and general average are dealt with by the General Adjuster. In a case decided by the General Adjuster appeal is made to the Helsinki District Court and from there, without any leave to appeal, directly to the Supreme Court.

(f) Jurisdictional rules as to limitation of liability

The Lugano Convention contains a provision, Article 6a, according to which the court which has jurisdiction in actions relating to liability arising from the use or operation of a ship by virtue of the Convention, also has jurisdiction over claims for limitation of such liability.

The Finnish Maritime Act does not contain a general provision regarding limitation of liability like Article 6a of the Lugano Convention. The provisions regarding jurisdiction in maritime claims do, however, apply also to cases regarding limitation of liability. A separate claim regarding limitation of liability would hardly be of any interest. Limitation of liability will be used as a defence when a claim regarding liability is raised.

Where the limitation of liability is to take place through a global limitation fund special provisions are found in Chapters 9 (general limitation fund), 10 (oil pollution) and 12 (procedural rules) of the Maritime Act. According to Chapter 9 a global limitation fund can be established when a claim for which a limitation can be applied has been raised or an application for arrest or for other legal measures has been made. The fund shall be established at the maritime court where the above-mentioned applications have been made. This means that the jurisdictional issue in regard to the fund is linked to the provisions on jurisdiction over maritime claims in Chapter 21 of the Maritime Act. The possibility to establish a limitation fund is thus dependent on the claims regarding liability.

However, when a global limitation fund is established for claims based on oil pollution, the fund shall be established at the court where a claim has been raised or can be raised. According to Article 3a of Chapter 21 of the Maritime Act, Helsinki District Court is the maritime court which has jurisdiction over claims based on oil pollution, if jurisdiction according to the said Article is vested with the Finnish courts.

3. SERVICE OF PROCEEDINGS

According to Chapter 11 of the Procedural Code, the court shall take care of the service of proceedings unless the plaintiff has asked the court to give him the right to take care of the service and the court finds it justified. Such an application is often made by the plaintiff and accepted by the court when the service is to take place abroad, in order to get the writ served on the defendant more rapidly.

If the court takes care of the service of a writ outside the jurisdiction, it will be done either by mail (which is also the main rule when service is done domestically) if it is allowed by the conventions mentioned hereafter, or through diplomatic channels in accordance with the Hague Convention of 1954, or according to the rules of the Hague Convention of 1965.

If the plaintiff himself wishes to effect the service he must, of course, have the documents translated into the language of the defendant and then serve them in accordance with the rules of the state where the service takes place. For practical reasons it is, however, advisable to effect service in such a way that both the local requirements and the Finnish requirements are fulfilled, when service to a court in Finland is effected in another state.

4. COSTS

(a) Court fees

In Finland there is no actual court fee. The only fee charged by the court is a charge for the minutes containing the judgment, which fee is negligible.

(b) Lawyer's fees

There is no fixed scale of fees to be applied. The fees are based on agreement between the lawyer and the client. Generally the fee is based on the time spent on the case.

According to the rules of the Finnish Bar Association contingency fees are allowed. Contingency fees are, however, rarely used by Finnish lawyers.

The Council of the Bars and Law Societies of the European Community (CCBE) has set out its own ethical rules which are to be applied in cross-border situations. According to these rules contingency fees are not allowed. The recommendation of the Finnish Bar Association thus is that contingency fees should not be applied to clients from the EU.

(c) Recovery of costs from unsuccessful party

The party successful in the proceedings can recover his legal expenses in full from the losing party. If both parties are partly successful they will suffer their own legal expenses.

(d) Security for costs

No security for costs is required.

5. INTERIM ARREST

(a) Measures permitted to provide security for domestic proceedings and proceedings in another jurisdiction

According to Chapter 7 of the Procedural Code a court can give an arrest order (seizure) in order to secure payment of a claim or in order to safeguard the applicant's so-called better right (e.g. of ownership or possession) to the property in question. The court can also order a variety of other measures in order to safeguard any other right of the applicant than the right of payment or proprietary/possessory rights. The court can:

- prohibit the defendant from taking specified measures or order him to take specified measures under the penalty of a fine;
- allow the applicant to take specified measures;
- order the property of the defendant to be taken into the possession and administration of a custodian;
- decide on other measures necessary to safeguard the rights of the applicant.

(b), (c) Criteria and limits on jurisdiction

As explained above in item 2(c) the general conditions for an arrest or other security measures are that the applicant can show:

1. *prima facie* evidence of a claim based on the right invoked (claim of payment, a so-called better right or any other right) and that the right of payment, the proprietary right or any other right can be established by a court decision or arbitral award enforceable in Finland; and
2. that there is a risk that the defendant will hide, destroy or dispose of his property or take any other measures which endanger the applicant's claim or right.

As for the first requirement reference is made to item 6 hereunder in regard to judgments enforceable in Finland. Even if Finnish law accepts that jurisdiction in the substance of the matter is abroad (as long as the judgment or award is enforceable in Finland) it should be mentioned that Article 24 of the Lugano Convention explicitly states that a plaintiff can apply for provisional, including protective, measures available in the Contracting State where the application is made, even if according to the Convention the courts of another Contracting State have jurisdiction as to the substance of the matter.

(d) Counter-security

According to Article 16 in Chapter 7 of the Execution Act an order regarding security measures cannot be enforced unless the applicant provides counter-security for any loss or damage which the defendant might suffer as a result of the measures. According to Article 7 of Chapter 7 of the Procedural Code the applicant for the security measures can, however, apply to the court that he be released from the obligation to provide counter-security. The condition for such a release is that the court finds that the applicant is unable to provide counter-security and that his claim is well-founded.

It is the bailiff enforcing the arrest who decides the amount of the security and what security is acceptable in each case. In general the only security accepted are bank guarantees by Finnish banks and guarantees given by Finnish individuals.

(e) Applications ex parte

According to Article 5 of Chapter 7 of the Procedural Code an application regarding security measures must not be accepted unless the defendant has been heard in the matter. It is, however, possible to get a so-called interim decision regarding a security measure *ex parte*, if it is likely that the whole purpose of the measure is at risk should the defendant be heard.

When the interim decision has been enforced and notified to the other party the applicant must, after a certain period of time, apply to the court for a final decision. When giving its final decision the court is not bound by its own interim decision. This means that in the light of the defendant's answer, which at this stage most likely has been submitted, the court may find that the conditions for a security measure are not fulfilled.

(f) How quickly can an order be made?

According to Article 7 of the Procedural Code an application for security measures should be dealt with urgently. This means that the decision, depending on the situation, should be given the very same day as the application is made, or at least within the next two working days.

In general the authorities involved, i.e. the court and the bailiff, are co-operative in matters regarding security measures. Therefore it should be possible to obtain an interim decision and get it enforced in one or two days, provided, of course, that the documentation and the counter-security are in order.

(g) Will the order bind third parties?

Yes.

(h) What are the consequences of breach of an order?

The Penal Code contains provisions according to which wilful breach of a security order is criminalised. Depending on the type of situation the penalty can at its maximum be either six months' or three months' imprisonment.

(i) Types of assets

In principle all types of assets can be the object of security measures, i.e. both account balances and physical assets. According to Article 5 of Chapter 7 of the Execution Act, assets which cannot be subject to execution cannot be subject to security measures either. Specific assets which cannot be subject to execution are personal belongings such as clothes and necessary furniture. It is worth mentioning, however, that of an individual's salary only one-third can be subject to execution. The same applies to pensions and certain types of social security payments.

According to a specific Act, aircraft cannot be subject to security measures. This applies *inter alia* to aircraft owned by the Finnish state or any other state and which are used only for state purposes and to aircraft in regular traffic and to aircraft in passenger traffic when the aircraft is ready to take off.

(j) What if third parties are affected?

An arrest can, of course, affect the rights of third parties—i.e. parties other than the owners of property under arrest or the applicant. A solution to a situation where the rights of a third party are affected can naturally be found amicably through co-operation. It should, however, be mentioned that a general principle expressed in the legislation regarding enforcement and executionary measures is that the rights of a third party should not be violated. For example, when a vessel is arrested the arrest cannot cover the cargo on board belonging to a third party. Thus, the third party is allowed to discharge the cargo (at his own expense). Should anyone interfere with the third party's right to discharge his property it most likely would be possible for him to apply for one of the measures mentioned under item 5(a) above.

(k) Other provisional measures

As mentioned above in item 5(a) the court can order the property of the defendant to be taken into the possession and administration of a custodian.

6. RECOGNITION OF JUDGMENTS/AWARDS

(a) Conventions which apply to enable judgments (i) to be enforced abroad and (ii) to enable enforcement of foreign judgments domestically

Since the conventions regarding enforcement of judgments which Finland has ratified are multilateral, i.e. work in both directions, enforcement of Finnish judgments abroad and enforcement of foreign judgments in Finland will not be dealt with separately.

As mentioned in item 1(f) above Finland has ratified the Convention on Jurisdiction and the Enforcement of Judgments in Civil and Commercial Matters done at Lugano on 16 September 1988, the so called Lugano Convention, in April 1993, and it entered into force in Finland on 1 July 1993. The Convention is a so called double convention which regulates jurisdiction as well as enforcement. The Convention applies in civil and commercial matters, however not to *inter alia* the status or legal capacity of natural persons, bankruptcy, social security or arbitration.

According to Article 55 of the Lugano Convention, the Convention supersedes the conventions mentioned in the Article, to the extent that the fields of application of the Lugano Convention and the other conventions overlap. This means that the Convention on Recognition and Enforcement of Nordic Judgments regarding Civil Matters of 1977 (Finland, Sweden, Norway, Denmark and Iceland) is applicable between the Contracting States only in the few situations where the Lugano Convention is not applicable.

There is also legislation based on international conventions and conventions between the Nordic countries regarding enforcement of certain decisions in family matters (adoption, paternity, maintenance) and a convention between the Nordic countries regarding certain decisions on bankruptcy and receivership. These conventions apply in full, since they fall outside the scope of the Lugano Convention.

(b) Procedure followed

(i) To enforce a foreign judgment governed by a treaty/convention

Since the other conventions regarding the enforcement of judgments are quite limited in scope the procedure according to the Lugano Convention only will be described briefly.

A judgment given outside the jurisdiction but in a Contracting State shall be recognised without any special procedure. In order to get the judgment enforced an application for the declaration of enforceability shall be made to the court of first instance of the district where the defendant (i.e. the party against whom enforcement is sought) is domiciled. The court applied to shall give its decision without delay. After the applicant has served the decision to the defendant, the defendant can appeal against the decision within one month. Within the time for appeal no measures of enforcement may be taken. When the decision regarding enforceability has become final the bailiff will enforce the judgment on application by the applicant.

Regarding the necessary documentation reference is made to Articles 46–49 of the Lugano Convention.

(ii) To enforce a foreign judgment not governed by a treaty/convention

According to Finnish law the main rule is that a foreign judgment is not recognised or enforced in Finland unless provided otherwise in the legislation (conventions, etc.). Thus a foreign judgment cannot be enforced in Finland unless the judgment is recognised and enforceable according to either convention-based or purely national legislation. A foreign judgment can, however, be given some effect in a Finnish court, for instance as evidence of the contents of foreign legislation.

(c) Foreign arbitration awards

Finland is a party to the 1958 New York Convention on the Recognition and Enforcement of Foreign Arbitral Awards.

(d) Exportability of proceeds of a judgment

The proceeds of a judgment are freely exportable.

7. OTHER REMARKS

Since it is of importance especially when considering the effect of Articles 21–23 (*lis pendens*) of the Lugano Convention it should be mentioned that according to Article 1 of Chapter 3 of the Procedural Code a court is seised with a matter when the application for a writ is handed in to the court.

CHAPTER 8

FRANCE

Béatrice Favarel-Veidig
Eurolegal, 77 Cours Pierre Puget, 13006 Marseille, France

1. JURISDICTION

The rules of jurisdiction are governed by the French Civil Code (Arts. 14 and 15) and the New Code of Civil Proceedings (hereinafter "NCCP") (Arts. 42 and 46).

France is a civil law country as opposed to a common law country.

(a) Domicile

Based on Article 42 of the NCCP the court of the defendant's domicile or of the place of a company's registered office has jurisdiction. Failing a domicile or personal address (where a private person is concerned) the court of the residence of such person has jurisdiction, and failing residence any other court which otherwise has jurisdiction.

In international matters one can elect the domicile of the office of one's lawyer, whereafter the court of the place where the lawyer's office is situated has jurisdiction.

(b) Place of business

Under French law there is no jurisdiction for the court of the place of an agency or non-head office of a company.

(c) Assets located within jurisdiction

In the case of real estate, the court where the real estate is situated has jurisdiction (Art. 44 NCCP).

For alimony and similar claims, the court of the plaintiff's domicile has jurisdiction (Art. 46 NCCP).

For the validation of an arrest of assets the court of the defendant's domicile has jurisdiction.

(d) Act complained of within the jurisdiction

The court of the place where a tort has been committed, or the court of the place where the damage occurred, has jurisdiction (Art. 46 NCCP).

(e) Contract governed by local law

The fact that local law governs a contract does not provide jurisdiction under French law.

(f) Conventions

France is a party to the Brussels Convention on Jurisdiction and Enforcement of Judgments 1968. The Convention overrides rules of national law.

(g) Clause attributing jurisdiction

Where the Brussels Convention applies, Article 17 sets out the rules for the validity of clauses attributing jurisdiction. Based on this article the parties may agree to designate a specific, exclusive forum, provided that such choice has been put in writing or has been confirmed in writing, or is in a form in accordance with the customs of the parties, or, in respect of international business matters, has been concluded in a manner which is common in the particular trade.

In French law this clause is known as *prorogation de compétence.*

French courts interpret Article 17 strictly and formally. Where a bill of lading is concerned, such clause will only be considered valid when it has been concluded at the time of concluding the contract of carriage. In order for the clause to be valid and binding upon a consignee (not being the shipper), the consignee must have accepted the contract by separate and independent documents when receiving the goods.

The mere fact that a bill of lading contains a jurisdiction clause is also not per se binding on the shipper, who may give evidence that no agreement has been reached in the above-mentioned manner.

Where the Convention is not applicable, the same strict rules apply.

(h) Other

(i) Nationality

French courts will assume jurisdiction with respect to contracts between a French national and a foreigner (Art. 14 NCCP). French courts will accept jurisdiction for claims under a contract against a French national, whether the agreement has been concluded within or outside France.

(ii) Sale of goods

In the case of sale of goods, the court of the place of the delivery of the goods has jurisdiction.

(iii) Contractual obligations

The court of the place where contractual obligations are to be performed has jurisdiction.

(i) Counterclaim/third-party proceedings

Where several defendants are involved, the court of the domicile of any one of the defendants has jurisdiction to hear the claim against all the defendants.

In the case of third-party proceedings, where an *appel en garantie* is issued by the defendant to be indemnified should the claimant succeed it is not possible for the third party to dismiss the clause attributing jurisdiction (Art. 17 of the Brussels Convention) concluded between the claimant and defendant. The third party must accept the jurisdiction.

2. MARITIME CLAIMS

(a) Special jurisdiction for maritime claims based on arrest of a vessel

There is no jurisdiction in France based on *forum arresti* (cf. Supreme Court, 17 January 1995).

(b) Specific

There is no special jurisdiction based on, for instance, the place of loading, collision or salvage. The claimant presents a petition to the president of the court where the vessel is anchored to obtain an order authorising arrest of the vessel.

(c) Grounds for arrest

For arrest of vessels under domestic law it will be sufficient, on the basis of the Law of 3 January 1967 and Article 27 of the Decree of 27 October 1967, to detain a ship if the claim appears serious and justified. This order is very easy to obtain.

For international arrest the petition is presented on the basis of the 1952 Brussels Convention on the Arrest of Ships. Article 1 requires a maritime claim arising out of one of the 17 causes provided for in the Convention.

The link between the claim and the vessel is governed by Article 3(1) and (2) of the Brussels Convention 1952.

(d) Connection between claim and vessel

The claim must be linked with the vessel arrested, but if it is a general claim against the shipowner any one of his vessels may be arrested.

If the shipowner decides to challenge the order for arrest, he must take legal action before the emergency judge of the Commercial Court to obtain release of the vessel.

It is possible to plead the day after the arrest and to obtain a special hearing before the president of the court without a special authorisation.

Then the magistrate will serve the court's decision the day after the pleadings ordering the release of the ship if the arrest is not justified, or, if it is, requesting a bank guarantee from the debtor.

(e) Procedural differences applying to special maritime jurisdiction

While there is no special maritime jurisdiction, there is a special Maritime Division in the commercial courts situated in ports (e.g. Marseilles, Dunkerque, Rouen, Le Havre). The judges of these courts are experienced in maritime matters.

The same procedural rules are applicable, except for auction sale of vessels and mortgages which come under a specific regime.

In contrast to other branches of commercial law, it is possible to obtain a specially urgent hearing for air and shipping matters without judicial authorisation from the Commercial Court.

It is also possible to obtain, after the arrest of a ship, an order from the Civil Court (Tribunal de Grande Instance) authorising the ship to depart port for a stipulated period against payment of a guarantee fixed by the judge, who will decide the amount according to the amount of the claim.

(f) Jurisdiction rules as to limitation of liability

There is no special court to settle this question. The Commercial Court is competent to settle the limitation of liability for maritime claims (London Limitation of Liability Convention 1976).

3. SERVICE OF PROCEEDINGS

France is a party to The Hague Convention 1965 on the service and notification abroad of judicial and extrajudicial documents in civil and commercial matters.

4. COSTS

(a) Court fees

Courts fees are 350 francs maximum to register a claim before the competent court.

Bailiffs' fees depend on the geographical location of the defendant. Typical fees could be 2,000 francs for arrest of the vessel and 500 francs for service of the writ of summons.

(b) Lawyers' fees

Lawyers' fees are generally calculated on the basis of an hourly rate of 1,000 to 1,200 francs for maritime and commercial claims.

(c) Recovery of costs from unsuccessful party

These will be compensated by an order in the court's judgment. The court will order a lump sum payment (usually very low) (Art. 700 NCP).

(d) Security for costs

There is no security for costs unless the claim concerns a secured claim (e.g. a lien on the vessel).

5. INTERIM ARREST

Interim arrest and provisional remedies are provided for by the Law of 9 July 1991 and its Decree of 31 July 1992.

(a) Are interim arrest/freezing of assets/other provisional measures permitted to provide security for domestic proceedings and/or proceedings in another jurisdiction?

(i) Garnishment

The *saisie-arrêt* (enforcement of a judgment against intangibles) allows all or any creditors, holding an enforceable judgment, to seize the assets of his debtor in the hands of a third party. *Saisie-arrêt* may be based on any money claim, whether due or liquidated. This is a provisional remedy as well as a means of execution.

Since 1991, the *saisie-arrêt* has been superseded by another remedy called *saisie-attribution* or garnishment.

The procedure is similar with three persons involved:

— a creditor (garnishor)
— a third party
— a debtor (garnishee).

It is now essential for the claimant to hold an enforceable judgment in order to seize the assets of his debtor in the hands of a third party.

The third party shall declare to the bailiff the amount of sums due or belonging to the debtor. After the garnishment the sums are frozen and unavailable to the debtor. The garnishee debtor has one month in which to challenge the measure.

If the debtor fails to challenge, or if his challenge is overruled, the garnished debt must be paid to the garnishing creditor.

(ii) Apprehension arrest

The apprehension arrest (*saisie-apprehension*) is applicable to all movable property by virtue of an enforceable title. Any creditor may seize effects or movable property in the hands of a third party or held by the debtor, except aircraft or assets placed in a strongbox.

This proceeding will be served by the execution judge of the Civil Court of the debtor's domicile.

(b) What criteria apply to this?

The claim must be certain, liquid and due.

(c) Is there a limit on jurisdictions whose proceedings are recognised for this purpose?

The creditor must have an enforceable judgment or a letter of credit to seize any assets and proceed to execution (levy procedure).

However, in cases of emergency the creditor may be authorised by the judge to obtain a provisional seizure of the assets of the debtor, without any previous order, if his claim seems to be reasonable and justified and when assets are in danger of disappearing.

(d) Is there a requirement for counter-security?

There is no special requirement for counter-security.

(e) Can applications be made ex parte?

Under French law, an *ex parte* order is a provisional decision rendered in a case where the claimant is not required to call the opposing party (Art. 493 Code of Civil Procedure).

The *ex parte* order is issued by the president of the Civil Court for civil matters or the Commercial Court for commercial matters. The president of the court may order all types of urgent measures and injunctions where the circumstances require that they not be contested.

(f) How quickly can an order be made?

The order can be notified and executed on the same day.

A compulsory proceeding upon the merits will follow one month after. The order becomes null and void after one month if it is not carried out.

(g) Will the order bind third parties?

The order will bind a third party in the case of a garnishment *saisie-attribution* or an apprehension arrest (see section 5 above).

After the claimant has obtained the order, the proceedings between the creditor and the debtor shall be notified by a bailiff eight days afterwards to the third party, which is generally a bank.

(h) What are the consequences of breach of an order?

The breach of an order by a debtor by destroying or diverting the assets is an offence and carries a penalty of up to three years imprisonment and a fine of 2,500 francs (Art. 314–5 New Criminal Code).

(i) Is there a limit to types of asset?

Normally, if the claim is justified, there is no limit on the assets if they have a sufficient link with the claim. However, some property cannot be seized:

- property which the law declares exempt from seizure;
- movable property necessary to the life and work of the garnishee and his family;
- credits, cash and allowances for maintenance;
- disposable property declared exempt from seizure by a testator.

(j) What if third parties are affected?

If a third party suffers any prejudice by the arrest, it will be possible to sue either the creditor or the debtor for damages in the proceedings on the merits that take place one month later.

(k) What other provisional measures may be ordered?

Generally, all types of provisional measures may be requested from the president of the court if the case is urgent and justified.

To complete the evidence it is also possible to be authorised to appoint:

- — a receiver or broker to sell goods if they are abandoned at the port;
- — a technical surveyor to check the general or particular average and explain its origin, causes, value of damages supported, accountancy, etc.

The surveyor will never be authorised to give a legal opinion about liabilities, only a technical opinion.

Emergency proceeding for provisional measure of payment

To obtain payment of his claim, if it is unquestionable, the creditor may issue a proceeding against the debtor through a writ of summons before the *juge des référés*. He will not be allowed to sue for damages before this judge since it is a summary proceeding permitting the president to render a provisional decision on issues whose adjudication cannot, without injury, admit delay.

This proceeding is authorised even if there is an arbitration clause, if the arbitrators have not yet been appointed.

6. RECOGNITION OF JUDGMENTS/AWARDS

(a) What treaties/conventions apply (i) to enable judgments to be enforced abroad and (ii) to enable enforcement of foreign judgments domestically?

France is a party to the Brussels Convention 1968.

(b) What procedure is followed to enforce a foreign judgment (i) governed by a treaty/convention and (ii) not governed by a treaty/convention?

For European judgments it is very easy to enforce them through an *exequatur petition* on the basis of the Brussels Convention 1968.

This proceeding merely requires that the judge be given a sworn translation of the decision, proof of notification by the bailiff and proof that the judgment is final and binding (without any appeal pending).

The petition is always presented to the Civil Court (Tribunal de Grande Instance) even for commercial matters.

For foreign judgments the proceeding is longer and requires a hearing with cross-examination of points of defence between the parties.

They should also bring a sworn translation of the judgment and proof of notification by the bailiff to the Civil Court.

However, the judge of *exequatur* will not have to re-examine the case on the merits. He will just have to check:

- the jurisdiction of the court
- the applicable law
- the validity of the proceedings
- whether it is against public policy
- whether there has been any fraud.

A foreign judgment without an *exequatur* order having been obtained, will have no effect and is not freely exportable.

(c) What about foreign arbitration awards?

Enforcement of arbitration awards is the same as that described above. If they are international the parties can invoke the New York Convention of 10 June 1958 (Art. 4).

(d) Exportability of proceeds of a judgment

Proceeds of a judgment are freely exportable.

7. OTHER REMARKS

It is possible to lodge an appeal against an *exequatur* order according to Article 37 of the Brussels Convention 1968. The time allowed is two months and begins from the day of service. No time extensions are allowed.

CHAPTER 9

GERMANY

Dr Christian Breitzke
Lebuhn & Puchta, Vorsetzen 35, D–20459 Hamburg, Germany

1. JURISDICTION

The general grounds on which German courts will accept jurisdiction are the following.

(a) Domicile

The domicile of the defendant (natural person).

(b) Place of business/residence/office

In the case of a company, its residence or the residence of its branch office as long as the contract was concluded via the branch office.

(c) Assets located within the jurisdiction

Assets located within the jurisdiction but only in cases where the person or company has no domicile or residence within Germany.

(d) Act complained of within the jurisdiction

For tort claims the place where the tort is committed, i.e. where the tortfeasor acts and/or where the damage occurs.

For contractual claims the place where a contractual obligation is to be fulfilled by a party.

(e) Contract governed by local law

No jurisdiction.

(f) Conventions

The Brussels and Lugano Conventions apply. Germany has ratified both conventions.

(g) Clause attributing jurisdiction

Jurisdiction clauses are in principle valid under German law unless some very few compulsory legal provisions provide for an exclusive jurisdiction in some special areas, such as for example, in real estate matters, in the area of tenancy law or in family law.

(h) Other

A not otherwise competent court will have jurisdiction if the defendant does not invoke the lack of jurisdiction, i.e. jurisdiction is by consent of the defendant.

(i) Counterclaims/third-party proceedings

Counterclaims will be heard to the extent that there exists a connection between the claim and the counterclaim.

Third-party proceedings by means of a third party action are not possible under German law. The claimant and/or the defendant have only the possibility to file a third-party notice, upon service of which the third party—at its own discretion—may decide whether or not to join the proceedings on the claimant's or on the defendant's side.

2. MARITIME CLAIMS

(a) Is there special jurisdiction for maritime claims based on arrest of a vessel in the jurisdiction?

There is no special jurisdiction for maritime claims based on an arrest of a vessel except the one provided for under Article 5, item 7 of the Brussels/Lugano Convention and under Article 7, 1(a)–(f) of the 1952 Arrest Convention.

Unless there exists an exclusive jurisdiction agreement and unless there is no other place of jurisdiction within Germany (domicile/residence) and subject to Article 3 of the Brussels/Lugano Convention an arrested vessel is an asset located within the jurisdiction and thereby creates jurisdiction for the court at the port where the vessel is arrested.

(b) Specific

For salvage: see Article 5, item 7 of the Brussels Convention.

For collisions: collisions create claims under the law of tort with the consequence that the place of collision as the place where the tort is committed gives jurisdiction.

(c) Grounds for arrest

An arrest order can be issued in cases where the conduct of the liable party/debtor gives rise to the assumption that the later enforcement of a judgment will be impeded or at least will be more difficult. The claimant/creditor has to substantiate this by *prima facie* evidence (affidavit).

(d) Need the vessel be connected with the claim or can other vessels in the same legal (or beneficial) ownership also be arrested?

Germany ratified the 1952 Arrest Convention. Thus a ship can only be arrested in connection with "maritime claims" within the definition of Article 1, subparagraph 1 of the Convention in all cases where the vessel runs the flag of a Convention State.

In connection with maritime claims German law allows arrest of all vessels that legally belong to the debtor. The arrested vessel need not be connected with the claim. On the other side vessels in the same beneficial ownership cannot be arrested.

(e) What procedural differences apply to special maritime jurisdiction?

No procedural differences apply to special maritime jurisdiction because there is no special maritime jurisdiction.

(f) What jurisdictional rules are there as to limitation of liability?

Germany is a party to the International Convention on Limitation of Liability for Maritime Claims, 1976. In accordance with that Convention the limitation of liability can either be effected by constituting a fund with the local court of Hamburg (Art. 11 of the Convention) or without a limitation fund having been constituted by invoking the limitation of liability in the course of ordinary legal proceedings (Art. 10 of the Convention). The constitution of the fund and its distribution is governed by the so-called "Seerechtliche Verteilungsordnung" dated 25 July 1986.

3. SERVICE OF PROCEEDINGS

Germany has been a party to the 1965 Hague Convention since 1979. In Germany each country (*Bundesland*) has its own and separate central authority which has to be contacted in accordance with the Convention for the purpose of serving of documents in Germany. In as far as German documents are to be served outside German jurisdiction, service of documents is usually automatically or in special cases on specific application effected by the German court in accordance with the Convention and/or specific bilateral treaties.

4. COSTS

When starting proceedings the claimant has to pay in advance to the court the court costs for the first instance. Court costs and lawyers' fees are charged in accordance with standard scales and are based on the value in dispute.

(a) Court fees

In the first instance the court costs for a claim of DM 100,000.00 amount to DM 2,865.00 plus disbursements, for a claim of DM 1 million DM 17,715.00 plus disbursements and for a claim of DM 10 million. DM 98,715.00 plus disbursements. In the second instance these costs increase by 50 per cent.

(b) Lawyers' fees

In the first instance one lawyer's fee for a claim of DM 100,000.00 amounts to DM 2,125.00, for a claim of DM 1 million to DM 6,225.00 and for a claim of DM 10 million to DM 33,225.00. Each lawyer earns in the first instance two or three of those fees depending on whether the court issues an evidence order or not. Should the case be settled an additional fee of the same amount is due to each lawyer.

Lawyers' fees can be agreed upon between the lawyer and his client in as far as they are not less than the standard scale fees. Contingency fees are prohibited.

(c) Recovery of costs from unsuccessful party

The unsuccessful party has to bear all court costs and all lawyers' fees including the fees of the lawyer of the winning party.

(d) Security for costs

Foreign claimants do not have to provide security for costs in as far as reciprocal treatment is granted. Otherwise security has to be provided for the fees of the defendant's lawyer, normally for the first instance, upon application of the defendant.

5. INTERIM ARREST

(a) Are interim arrest/freezing of assets/other provisional measures permitted to provide security for domestic proceedings and/or proceedings in another jurisdiction?

Arrests are permitted to provide security for proceedings and judgments in other jurisdictions in as far as the applicant is able to make credible to the court the existence of an urgent reason for granting an arrest order. Such reasons are usually accepted in cases where it can be substantiated by *prima facie* evidence (affidavit) that the debtor will otherwise prevent a later enforcement of the judgment by transfering his assets abroad or by otherwise secreting his assets (see above 2(c)).

According to section 917, subsection 2 of the German Procedural Law (ZPO) a sufficient reason for an arrest order is accepted in cases where a domestic judgment—without arrest order—would have to be enforced outside Germany. However, it is disputed whether the EU territory is to be considered outside Germany or not. Therefore, in cases of non-domestic judgments or in cases where the enforcement of the future judgment can be effected in Germany or even within the EU an arrest order will only be granted on the general rule that the conduct of the debtor gives rise to the assumption that the later enforcement of the judgment will be impeded or will be more difficult if not impossible. This has to be substantiated by *prima facie* evidence, i.e. by an affidavit.

(b) What criteria apply to this?

See above (a).

(c) Is there a limit on jurisdictions whose proceedings are recognised for this purpose?

No.

(d) Is there a requirement for counter-security?

A counter-security is—at the judge's discretion—very often requested, in particular in cases where the claim to be secured by an arrest order seems not to be clear or seems not to be without doubts.

(e) Can applications be made ex parte?

Applications can be made and are usually made *ex parte*. However, the respondent may file an objection against the arrest order which will then automatically lead to a hearing.

(f) How quickly can an order be made?

To prepare the application for an arrest order may need some time. An affidavit/a declaration in lieu of oath, a Power of Attorney and some supporting documents (invoices, contracts, etc.) are needed. Once the application has been filed the judge can be expected to issue the arrest order within two or three hours.

(g) Will the order bind third parties?

In principle, the arrest order will not bind third parties. The arrest order is a general court order by which the arrest of all the debtor's domestic assets is directed. This arrest order has to be enforced either by additional court orders, for example by an order of attachment of garnished claims, or by the assistance of the bailiff in attaching assets. Third parties will only be bound by these additional enforcement acts.

In the case of an attachment of a payment claim against a bank the attachment order actually consists of two orders. The first requires the debtor not to collect the money and/or to otherwise dispose of the payment claim whereas the second order directs the third debtor/bank not to pay any amount to the debtor. If an arrest order is rendered against the charterer of a vessel the claimant may ask the bailiff to attach the bunkers which belong to the charterer. Since the bunkers are in the possession of a third party, i.e. in the possession of the owner of the vessel, the bailiff has to ask the owner/master whether he agrees to the attachment of the bunkers. Should the master disagree, the bailiff is not allowed to attach the bunkers. Should the master agree, the bailiff will attach the bunkers and will pump them out of the vessel.

(h) What are the consequences of breach of an order?

An arrest order must not be breached. Once the arrest order has been enforced the breach of any attachment under the arrest order will be considered a criminal act and will be punished by pecuniary penalty or prison sentence.

(i) Is there a limit to types of asset?

In principle, there is no limit to types of asset. However, usually objects for personal use and things necessary for basic requirements cannot be attached. In principle, all physical assets can be attached. As regards accounts it is not possible under German law to attach account balances. Under German law the payment claim of the debtor against his bank or against a third party can be attached.

(j) What if third parties are affected?

See above (g).

(k) What other provisional measures may be ordered?

By means of an arrest order only claims and physical assets can be attached. A further provisional possibility is the interim injunction which allows the judge to order all kinds of provisional actions and measures and/or to issue prohibitory orders. Finally, German law has special proceedings for the preservation of evidence. Within such proceedings, which are also provisional, the judge may order the survey of a certain object by an expert or the hearing of a witness.

6. RECOGNITION OF JUDGMENTS/AWARDS

(a) What treaties/conventions apply (i) to enable judgments to be enforced abroad and (ii) to enable enforcement of foreign judgments domestically?

Germany is a party to the Brussels and Lugano Conventions as well as to several bilateral treaties.

(b) What procedure is followed to enforce a foreign judgment (i) governed by a treaty/convention and (ii) not governed by a treaty/convention?

In as far as the enforcement of a foreign judgment is governed by a treaty or a convention the provision of such treaties/conventions are to be complied with. In as far as no treaties and conventions apply a foreign judgment may be acknowledged and declared enforceable in Germany in accordance with section 328 German Procedural Law (ZPO) in as far as reciprocity is guaranteed and always provided that the foreign court had jurisdiction, that the defendant—in case of a judgment by default—had been summoned in due time, that the judgment is not in contradiction to an earlier judgment and that the judgment is not against the German *ordre publique*.

(c) What about foreign arbitration awards?

Germany is a party to the New York Convention regarding the enforcement of arbitration awards.

(d) Will proceeds of a judgment be freely exportable?

Proceeds of a judgment will, as a rule, be freely exportable.

CHAPTER 10

GREECE

Nick Anagnostopoulos
Lallis Voutsinos Anagnostopoulos, 100 Kolokotroni Street, 185 35 Piraeus, Greece

1. JURISDICTION

According to Article 3 of the Greek Procedural Code (CPC), "the Greek Courts have (international) jurisdiction over Greek citizens and foreigners, provided they are competent ('competency *ratione loci*') to try the case." Once the Greek courts find that they are competent *ratione loci* to try a case, then the international jurisdiction is automatically established. The jurisdictional grounds provided for in the CPC relate always to the defendant and never to the plaintiff.

(a) Domicile—Residence

Articles 22 and 23 of CPC provide that the court, within the district of which the defendant (a physical person) has his domicile or his residence, is competent and, consequently, has jurisdiction to try a case against him.

(b) Place of business—office

In respect of a body corporate, Article 25 of CPC provides that the Greek courts have jurisdiction where a defendant body corporate has its seat or its principal place of business in Greece. Greek law, for establishing the situs of a company, looks to the place where the business of a company is principally conducted (principal place of business), irrespective of the place of its incorporation/registered address. Therefore, a foreign company, having its principal place of business in Greece (and not in the place of its incorporation) shall be treated—for the purposes of jurisdiction—as a Greek company and, then, the jurisdiction of the Greek courts is established.

(c) Assets located within the jurisdiction

In the case of defendant persons or bodies corporate not having domicile or seat in Greece, the Greek courts may have jurisdiction, in respect of its pecuniary claims, if such person or a body corporate has assets within Greece (Art. 40 of CPC).

However, it should be noted that this jurisdictional ground is not recognised by the International Convention on Civil Jurisdiction and Enforcement of Foreign Judgments signed in Brussels in 1968, which came into force in Greece on 1 April, 1989. Therefore, whenever the Brussels Convention 1968 applies to a case, the Greek courts shall not entertain jurisdiction on the above ground (location of the defendant's assets).

In this respect, Article 29 of CPC should be noted; it provides that the situs of an immovable property provides jurisdiction to the Greek courts in respect of disputes over the ownership of such property or in the case of disputes over the lease of such property.

(d) Act complained of within the jurisdiction

Article 35 of CPC provides that in the case of a claim arising out of a criminal act punishable by the Greek Penal Code, the courts of the place where such criminal act was committed have jurisdiction to hear such claims.

In respect of disputes arising out of a contract, the Greek courts may have jurisdiction on two grounds, namely, if the place the contract was concluded or the place the contract is to be performed is in Greece (Art. 33 of CPC). (It should be noted that the place the contract was concluded is not recognised under the Brussels Convention 1968.)

(e) Contracts governed by local law

The fact that a contract is governed by Greek law is not sufficient to render a Greek court competent to try claims arising out of such contract. The jurisdiction of the Greek courts should be obtained on other grounds, provided for by the relevant provisions of CPC.

(f) Conventions

Apart from the jurisdictional grounds provided for in the relevant provisions of CPC, Greece has ratified certain international conventions, which give jurisdiction to the Greek courts on other grounds.

The most important of the conventions is the Brussels Convention 1968, which provides for further jurisdictional grounds than the provisions of CPC and, in particular, in Section 2 ("Special Jurisdiction"), Section 3 ("Jurisdiction on matters relating to insurance") and Section 4 ("Jurisdiction over consumers contracts"). It should be noted that Greece has recently (February 1997) ratified the Convention of Lugano 1988, on Civil Jurisdiction and Enforcement of Judgments on Civil and Maritime Matters.

(g) Clause attributing jurisdiction

The Greek courts have jurisdiction in cases whereby the parties have agreed in their contractual documents that their disputes shall be referred for determination to the Greek courts. For such an agreement to be valid it should be reduced in writing and should, specifically, refer to the contract/relation in question.

(h) Other

Other jurisdictional grounds provided for in CPC, are the following:

(i) the seat or the principal place of business of a body corporate in respect of company disputes (Art. 27 of CPC);
(ii) the residence of the inheritor in cases of disputes over estate (Art. 30 of CPC);
(iii) the place of the court which is seised of the main action, where an ancillary action is instituted subsequently (i.e. guarantee claim, intervention, etc.) (Art. 31 of CPC);
(iv) the place of the court first seised of the matter in respect of interrelated claims (Art. 31 of CPC).

(i) Counterclaim/third-party proceedings

Article 34 of the CPC provides that a counterclaim may be brought for determination before the court which is seised of the main action, provided that the parties have not agreed on an exclusive jurisdiction on such counterclaim.

The same applies *mutatis mutandis* with respect to third-party proceedings.

2. MARITIME CLAIMS

(a) Jurisdiction through arrest of a vessel

The mere fact that an arrest of a vessel has been made in Greece does not give jurisdiction to the Greek courts to try the case on its merits.

However, if a vessel has been arrested within Greece, it may be argued that the Greek courts have jurisdiction to determine the merits of the case on the basis that the defendant has assets within Greece (Art. 42 of CPC). However, as mentioned above, such jurisdictional ground is not available when the Brussels Convention 1968 applies.

Further, Greece has ratified the International Convention for the Unification of Certain Rules Relating to the Arrest of Seagoing Ships, signed in Brussels in 1952, which has become domestic law since 1966.

Article 7 of the above Convention provides as follows:

"The Courts of the country in which the arrest was made shall have jurisdiction to determine the case upon its merits if the domestic law of the country in which the arrest is made gives jurisdiction to such Courts, or in any of the following cases, namely:

(a) if the claimant has his habitual residence or principal place of business in the country in which the arrest was made;
(b) if the claim arose in the country in which the arrest was made;
(c) if the claim concerns the voyage of the ship during which the arrest was made;
(d) if the claim arose out of a collision or in circumstances covered by Article 13 of the International Convention for the unification of certain rules of law with respect to collisions between vessels, signed at Brussels on September 23, 1910;
(e) if the claim is for salvage;
(f) if the claim is upon a mortgage or hypothecation took place in the Greek territorial waters."

(b) Specific

(i) Place of loading/discharge

The place of loading or discharge does not by itself give jurisdiction to the Greek courts unless—and especially the place of discharge—it can be considered as the place where the contract was concluded or was to be performed, in which case Article 33 of CPC shall apply.

(ii) Collision

Special jurisdiction in respect of maritime claims applies in respect of collision cases according to Article 242 of the Greek Private Maritime Code which provides that "Greek courts, in cases of collision, have jurisdiction (a) if the defendant is resident in Greece, (b) if the vessel flies the Greek flag, (c) if the collision took place in the Greek territorial waters and (d) if Greece was the place where the vessel was arrested even before the institution of the main proceedings, the arrest was revoked."

(iii) Salvage

If salvage services have been rendered within Greece, and the parties to the salvage agreement have not agreed otherwise, the Greek courts shall have jurisdiction mainly on the basis that the salvage agreement was concluded in Greece and/or the salvage services were performed within Greece (Art. 33 CPC). Of course, other jurisdictional grounds (such as the residence or principal place of business of the defendant) are always available.

(c) What are the grounds for arrest?

For the Greek courts to order the arrest of a vessel (like, of course, any other security measure), the applicant must satisfy two basic requirements:

(1) He has to show an arguable case on the merits;
(2) He has to show that there is an imminent risk to the eventual satisfaction of his claim, or an urgent need justifying the granting of the arrest required.

(d) Connection between arrested ship and claim

According to Greek law, a debtor is answerable to his creditors through all his property, including ships.

Therefore, the principle is that any vessel is subject to arrest, provided that such vessel is in the same legal ownership as the vessel in respect of which the claim arose. The Brussels Convention 1952 on Arrest of Seagoing Vessels in Article 3(1) follows this principle, with the exception that arrest of another vessel (not connected with the claim), which is in the same legal ownership, is not allowed with respect to the maritime claims enumerated in Article 1(l), (o), (p), (q) of the Convention (i.e. disputes on the ownership of a vessel, disputes between co-owners and disputes over mortgage).

Furthermore, in the case of a bareboat charter, the registered owner is liable, only through his vessel (*in rem*), for any claim arising out of the employment of the vessel by the bareboat charterer. (The same principle is followed by Article 3(4) of the Brussels Convention 1952.)

The arrest of an associated vessel (i.e. not belonging to the same legal ownership as the vessel connected with the claim) is not possible under Greek law. Such arrest could be effected, theoretically, on the principle of lifting the corporate veil of a company, which is, of course, very difficult.

(e) Procedural differences with respect to special maritime jurisdiction

The procedural rules provided for by CPC apply, also, to maritime claims. It is relevant to note here that the Piraeus Court (maritime session) is exclusively competent to hear all maritime claims falling within the jurisdiction of the Athens Court.

(f) Limitation of liability

Greece ratified in 1991 the London Convention 1976 on Limitation of Liability for Maritime Claims. This Convention applies whenever the persons mentioned in Article 1 of the Convention seek to limit their liability in respect of claims mentioned in Article 2 of the Convention, irrespective of whether the persons are Greek or foreigners and irrespective of whether the vessel flies a foreign or a Greek flag.

Whenever the London Convention 1976 does not apply, then, the Greek Code of Private Maritime Law provides that the shipowner may limit his liability in respect of claims arising out of contracts made by the master during the course of his employment or for torts committed by the master, crew or pilot during the course of their employment. The shipowner may limit his liability by (i) assigning the vessel and the gross freight or (ii) paying three-tenths of the value of the vessel for each voyage. The value of the vessel is estimated by reference to the commencement of the material voyage. The right of limitation is not available in respect of (i) contractual obligations which the owners specifically consented to or approved or (ii) crew and master's claims.

Greece signed and ratified in 1991 the Athens Convention 1974 in relation to the sea carriage of passengers and their personal effects signed in Athens as well as the Athens Protocol, which was signed in London in 1976. The Convention and the Protocol apply in international carriages, as provided for in Article 2 of the Convention, i.e. when (a) the ship is flying the flag of, or is registered in a State Party to this Convention, or (b) the contract of carriage has been made in a State Party to this Convention, or (c) the place of departure or destination, according to the contract of carriage, is in a State Party to this Convention. The issue of limitation of the liability of the carrier is dealt with in Article II of the Protocol, which amends the Articles 7, 8 and 9 of the Convention.

3. SERVICE OF PROCEEDINGS

In accordance with Article 134 of CPC, if court proceedings are to be served out of Greece, then the service is made on the Public Prosecutor of the court in which the proceedings are pending, who, in turn, passes the documents to the Greek Foreign Ministry for further transmission abroad. The service is considered to be effected at the time the proceedings are served on the Public Prosecutor.

Greece ratified in 1983 the Hague Convention 1965 regarding the service of judicial documents abroad. If service is to be made to a country that is a member of the Hague Convention, then the provisions of such Convention shall apply. The proceedings are, again, served through the Public Prosecutor of the court in which the proceedings are pending, on the Greek Foreign Ministry, which, in turn, passes the documents to the appropriate authority of the foreign country. Also, the service may be effected in accordance with Article 10 of the Convention. According to the Hague Convention, for a service to be considered valid, evidence should be produced to the Greek court to the effect that the document was in fact served on the party intended. For serving proceedings abroad no previous permission or order of the court to the plaintiff is required.

4. COSTS

(a) Court fees

For pursuing a recovery claim in Greece, the following amounts should be paid to the court:

(1) an amount of about Drs 20,000 for filing the writ of action with the court and for serving the proceedings on the opponent;
(2) at the hearing date, approximately 1 per cent of the amount claimed (comprising the capital and interest calculated up to the hearing date) as stamp duty and approximately Drs 40,000 for petty expenses;
(3) if witness examination follows the hearing of the case, approximately Drs 80,000 as additional costs;
(4) once a final judgment is issued, then, for obtaining an enforceable copy of the final judgment, 2 per cent on the capital awarded, plus interest, and, in respect of unpaid invoices, only 2 per cent of the interest;
(5) if an appeal is filed, about Drs 60,000 for various expenses in respect of the appeal proceedings; and
(6) if the matter is taken to the Supreme Court, a further amount of about Drs 100,000 should be paid.

The above amounts do not include the lawyers' fees and expenses.

For applying to court for interim relief (security measures proceedings) no court fees are paid and the relevant costs do not exceed Drs 50,000.

(b) Lawyers' fees

The party who instructs a lawyer is responsible for the payment of his fees, including any expenses, which have been incurred in the conduct of the action. Normally, the costs of legal representation are discussed and agreed between the client and the lawyer in advance. The basis of the payment of the costs may be one of the following:

(1) On an hourly rate;
(2) On a fixed-fee; or
(3) On a contingency fee.

If no agreement is made between the lawyer and the client, then the lawyer's fees are calculated in accordance with the tariffs provided for in the Code on Legal Profession, which are very low.

(c) Recovery of costs from the losing party

The issue as to which party shall bear the legal costs of the proceedings is decided by the final and unappealable judgment on the basis of the so-called "defeat principle", which provides that the losing party pays the legal costs of the winning party.

If the debtor has not caused the institution of the proceedings and, once the proceedings were commenced, the debtor admitted the claim, then the legal costs are borne by the creditor. If the proceedings are partially successful, it might be decided that each party bears his own costs. If the losing party had reasonable doubts regarding the outcome of the case, then the court may reduce the costs of the winning party, payable by the losing party, or it may order that each party bears its own costs.

(d) Security for costs

Article 169 of the CPC provides as follows:

"The court, following a request of the defendant, may order the plaintiff to provide security for the costs of the proceedings pending before the same court, if it is considered that there is an apparent risk that the recovery of the costs shall be impossible."

In case the security is not provided by the plaintiff, within the time ordered by the court, then the proceedings are revoked.

According to the prevailing practice, the Greek courts very rarely order the plaintiff to provide security for costs.

5. INTERIM ARREST

(a) Interim relief and the main proceedings

Any foreigner, whether a physical person or a body corporate, is entitled to apply to the Greek courts requesting interim relief in the same way and to the same extent and degree as a Greek national, provided that the Greek court has jurisdiction. The Greek courts will grant interim relief to a foreign creditor irrespective of whether the litigants are foreigners or whether the main proceedings will be tried in Greece or not, or the substantive right in respect of which the Greek courts are requested to provide interim relief has been acquired by virtue of a foreign legal system or the domestic law. The same principle is followed by Article 24 of the Brussels Convention 1968 on Civil Jurisdiction and Enforcement of Foreign Judgments.

(b) Criteria for providing an arrest order

For the Greek courts to grant a security measure, the applicant must satisfy two basic requirements:

(1) He has to establish an arguable case on their merits;
(2) He has to show that there is an imminent risk to the eventual satisfaction of his claim, or an urgent need justifying the granting of the security measure requested.

The issue of the imminent risk or the urgent need are fundamental prerequisites for the court to grant a security measure. If the court finds that the claim of the applicant, although *prima facie* established, is not at risk or there is no urgent case, then no security measure shall be granted and the court will let the case be decided on the merits in the course of the main proceedings.

(c) Limit on jurisdiction whose proceedings are recognised for the purpose of arrests

In regard to the security measures of arrest, sequestration or provisional adjudication of a debt, the arresting party should initiate main proceedings in the appropriate forum, within a period of 30 days. The court has, always, the discretion to fix a period for the issuance of main proceedings, when ordering a security measure.

(d) Requirement for counter-security

According to Article 694 of the CPC the court has the discretion, in ordering a security measure, to make it subject to the applicant's providing counter-security. If no counter-security is lodged, then the security measure is *ipso jure* revoked. According to the prevailing practice, such discretion is exercised very exceptionally.

(e) Can applications be made ex parte?

The application for a security measure is heard by the court *inter partes*. This is based on a fundamental principle of Greek law (Article 20 of the Greek Constitution), since no one may be condemned unheard. In exceptional cases whereby serious urgency or irreparable damage is imminent, the court may hear an application *ex parte*.

However, in cases of serious urgency, the court has the discretion, upon the filing of an arrest application, to issue a provisional order, valid until the *inter partes* hearing of the application, by which the applicant's claim is temporarily secured in the meantime (for example: upon the filing of an application for the arrest of a vessel, the court may issue a provisional order prohibiting the sailing of the vessel until the *inter partes* hearing date).

(f) How quickly can an order be made?

Depending on the urgency of the matter, orders on arrest applications may be issued shortly after the hearing or one to two weeks after.

However, in cases of serious urgency, the courts may issue a provisional order which may be given on any day and at any time, even during weekends and bank holidays.

(g) Will the order bind third parties?

Article 692, paragraph 5 of CPC provides that the security measures should not affect rights of innocent third parties.

(h) The consequences of breach of an order

According to Article 232 of the Greek Penal Code, he who has intentionally failed to comply with a provisional order of a court or a judge or with a court judgment, by which he has been ordered to do or omit something, is subject to up to one year imprisonment.

Furthermore, Article 715 of CPC provides that "any disposal of the arrested assets or the claim, made by the respondent, is forbidden and void, in favour of the arresting party".

(i) Limit of types of assets

A debtor is answerable to his creditors through all his assets. However, there is one serious exception, which is bank accounts.

In law, the conservative attachment of bank accounts may be affected by following the steps for attaching property in the hands of a third party (garnishee). The third party, once the court's judgment is served on him, is obliged to make a declaration stating whether he possesses the goods so attached. In respect of attachment of bank accounts, the bank in its capacity as third party should declare to the applicant the details of the material account(s); in the case of a positive declaration, the attachment is effected. However, according to Law Decree 1059/71, bank accounts in banks operating in Greece are confidential. Furthermore, the disclosure by banks of information concerning accounts to a third party is a criminal offence. (The disclosure is, basically, permitted in case of a criminal offence committed in Greece, provided such disclosure is necessary to the investigation and punishment of such offence.) In view of the above, the judiciary unanimously accepts that Greek banks (including foreign banks doing business in Greece) have no obligation to make an declaration with regard to the accounts kept by them. Therefore, the Greek courts decline to order the conservative attachment of bank accounts in view of the fact that the third party (i.e. the banks) is not allowed to make the necessary declaration. This view has been strongly criticised by many commentators, who agree that the conservative attachment of bank accounts is perfectly possible. However, the situation, as it stands today, is to the effect that conservative attachment of bank accounts in a Greek or foreign bank operating in Greece does not appear to be possible.

Finally, there are certain assets which may not be arrested, such as the personal effects of the debtor (furniture, clothes, books, etc).

(j) What if third parties are affected?

If a third party is affected by an arrest order, he may apply to the court for the modification of the order or even its revocation.

(k) Other provisional measures

According to Greek law, interim relief is provided by the granting of any of the following security measures, and in particular:

(1) *conservative attachment*: the conservative attachment of a property is a security measure granted by the court aiming at the "preservation" of the attached property until a final judgment is issued on the merits of the claim;
(2) *charging order on land or property, known as prenotation of hypothec*: the prenotation of hypothec is a charging order registered on the defendant's immovable property, which gives priority over other creditors in case such property is sold by a public auction;
(3) *judicial sequestration*: this security measure is granted in case of disputes as to the ownership or possession of a property;
(4) provision of guarantee;
(5) *provisional regulation of a transaction or relationship*: the court may issue an order, by which the defendant is provisionally ordered to perform, omit or tolerate the performance of a specific act;
(6) provisional adjudication of a debt; and
(7) seal, unseal, inventory or public deposit.

The above security measures are "*numerus clausus*" but we can say that the creditors' claims may be sufficiently secured by taking any of the above measures, as the court has wide discretion to make an order falling within the ambit of any of the above measures.

Also, the Greek courts may make orders for conservative survey or provisional examination of witnesses in case of urgency for preserving the evidence.

6. RECOGNITION OF JUDGMENTS

(a) Treaties/conventions—court judgments

Greece ratified the Brussels Convention 1968 on Civil Jurisdiction and the Enforcement of Foreign Judgments, in force as from 1 April 1989. Therefore, all judgments issued in a EU country shall be declared enforceable in Greece in accordance with the provisions provided for in this Convention.

Apart from the Brussels Convention 1968, Greece has signed bilateral agreements relating to the recognition and enforcement of judgments with the following countries: Yugoslavia (Law Decree 4007/1959); Romania (Law 429/1974); Bulgaria (Law 841/1978); Lebanon (Law 1099/1980); Hungary (Law 1149/1981); Poland (Law 1184/1981); the former USSR (Law 1242/1982); Czechoslavakia (Law 1323/1983); Syria (Law 1450/1984) and Cyprus (Law 1548/1985).

(b) The procedure

The procedure for declaring enforceable in Greece a foreign judgment, irrespective of whether it is governed or not by a treaty/convention, may be outlined as follows:

- (i) An application is filed with the one-member court of first instance (summary proceedings) and a hearing is fixed in about one to two weeks time.
- (ii) At the hearing date, the applicant submits to the court an official copy of the foreign judgment plus other supporting documentation.
- (iii) Judgment is normally given very shortly after the hearing date (one to three weeks time).
- (iv) Upon the issuance of the Greek judgment, the foreign judgment becomes immediately enforceable. However, the Greek judgment is subject to appeal. The lodging of the appeal does not stay the execution, unless the defendant obtains a stay of execution order, pending the determination of his appeal.

For declaring a foreign judgment enforceable in Greece, in accordance with the Brussels Convention 1968, the applicant should satisfy the requirements provided for in Articles 46 and 47, i.e. he has to submit to the court an official copy of the judgment plus evidence to the effect that the judgment is enforceable in the country of its origin and that a copy of the judgment has been served on the defendant. (In the case of a judgment in default, evidence should be produced to the effect that the proceedings were served on the defendant.)

For declaring a foreign judgment enforceable in Greece, in accordance with the general principles of Greek law, the applicant should satisfy the following criteria:

- (i) the foreign judgment is enforceable in the country where it was issued;
- (ii) the foreign court had jurisdiction to try the case in accordance with the provisions of Greek law;
- (iii) the losing party was not deprived of his right to defend the case;
- (iv) the judgment does not contradict a Greek judgment issued between the same litigants on the same case; and
- (v) the foreign judgment is not against Greek public policy or *bonae mores*.

(c) Foreign arbitration awards

Foreign arbitration awards may be declared enforceable in Greece provided the applicant satisfies the following criteria:

(i) the arbitration agreement is valid under the law which governs it;
(ii) the object of the foreign arbitration award can be also the object of a Greek arbitration award;
(iii) the foreign arbitration award is final and not subject to any opposition in the country where it was issued;
(iv) the defendant was not deprived of his right to defend himself in the arbitration proceedings;
(v) the arbitration award does not contradict a Greek court judgment issued on the same case between the same litigants;
(vi) the foreign award is not against the Greek public policy or *bonae mores*.

Greece ratified in 1961 the New York Convention of 1958 on the Recognition and Enforcement of Foreign Arbitral Awards. In case this Convention applies the enforcement follows the prerequisites provided for in Articles 4, 5 and 6 of the Convention.

The court procedure for declaring a foreign award enforceable in Greece is identical to the one outlines above in respect of foreign judgments.

(d) Exportability of proceeds

The proceeds of a judgment are freely exportable.

CHAPTER 11

IRELAND

Frank Nowlan
Matheson Ormsby Prentice, 30 Herbert Street, Dublin 2, Ireland

1. JURISDICTION

(a) Domicile

The courts will accept jurisdiction where any relief is sought against any person or body corporate domiciled within the jurisdiction. (A company is domiciled in Ireland if it is incorporated in Ireland.)

(b) Place of business/residence/office

The courts will accept jurisdiction where this means that the person or body corporate is ordinarily resident within the jurisdiction. (The test of residence for a company is not where the company is registered, but where it keeps house and does its real business; and the real business is carried on where the central management and control actually abides.)

(c) Assets located within the jurisdiction

Jurisdiction is accepted where the whole subject matter of the action is land situate within the jurisdiction (with or without rents or profits), or the perpetuation of testimony relating to land within the jurisdiction; or any act, deed, will, contract, obligation, or liability affecting land or hereditaments situate within the jurisdiction, is sought to be construed, rectified, set aside, or enforced in the action.

Also, where the proceeding is an interpleader proceeding relating to property within the jurisdiction.

(d) Act complained of within the jurisdiction

Jurisdiction is accepted if the action is founded on a tort committed within the jurisdiction.

(e) Contract governed by local law

Where the action is one brought to enforce, rescind, dissolve, annul, or otherwise affect a contract, or to recover damages or other relief for or in respect of the breach of a contract:

(a) made within the jurisdiction; or
(b) made by or through an agent trading or residing within the jurisdiction on behalf of a principal trading or residing out of the jurisdiction; or
(c) by its terms or by implication to be governed by Irish law, or is one brought in respect of a breach committed within the jurisdiction of a contract wherever made, even though such breach was preceded or accompanied by a breach out of the jurisdiction which rendered impossible the performance to the part of the contract which ought to have been performed within the jurisdiction.

(f) Conventions

Ireland has implemented the Brussels Convention on Jurisdiction and the Enforcement of Judgments in Civil and Commercial Matters 1968, as amended by the San Sebastian and Lugano Conventions.

(g) Clause attributing jurisdiction

The parties to any contract may agree:

(a) that the court shall have jurisdiction to entertain any proceeding in respect of such contract, and also, or in the alternative
(b) that service of any summons in any such proceeding may be effected at any place within or out of the jurisdiction on any party or on any person on behalf of any party or in any manner specified or indicated in such contract.

(h) Other (e.g. instruction)

— At common law any person may be made subject to the jurisdiction of the Irish courts provided that personal service of an originating summons has been duly effected within the jurisdiction.

— Where the action is for the administration of the personal estate of any deceased person, who, at the time of his death, was domiciled within the jurisdiction, or for the execution (as to property situate within the jurisdiction) of the trusts of any written instrument, of which the person to be served is a trustee, which ought to be executed according to the law in Ireland.

— Where any injunction is sought as to anything to be done within the jurisdiction, or any nuisance within the jurisdiction is sought to be prevented or removed, whether damages are or are not also sought in respect thereof.
— Where the proceeding relates to an arbitration held or to be held within the jurisdiction.
— Where the proceeding relates to the enforcement of an award under Part III of the Arbitration Act 1980 or of the pecuniary obligations imposed by an award under Part IV of the Arbitration Act 1980.
— Where the proceeding is by a mortgagee or mortgagor in relation to a mortgage of personal property within the jurisdiction and seeks relief of the nature or kind following, that is to say sale, delivery of possession by the mortgagor, redemption, reconveyance, delivery of possession by the mortgagee.
— Where the proceeding is brought under the provisions relating to carriage by air of the Air-Navigation and Transport Act 1936.
— Where the proceeding relates to a ship registered or required to be registered under the Mercantile Marine Act 1955, or any share or interest therein.
— Where the proceeding relates to the ownership of a trade mark registered or sought to be registered in the Industrial and Commercial Property Registration Office.
— Where the proceeding is brought to enforce any foreign judgment or foreign arbitral award.
— Even if a defendant is not personally present in Ireland so as to enable personal service of process on him, he may submit to the jurisdiction to the Irish courts. Submission may come about in a number of ways:

(a) by instructing a solicitor to accept service
(a) by entering an unconditional appearance
(c) by commencing an action as a plaintiff
(d) by seeking interlocutory relief that is consistent only with an intention to contest on the merits.

(i) Counterclaim/third-party proceedings

A person who brings an action as plaintiff gives the court, in general, jurisdiction to entertain a counterclaim against him in some related matter.

Where any person out of the jurisdiction is a necessary or proper party to an action properly brought against some other person duly served within the jurisdiction, Irish courts will have jurisdiction.

2. MARITIME CLAIMS

(a) Is there special jurisdiction for maritime claims based on arrest of a vessel in the jurisdiction?

Yes. In this context presence "within the jurisdiction" means, of course, presence in internal waters or within territorial waters of the state. It is not settled whether a ship must be anchored within territorial waters or whether a ship in the course of navigation may be arrested. An originating summons in an action *in rem* cannot be served out of the jurisdiction.

(b) Specific?

The jurisdiction of the High Court extends to such matters as claims for the sale of a ship, or in respect of a mortgage of or charges on a ship, claims arising out of bottomry or pilotage.

Both the International Convention relating to the Arrest of Seagoing Ships 1952 ("the Arrests Convention"), and the International Convention on certain rules concerning Civil Jurisdiction in matters of Collision 1952 ("the Collisions Convention") have been implemented in Ireland.

The Collisions Convention represents little or no change in the jurisdiction of the Irish courts in cases of collision. Ships flying the Irish flag will benefit from the protection afforded by the Convention in other Contracting States.

The Collisions Convention applies even where there has not been actual contact but damage has occurred as a result, for example, of evasive action.

(c) What are the grounds for arrest?

Under the Irish Act of 1989 which implements the Arrests and Collisions Conventions, the High Court has the jurisdiction to hear and determine in admiralty proceedings *in rem* any of the maritime claims in Article 1(1) of the Convention relating to the Arrest of Seagoing Ships. These are the only claims in regard to which a ship may be arrested. A number of these maritime liens will, in fact, be the same as those under the original Irish Court Rules, but there are a couple more which give rise to a right of arrest.

(d) Need the arrested vessel be connected with the claim or can other vessels in the same legal (or beneficial) ownership also be arrested?

Under the 1989 Act, the arrest of sister ships is permitted where the claim involves Contracting States, and it is to be noted that the Act expands the definition of ownership of vessels in this respect to include "beneficial" ownership. Subject to this statutory sister-ship provision, the only property liable to arrest is the ship, cargo or freight which is the focus of the action *in rem*.

(e) What procedural differences apply to special maritime jurisdiction?

In admiralty actions *in rem* service of a summons or warrant of arrest must be effected by the Admiralty Marshal or his substitutes by nailing or affixing the original for a short time on the main or on the single mast or some other conspicuous part of the vessel and by leaving a true copy nailed or affixed in its place when the original is taken off. If the *res* is cargo and it has been landed or transhipped, service of the summons or warrant is to be effected by placing it for a short time on the cargo and leaving a true copy of it on the cargo. Failure to follow the prescribed method of serving a writ against a ship vitiates the service. Therefore, service on the captain or master, even on board the ship, is not sufficient. If on the other hand cargo is in the custody of a person who will not permit access to it, service of the summons or warrant may be made upon that person. No warrant for the arrest of property in admiralty actions *in rem* is to be issued until an affidavit by the party seeking it or his agent has been filed containing certain specified particulars, including, the name and description of the party at whose instance the warrant is to be issued, the nature of the claim or counterclaim, the name and nature of the property to be arrested, and a statement that the claim or counterclaim has not been satisfied.

It is necessary now, since 1989, when making application for an arrest, to inform the court whether one is making the arrest on the basis of a claim for necessaries under the common law effectively and the Rule of Court or whether the claim is being made under the Convention. The reason is that if the claim is specified as being made under the Convention and reliance is placed on the Convention for the arrest, then application has to be made to the Admiralty Judge rather than the Master. Accordingly, what one has to look at is the nature of the maritime claim and if one is going to rely on the Convention for the arrest then one can go to the judge and if one can justify the claim as being necessaries or other matters covered by the 1867 Act or the Irish Court Rules, then one can go to the Master. If you plead *both*, then the application will have to go to the judge.

A party may obtain an order for the release of any property by paying into court the sum in respect of which the action was commenced and a sum for costs but there is a procedure whereby a party desiring to prevent this release can file a caveat, against release. If an action *in rem* is stayed, the arrested property or other security cannot be retained by the court as security for the other proceedings (such as arbitration proceedings) in whose favour the stay is granted. However, in the case of a discretionary stay the court can get round this lack of power to retain security by making the stay conditional on the provision of alternative security by the defendant.

(f) What rules are there as to limitations of liability?

Section 46 of the Irish Civil Liability Act 1961 provides that:

> "where, by the fault of two or more vessels, damage is caused to one or more of those vessels or to another vessel or to the cargo of any of those vessels or any property on board, and an action is brought for such damage, the liability of each vessel in respect of such damage shall be in proportion to the degree in which such vessel was in fault and accordingly there shall be no right of contribution in respect of such apportioned liability: provided that—
>
> (i) if, having regard to all the circumstances of the case, it is not possible to establish different degrees of fault, the liability shall be apportioned equally among the vessels in fault;
>
> (ii) nothing in this subsection shall affect the liability of any person under a contract of carriage or any contract, or shall be construed as imposing any liability upon any person from which he is exempted by any contract or by any provision of law, or as affecting the right of any person to limit his liability in the manner provided by law."

In 1996 Ireland implemented the following international conventions by virtue of the Irish Merchant Shipping (Liability of Shipowners and Others) Act 1996:

1976 Convention on Limitation of Liability for Maritime Claims
1974 Convention relating to the Carriage of Passengers and their Luggage by Sea (and 1976 Protocol).
1924 Convention for the Unification of Certain Rules of Law relating to Bills of Lading (Law 1968 and 1979 Protocols).

Article 6 of the 1976 Convention therefore applies in Ireland.

3. SERVICE OF PROCEEDINGS

What rules apply to service of proceedings outside the jurisdiction?

(i) Hague Convention

The 1965 Hague Service Convention entered into force in Ireland on 4 June 1994.

The Master of the High Court is the Irish "Central Authority". In Ireland the "competent authorities" are:

(a) The Central Authority
(b) A practising solicitor

(c) A County Registrar
(d) A District Court Clerk.

(ii) Service of Irish process outside the Republic of Ireland

Leave of the court for service of the summons must be sought in order to serve in countries which are not Contracting States to the Hague Convention.

For those states which are party to the Hague Convention, the Irish Rules provide for two ways to forward documents from Ireland to a Central Authority in another State:

1. If you are not a competent authority you may lodge a request with the Master. He is then obliged to forward the document for you.
2. If you are a competent authority you may lodge a similar request with the Master who may certify that you are a competent authority, and you may then forward the documents along with the certificate directly to the Central Authority in the destination state.

(iii) Service of foreign process in the Republic of Ireland

The Master of the High Court is the Central Authority for the acceptance of the service of foreign processes from States which are party to the Hague Convention. Further, where the Hague Convention applies, alternative methods of service can be used:

(a) Consular/diplomatic channels can be used to serve directly on the other party.
(b) Postal channels can be used to serve directly on the other party.
(c) Service can be effected directly through a solicitor in Ireland.

These are in fact the most convenient methods of service.

Both Contracting States and foreign countries which are not Contracting States to the Hague Convention can serve a foreign process on any person in the Republic of Ireland where the Master of the High Court:

(a) has received a written request for service on that person from the Central Authority of another Convention country or from an authority or judicial officer competent under the law of the state in which the documents originate, or
(b) has received from the Department of Foreign Affairs a letter of request for service of process from a court or tribunal of a foreign state on a person in the state with a recommendation from the Minister for Foreign Affairs that it is desirable that effect should be given to such request.

If the request is not a Convention request and is not in English then it shall be accompanied by a translation thereof, and all requests shall also be accompanied by two copies of the document to be served and two copies of the translation thereof and by two summaries of the document to be served and two copies of the translations thereof, such translations to be certified as correct by a person competent to do so.

If the foreign State is a Contracting State then one of the alternative methods of service as outlined above is more convenient.

4. COSTS

(a) Court fees

A fixed fee is payable by way of stamp duty on initiating proceedings in each of the three courts. The fee for issuing proceedings in the High Court is IEP£60, regardless of the size of the claim. In the Circuit Court it is IEP£25 on the issue of a Civil Bill, and in the District Court it is IEP£12 for a Civil Process.

(b) Lawyers' fees

Lawyers' fees are usually agreed between the lawyer and the client.

(c) Recovery of costs from unsuccessful party

The judge has a discretion to order that legal costs be paid by the losing party. There is often a shortfall between actual and recoverable costs. The recoverable figure is based on the number of hours reasonably spent on the case, and the complexity and size of the case are also factors determining the reasonable charge per hour. For the District Court there are fixed costs as to scales.

Recoverable legal expenses are assessed by agreement between the parties or on taxation by a court official. Included are costs reasonably incurred by the claimant in prosecuting his action (these costs are known as party and party costs).

Liability can be apportioned among a number of unsuccessful defendants either by the trial judge, or by agreement among the unsuccessful defendants.

(d) Security for costs

When a party shall require security for costs from another party, he may apply by notice to the other party for this security, and if the other party does not within 48 hours undertake to comply with this requirement, the party requiring the security may apply to the court for an order directing security for costs.

Where the court makes an order for security for costs in the exercise of its discretion, the amount of the security and the time and manner in which it is to be given and the person(s) to whom it is to be given are generally determined by the Master of the High Court.

5. INTERIM ARREST

(a) Are interim arrest/freezing of assets/other provisional measures permitted to provide security for domestic proceedings and/or proceedings in another jurisdiction?

Yes. An injunction to restrain the defendant from disposing of the assets or removing them from the jurisdiction is known in Ireland as a Mareva injunction. It can be sought in respect of domestic proceedings or proceedings in certain other jurisdictions (see (c) below).

(b) What criteria apply to this?

Five criteria should be established prior to Mareva-type injunctions being granted:

(a) The plaintiff should make full and frank disclosure of all matters in his knowledge which are material for the court to know;
(b) The plaintiff should give particulars of his claim and the amount thereof, fairly stating the points made against it by the defendant;
(c) The plaintiff should give some grounds for believing the defendant has assets within the jurisdiction: the existence of a bank account is normally sufficient;
(d) The plaintiff should give some grounds for believing that there is a risk of the assets being removed or dissipated;
(e) The plaintiff must give an undertaking in damages, in the event that he should fail.

A Mareva-type injunction will only be granted by the court, when it is established by the plaintiff:

(a) that he has an arguable case that he will succeed in the action, and
(b) the anticipated disposal of the defendant's assets is for the purpose of preventing the plaintiff from recovering damages and not merely for the purpose of carrying on a business or discharging lawful debts.

(c) Is there a limit on jurisdictions whose proceedings are recognised for this purpose?

Prior to the enactment of the 1968 Brussels Convention, if the main cause of action lay in some other country, then the fact that the defendant had assets in Ireland would not warrant the granting of an injunction to freeze those assets.

However, section 11 of the 1988 Act (which implements the 1968 Brussels Convention) specifically says that where proceedings have been commenced in a Contracting State, the High Court may, under Article 24 of the Convention, grant Orders in Aid to assist those proceedings. This applies where the subject matter of the litigation is within the scope of the Convention as defined by Article 1 (i.e. it must be a civil or commercial matter).

It should be noted that the granting of section 11(1) injunctions lies in the discretion of the court.

(d) Is there a requirement for counter-security?

The plaintiff must give an undertaking in damages, supported in certain cases by a bond or security (stronger than the usual security for costs). This is an undertaking by the applicant that if an injunction is awarded and it subsequently appears to the court that an injunction should not have been granted the plaintiff will be obliged to pay damages to the person injuncted.

(e) Can applications be made ex parte?

Yes, and this is normally the case.

(f) How quickly can an order be made?

The injunction is sought at the interim or interlocutory stage of the proceedings, and can be obtained virtually instantaneously, subject to the availability of a judge, and provided the urgency of the situation can be shown and the relevant documents accurately completed.

(g) Will the order bind third parties?

Once a third party has been notified of an injunction, he will be restrained from dealing with assets in a manner contrary to its terms, otherwise he may be in contempt of court. It is therefore in the plaintiff's interest to notify any third parties, such as banks who may be holding assets belonging to the defendant, of the terms of the order as soon as it is made.

(h) What are the consequences of breach of an order?

The party who breaches the order will be guilty of contempt of court. In practice the remedy of the Mareva injunction is likely to be most effective in relation to assets within the jurisdiction (or a company with offices in the jurisdiction) or if the defendant has a real interest in defending the substance of the Irish action or (as the case may be) in appealing the Irish judgment. It is possible that these are the only cases in which the remedy will be effective.

(i) Is there a limit to types of asset, e.g. physical asset/account balances?

There is no limit to the type of asset over which the injunction can take effect, although what is usually obtained is an order freezing the defendant's bank account. However, the Mareva injunction should be limited to assets within the jurisdiction of the court if these are sufficient to meet the plaintiff's claim, although it is possible for an order to be obtained on a worldwide basis where this is warranted by the facts.

(j) What if third parties are affected, e.g. airliner?

A Mareva injunction operates *in personam* to restrain the defendant from dealing with the assets to which the order relates and it gives no proprietary right over these assets nor priority over other creditors. Therefore the rights of third parties with an interest in the asset will not be prejudiced.

The injunction may not be granted if an innocent third party is affected and the judge will decide this on the balance of convenience.

(k) What other provisional measures may be ordered, e.g. appointment of surveyor or receiver, security?

Measures such as the appointment of an equitable receiver can be invoked only after judgment is obtained.

6. RECOGNITION OF JUDGMENTS/AWARDS

(a) What treaties/conventions apply (i) to enable judgments to be enforced abroad and (ii) to enable enforcement of foreign judgments domestically?

The Brussels Convention on Jurisdiction and the Enforcement of Judgments in Civil and Commercial Matters 1968, as implemented in Ireland, governs both the enforcement of Irish judgments abroad and the enforcement of foreign judgments in Ireland, once the matter is one which is covered by the Convention and the states are party to the Convention.

The Maintenance Orders Act 1974 makes provision for the enforcement on a basis of reciprocity of maintenance orders made in the state, in Northern Ireland, England and Wales and Scotland. The Act is largely modelled on the provisions of the Brussels Convention.

Under Articles 187 and 192 of the EC Treaty, judgments of the Court of Justice of the EC and decisions of the Council or of the Commission which impose a pecuniary obligation on persons other than the States are enforceable.

(b) What procedure is followed to enforce a foreign judgment (i) governed by a treaty/convention and (ii) not covered by a treaty/convention?

(i) Governed by a treaty/convention

Brussels Convention

An application for the enforcement of a judgment is made to the Master of the High Court. The application is made *ex parte* on affidavit. There is a Foreign Judgments Cause Book opened in the Central Office and an Application for an Enforcement is given a record number under this heading.

The Master is required to give his decision without delay and may refuse the application only on one of the grounds specified in Articles 27 and 28. Since the application for an enforcement order is made *ex parte* it is difficult to envisage circumstances in which the Master would be required to consider the defences at this stage.

APPLICATION GRANTED

If the enforcement order is granted, notice of the enforcement order should be served on the defendant in accordance with the Irish Court Rules. The defendant may appeal against the decision within one month of service of the notice of enforcement. In the event that the defendant is domiciled outside the Contracting State in which enforcement is being sought, he is permitted two months to appeal running from the date of service.

During the time available for appeal, no measure of enforcement of the judgment is permissible. However, protective measures can be taken against the defendant's property.

WHERE AN APPLICATION FOR ENFORCEMENT HAS BEEN REFUSED

The applicant may appeal to the High Court. The defendant shall be notified of the refusal. Such an appeal must be brought within five weeks from the perfection of the Master's Order. The appeal is by way of Notice of Motion and the Grounding Affidavit must set out that the party against whom enforcement is sought has been notified of the appeal and the date specified for the hearing of the appeal in sufficient time to enable him to arrange his or her defence, or alternatively, that all necessary steps have been taken to defend.

An appeal from a decision of the High Court (on appeal from the Master) shall be on a point of law only to the Supreme Court. Such Notice of Appeal must be served within five weeks from the perfection of the Order of the High Court.

GROUNDS FOR RESISTING ENFORCEMENT

Once the applicant has satisfied the Master that the documentation is in order and the necessary information has been supplied, the Master may only refuse the application in the following circumstances:

1. Where it would be contrary to public policy to grant enforcement of the judgment;
2. If the recognition and enforcement of a foreign judgment would breach the rules of natural justice;
3. Where the judgment is irreconcilable with a judgment given in a dispute between the same parties in the state in which enforcement is being sought.

EC Treaty

Where the judgment is one of the European Court of Justice, enforcement is governed by the rules of civil procedure in force in the state in the territory of which it is carried out. The order for enforcement is appended to the judgment or decision, without formality other than verification of the authenticity of the decision, by the national authority which the government of each Member State must designate for this purpose. The Master of the High Court is the Irish national authority for this purpose. On application duly made by the person entitled to enforce a community judgment, the Master must make an order for the enforcement of the Community judgment and append the order on it.

(ii) Not governed by a treaty/convention

In this case one has a choice of either suing in Ireland on the judgment which has been obtained abroad or suing here on the original cause of action.

An order of a foreign court will not be recognised and enforced automatically. Certain conditions have to be fulfilled before a foreign judgment will be regarded by our courts as having created a duty or obligation with which the defendant is bound to comply:

(a) The foreign court must be of competent jurisdiction;
(b) The foreign judgment must be final and conclusive.

At common law a foreign judgment can be enforced in Ireland only by bringing an action here on the obligation which it creates. The common law does not allow for direct enforcement by a process of registration or otherwise. Hence, in order to seek enforcement of a foreign judgment, the plaintiff will have to commence proceedings here, by way of Plenary Summons in which the foreign judgment will be pleaded. These proceedings will have to be served on the defendant, to which he would be entitled to enter an appearance and a defence. The grounds of defence will not extend to reopening the merits of the original action.

(c) What about foreign arbitration awards?

A foreign arbitral award may be enforced in Ireland in a number of different ways: it may be sued upon in an action at common law or it may be enforced under the Arbitration Act 1954 or the Arbitration Act 1980.

(i) Enforcement at common law

Enforcement at common law is always available, regardless of whether the arbitration award may also be enforced under one of the Acts.

1. The defendant must have validly submitted to arbitration. The validity of any clause in a contract agreeing to submit any disputes to arbitration is governed by the proper law of the contract. Where the parties enter into a contract containing an arbitration clause to cover future disputes that may arise under the contract, there is a strong presumption that the proper law is that of the country where the arbitration is to be held.
2. The arbitration must also have been conducted in accordance with the submission.
3. To be enforceable in Ireland, the foreign arbitration award must be valid by the law governing the arbitration proceedings, which will in most cases be the law of the country in which the arbitration is held.

The award must also be final and conclusive under the law governing the arbitration proceedings.

It appears from case law that a foreign arbitration award, like a foreign judgment, will not be recognised or enforced if the arbitrator had no jurisdiction to make it, or it was obtained by fraud, or its recognition or enforcement would be contrary to public policy, or the arbitration proceedings were contrary to natural justice.

(ii) Enforcement under the Arbitration Act 1954

Part V of the Arbitration Act 1954 provides for the enforcement of certain foreign arbitration awards. The awards in question are those that are governed by the 1923 Geneva Protocol on Arbitration Clauses or the 1927 Geneva Convention on the Execution of Foreign Arbitral Awards. The award must have been made in pursuance of an agreement to which the 1923 Protocol applies and between persons who are subject to the jurisdiction of two different states which, on a basis of reciprocity, have been declared by government order to be parties to the 1927 Convention; the agreement must also have been made in the territory of a state party to the 1927 Convention. Any foreign award that is enforceable under Part V of the Act must be treated as binding for all purposes on the persons between whom it was made, and may be relied on by any of them by way of defence, set-off or otherwise in any legal proceedings in Ireland.

To be enforceable the foreign award must have:

(a) been made in pursuance of an agreement for arbitration which was valid under the law by which it was governed;
(b) been made by the tribunal provided for in the agreement or constituted in the manner agreed upon by the parties;
(c) been made in conformity with the law governing the arbitration procedure;
(d) become final in the country in which it was made;
(e) been in respect of a matter which may lawfully be referred to arbitration under the law of Ireland;

and the enforcement of the award must not be contrary to the public policy or the law of Ireland.

The party seeking to enforce a foreign award must produce certain specified evidence, including the original award or a duly authenticated copy and evidence proving that the award has become final (section 57(1)).

(iii) Enforcement under the Arbitration Act 1980

The Arbitration Act 1980 gives effect to two international conventions on arbitration: the 1958 New York Convention on the Recognition and Enforcement of Foreign Arbitral Awards and the 1965 Washington Convention on the Settlement of Investment Disputes between States and Nationals of Other States.

An award is enforceable as a New York Convention award if it is made, in pursuance of an arbitration agreement in writing, in the territory of a state, other than Ireland, which is party to the Convention. The Act enables the Minister for Foreign Affairs to make an order declaring that any specified state is a party to the Convention and the order is to be evidence that that state is a party to the Convention.

The person seeking enforcement of an award must produce the duly authenticated original award or a duly certified copy, and a certified translation if either of these is in a language other than English or Irish. When he does this the award will be enforced, unless the defendant can establish one or more of the limited policy grounds specified on the 1980 Act, which are the only ones on which recognition and enforcement can be refused. These are that:

(a) a party to the arbitration agreement was (under the law applicable to him) under some incapacity, or

(b) the arbitration agreement was not valid under the law of the country to which the parties subjected it or, failing any indication thereon, under the law of the country where the award was made, or
(c) the defendant proves that he was not given proper notice of the appointment of the arbitrator or of the arbitration proceedings or was otherwise unable to present his case, or
(d) the award deals with a difference not contemplated by or not falling within the terms of the submission to arbitration or contains decisions on matters beyond the scope of the submission to arbitration, or
(e) the composition of the arbitral authority or the arbitral procedure was not in accordance with what the parties had agreed or, failing an agreement, with the law of the country where the arbitration took place, or
(f) the award has not yet become binding on the parties or has been set aside or suspended by a competent authority of the country in which, or under the law of which, the award was made.

Enforcement of an award may also be refused if the award is in respect of a matter which is not capable of settlement by arbitration under the law of Ireland, or if it would be contrary to public policy to enforce the award.

The 1980 Act also gives effect to the Washington Convention. The pecuniary obligations imposed by an award of the International Centre for the Settlement of Investment Disputes (which was established under the Convention) are, by leave of the High Court, enforceable in the same manner as a judgment order of that court to the same effect. Where leave is so given, judgment may be entered for the amount due or outstanding under the award. A person applying for enforcement must lodge with his application a copy of the award certified in accordance with the Convention.

(d) Will the proceeds of a judgment be freely exportable?

Yes, provided they are not affected by UN sanctions. There are no Exchange Control Regulations.

CHAPTER 12

ISRAEL

Doron Shinar & Marcelle Saul-Sheiman
Shinar Shachor Weissberger, 5 Beit Hillel Street, Tel Aviv 67017, Israel

1. JURISDICTION

Israel is divided into six administrative districts, and in each one there are a few magistrates' courts having concurrent local jurisdiction and one district court having unique local jurisdiction. The Supreme Court has jurisdiction over the whole country, sitting as an appeal court or the High Court of Justice with jurisdiction in most administrative law and constitutional law matters.

In terms of the Civil Rules of Procedure, 1984, Israeli district and magistrates' courts have jurisdiction in matters of a civil nature where one of the following jurisdictional grounds is present, namely:

(a) Residence

The defendant in the action resides within the area of jurisdiction of the court.

(b) Place of business

The defendant has his place of business within the area of jurisdiction of the court.

(c) Assets located within the jurisdiction

In an action involving land, the court in which area of jurisdiction such land is situate.

(d) Act complained of within the jurisdiction

The place where the obligation created between the parties to an action or the place assigned or intended for the carrying out of such obligation is within the area of jurisdiction of the court; or the place of delivery of the subject matter of the action is within the area of jurisdiction of the court; or the place of the act or omission sued upon is found within the area of jurisdiction of such court.

(e) Contract and choice of law

Contract and its various aspects are governed by different choice of law rules. Choice of law rules in Israel are based on the common law, being mainly of English origin. In matters of a procedural nature as they relate to contract, the local law namely the *lex fori* applies. Matters of substance however are generally governed by the proper law, the court utilising whichever law governs the contract. The form of a contract is considered a procedural matter whereas the value of the claim, the validity of the contract and the expiry of the contract are considered as substantive matters.

(f) Conventions

Israel is furthermore party to numerous international Conventions which regulate civil procedures including the Hague Convention governing Civil Procedure of 1905, the Hague Convention governing Civil Procedure of 1954, and the Hague Convention governing the Taking of Evidence abroad in Civil and Commercial Matters 1970. The execution of these Conventions is usually within the jurisdiction of the court administration. The Conventions do not detract from the Israeli law; but will apply in spite of Israeli law.

(g) Clause attributing jurisdiction

Parties may agree as to the place of jurisdiction. In this instance, the action is filed in the court in whose area of jurisdiction that place is. Where the parties have not agreed that the agreed place shall be the sole place of jurisdiction, the action may be filed in the court of that place or another court having jurisdiction in terms of the rules. In this way parties may add to the jurisdiction of the Israeli courts, however, they may not detract from the authority legislated to the Israeli courts and they may not place conditions thereupon. One has to differentiate in this regard from the rules as they apply to substantive jurisdiction as opposed to those applicable to local jurisdiction as the former may not be made conditional, waived or made subject to agreement. Substantive law, for example the law applicable to contracts, may indeed be made conditional, waived or made subject to agreement by the parties to an action.

Israeli parties may also agree as to a foreign court having jurisdiction in a matter. In such circumstances, an Israeli court always has jurisdiction to hear the matter, however, it will adhere to the parties' agreement. The court will adjudicate upon the matter in special circumstances including where the plaintiff will not be able to obtain his proper relief in the court agreed upon or where the contract is in itself defective according to Israeli law. Where a foreign court has concurrent jurisdiction with an Israeli court, the latter will always assume jurisdiction. *Forum non conveniens* rules will however still apply and the final jurisdiction will be chosen.

Non-resident parties may agree as to an Israel court being the proper forum to adjudicate upon a matter. The Israeli court will in general respect such parties' agreement and adjudicate upon the matter other than where there is another *forum conveniens*. This rule also applies to an order staying arbitration proceedings.

(h) Other grounds of jurisdiction

(i) Transference of matters between local courts

A matter may be transferred to another court where a court finds that it is unable to deal with a matter for lack of jurisdiction either *ratione loci* or *ratione materiae* and it is in another court's jurisdiction. It may not thereafter be transferred again.

(ii) Incidental jurisdiction

Furthermore the issue of incidental jurisdiction comes to the fore where a matter has been lawfully brought before any court and a question arises, the decision of which is necessary for the trial of the matter. In this instance the court may decide such question for the purpose of that matter even if the subject of the question is under the exclusive jurisdiction of another court.

(i) Counterclaims and third party proceedings

In so far as counterclaims are concerned, Israeli district courts have jurisdiction over counterclaims even if they fall within the jurisdiction of the magistrates' court and flow from different circumstances than those of the main action. An Israeli magistrates' court, on the other hand, has jurisdiction to hear counterclaims in civil matters where the subject matter of the claim and the counterclaim, or the circumstances from which the claim and counterclaim arise, is or are the same whatever the value of the subject matter of the counterclaim.

In circumstances where an action was commenced by delivery of a statement of claim, the defendant may serve a third-party notice on a third party without obtaining leave of the court. The defendant is, however, required to obtain court approval prior to service of a third-party notice for claims originating otherwise than by way of the delivery of a statement of claim, namely by way of originating motion or in summary judgment proceedings.

2. MARITIME CLAIMS[1]

(a) Special jurisdiction for maritime claims based on arrest of a vessel in the jurisdiction

Arrest proceedings must be brought in the Maritime Court. The jurisdiction of the court is derived originally from the English Admiralty Court Acts of 1840 and 1861 and the Vice Admiralty Rules, 1883 ("VAR") as extended by virtue of the Palestine Admiralty Jurisdiction Order 1937 ("PAJO") (enacted under the English Colonial Courts of Admiralty Act (1890)), which were automatically accepted by Israel upon its establishment. These jurisdictional powers were then vested in the Supreme Court. Section 2 of the Maritime Court Law transferred these jurisdictional powers to the District Court of Haifa, sitting as the Maritime Court. Section 5 of the Maritime Court Law stipulates that all registrars of the District Court of Haifa shall be vested with the powers of a registrar of the Maritime Court.

By virtue of the Admiralty Court Acts and the Israeli Shipping (Vessels) Law 5470-1960, cases in which a party has a cause or right of action in the Maritime Court, may generally be heard in the said court in the form of either *in rem* or *in personam* proceedings.

An *in personam* cause of action is not restricted to the mandatory jurisdiction of the Maritime Court, and can be submitted to any court in Israel, according to the said court's jurisdictional and substantive powers. Obviously, in such cases the claimant cannot pursue arrest proceedings, although he may pursue an attachment order (on a vessel or other property), according to the Civil Rules of Procedure. In this latter instance he shall be required to provide a personal guarantee (and usually in addition thereto, a third party's guarantee).

In respect of arrest proceedings and in the case of *The Arctic Hunter* CA 168/93, the Supreme Court held (contrary to the then prevailing view), that a Maritime Court should have discretion to compel an arresting claimant to provide security as a precondition for the arrest.

Section 2(1) of the PAJO provides that Maritime Court jurisdiction extends to shipping on the high seas.

(b) Jurisdiction—loading/discharge; collision; salvage

The jurisdictional rules governing maritime claims based on arrest of vessels in jurisdiction apply likewise to loading/discharge, collision and salvage of vessels.

(c) Grounds for arrest

In addition to the Shipping (Vessels) Law 5720-1960, sections 3, 4 and 6 of the Admiralty Court Act 1840, and sections 4 to 8, 10 and 11 of the Admiralty

1. With the assistance of Dan L. Zaum.

Court Acts 1861 (which apply *mutatis mutandis* to the "Israeli Maritime Court") define the scope of the court's maritime jurisdiction in cases of *in rem* claims. All vessels, whether foreign or Israeli, must be in Israeli territorial waters before proceedings *in rem* can be pursued against them. The aforesaid sections of the Admiralty Court Acts (except to section 8 of the 1861 Act) apply to foreign-owned vessels.

The list of claims is as follows:

- in respect of any mortgage of such ship or vessel ("that has been arrested by process issuing from the . . . Court");
- questions as to "title to or ownership of any ship or vessels, or the proceeds thereof . . . arising in any cause of possession, salvage, damage, wages or bottomry . . .";
- salvage for services rendered to or damage received by any ship or vessel, or towage, or necessaries supplied to any foreign ship or vessel, and the enforcement of payment thereof (whether such vessel is or is not within the territorial waters of Israel at the time services were rendered);
- claim by the owners or consignee or assignee of any bill of lading of any goods carried into any port in Israel, for damage to the goods, by negligence, misconduct, breach of duty or breach of contract, on the part of the owner, master or crew of the ship, subject to proof that at the time of institution of the cause, any owner or part owner of the ship is domiciled in Israel (this section applies only to cargo being imported into Israel (see: CA 579/70 *The Fede*, PD 25(2) 733));
- damage done by any (Israeli or foreign) ship;
- questions arising between co-owners touching the ownership, possession, employment and earnings of ship registered at any port in Israel;
- provisions of the Merchant Shipping Act 1854, in regard to salvage of life or boat (note also the Wrecks and Salvage Ordinance);
- claims by seamen for wages (both Israeli and foreign vessels);
- claims in respect of mortgage duly registered according to the Merchant Shipping Act 1854 (s.11 1861 Act) (see s.72 of the Shipping (Vessels) Law 5720-1960 confers on a mortgagee the right to institute before the Maritime Court an action *in rem* for the realisation of the mortgage. In Maritime File 2/59 *The Pacific Wave* the Maritime Court held that the aforementioned law applies to foreign vessels actually registered in Israel);
- to investigate the nationality of a vessel (s.92 of the Shipping (Vessels) Law);
- Israeli law does not permit the arrest of vessels in respect of liens created in favour of charterers, except in two cases: (i) a lien arises over all salved property as a result of salvage services (s.41(5) Shipping (Vessels) Law; s.22 Wrecks and Salvage Ordinance); (ii) the crew of a

vessel have a lien over the vessel to which they performed services (s.41(4) Shipping (Vessels) Law).

(d) Arrest of associated vessels

Israeli law permits the arrest of a "sister" vessel (i.e. one belonging to the same owner) or an "associated" vessel (i.e. to some extent in the same beneficial ownership).

(e) Procedure in respect of special maritime jurisdiction

As to Israeli procedural law, the rules of the VAR govern the procedure of the Maritime Court. However, in situations where the VAR does not provide specific procedure, the Maritime Court may refer to the procedure stipulated in the Civil Rules of Procedure, 1984. In this regard certain procedural differences will apply, namely in respect of attachment applications brought in terms of the Civil Rules of Procedure.

The provisions of the International Convention for the Unification of Certain Rules Relating to Maritime Liens and Mortgages, Brussels, 1926, with regard to maritime liens are included in the Shipping (Vessels) Law, 5720-1960, Chapter 4, sections 40–55. The Israeli Supreme Court held that the existence of maritime lien is subject to the *lex causae*, while the question of priorities between maritime liens is subject to the *lex fori*. The order of ranking of such liens follows the order in the Conventions. Section 57 of the Shipping (Vessels) Law provides that, besides a "lien with respect to supplies or services provided to the vessel under agreements or transactions", all maritime liens have priority in ranking over a mortgage.

(f) Liability of vessels

Until 1992 the Hague Rules 1924 governed the liability of vessels in relation to carriage of goods by sea. In 1992 the Carriage of Goods by Sea Ordinance, 5752-1992 ratified the Hague-Visby Rules 1968. The Ordinance applies (i) to outgoing and incoming cargoes, or (ii) from a port of a Contracting State to the Hague or Hague-Visby Rules or, where the bill of lading was issued in such Contracting State, or (iii) where the contract of carriage is subject to the Ordinance or the bill of lading is subject to the proper law of the contract of carriage, or (iv) to an Israeli port where Israeli law governs the carriage.

The Ordinance provides that there is no importance regarding the nationality of the vessel, carrier, forwarder, consignee or any other person connected therewith. Section 5 omits the second paragraph to the Visby Rules (i.e. as if the section complies with all cargoes). Section 6 specifies that the stipulated weight of bulk cargo shall not be a *prima facie* evidence against the carrier. Section 8 provides that without prejudice to Article I(b) and Article III(4) of the Visby

Rules, the consignee shall have the same rights and liabilities as the shipper to the bill of lading.

Israel has not ratified the Convention for the Unification of Certain Rules Concerning the Immunity of State-Owned Ships, Brussels, 1926, and has not subscribed to the Convention relating to the Arrest of Seagoing Ships, Brussels, 1952. Israel is not a party to any bilateral agreements relevant to the arrest of vessels.

3. SERVICE OF PROCEEDINGS[2]

Acquisition of local jurisdiction is attained by service of process. A person including a juristic person's residence in Israel is sufficient for purposes of service of proceedings upon him and for litigation purposes. A foreigner's presence in the country, notwithstanding that it is only for a very short while, irrespective of where he is resident or domiciled, is sufficient for the aforesaid purposes. This may even be implemented by way of an order attaching his person prior to his departure from the country, against his will. The acquisition of jurisdiction on the part of the court does not however derogate from the discretion given to such court to refer the matter to a more suitable forum.

A non-resident who brings a claim in Israel, automatically subjugates himself to Israeli jurisdiction and to any counterclaim which may be brought against him in the country.

The Rules provide for service on an authorised business manager in an action brought before a court on a matter of business or work against a person who does not reside within the jurisdiction of such court. The definition of "Authorised Business Manager" has been widely interpreted in Israeli case law and no formal test has been applied to the interpretation thereof.

A foreign company, in order to set up a place of business in Israel, is required to register with the Registrar of Companies as a foreign company. Such company shall be required to furnish the registrar with various documents including the name and address of a person resident in Israel and authorised to accept service on the company's behalf. Service of any legal document or notification to be served upon a foreign company registered in Israel, shall be deemed to have taken place if it was addressed to the authorised person of whom notification was made to the Registrar and left at the address so announced or sent there by mail.

Service outside the jurisdiction of the state

The Rules provide for service of process outside the jurisdiction of Israel and the enactment thereof in terms of the Rules reinforces the idea of the supremacy of the Israeli court over matters allied to its sovereignty. In terms of the Rules,

2. With the assistance of Sharon Stein.

service of process outside the jurisdiction of the state may be permitted in any one of the following cases, namely:

(i) Where application is made for relief against a person whose ordinary domicile or residence is within the territory of the state;
(ii) The whole subject of the action is land situate therein;
(iii) Application is made to construe, amend, set aside or enforce any act or deed, will, contract, obligation or debt relating to land situate therein;
(iv) Action is brought to enforce, rescind, set aside, cancel or otherwise deal with a contract or to recover damages or other relief in respect of breach thereof and the contract was made within the said territory, or through an agent trading or residing therein on behalf of a principal trading or residing outside the territory, or the laws of the State of Israel are applicable to the contract as provided or implied;
(v) A claim is made for breach of contract within the territory of the state regardless of where the contract is made and notwithstanding that prior to or simultaneously with such breach a breach occurred outside the territory which negated the possibility of performing that part of the contract which ought to have been performed in the territory;
(vi) An injunction is claimed as to any thing done or about to be done in the territory of the state or to prevent or remove any nuisance in the territory of the state whether or not damages are also claimed in respect thereof;
(vii) An action is founded upon any act or omission in the territory of the state (designated in general for damages claims);
(viii) Application is made to enforce a judgment within the meaning of the Foreign Judgments Enforcement Law of 1958 or a foreign arbitration award within the meaning of the Israel Arbitration Law of 1968;
(ix) An application is made under the Matters of Dissolution of Marriage (Jurisdiction in special cases) Law of 1969;
(x) A person outside the territory of the state is a necessary or proper party to an action rightfully brought against another person duly served with a summons within the territory of the state. Usually an application for service outside the jurisdiction of the state is brought in terms of this latter case.

The Rules as they apply to service outside the jurisdiction of Israel apply to service of third-party notices.

Service of process outside the territory of the state activates the sovereignty of the state within that of another and accordingly has been restricted to the extent that one requires leave for service of process outside the territory of the state. Once leave has been attained, a date for filing pleadings is prescribed and a copy of the leave is delivered to the addressee.

The party who has been served outside the territory of the state may no later than the day on which he first pleads on the merits of the actions apply to set aside the order allowing service or deny in the pleadings the authority of the court to hear the action. In these circumstances a Power of Attorney given for purposes of denying the above, will circumvent any further service on the defendant should his application to set aside the order be denied. A Special Power of Attorney given for certain purposes may further be limited to the extent that it does not provide for the person in whose favour it is given, to accept service on behalf of the person so giving it.

There are special regulations which govern service of process within the administered territories of Israel (those parts not yet handed over to the control of the Palestinian Authority). Such service is akin to service in Israel; however, one is required to attach an Arabic translation to the documents, where they are to be served upon an Arabic-speaking defendant. Other procedural matters are governed by certain orders of the Military Authorities of Israel.

As to the territories currently under the Palestinian Authority, there is to date no secondary legislation governing matters including service and legal aid.

4. COSTS

(a) Court fees

Cost implications of starting proceedings

On commencing proceedings before court whether in writing or orally, a court fee as set out in a schedule to the Court Regulations (Fees) of 1987 is required to be paid. Where a fee has been prescribed and it has not been paid the matter will not be filed and the court will not deal with such matter unless an application for exemption for payment of the fee has been made. In principle, non-payment of the fee will result in a striking out of the action by the court. Certain fees have furthermore been designated for those procedures stated as not being capable of expression in monetary terms and others are exempt from payment. Certain fees may furthermore be returned under certain circumstances, including where a proceeding ends in a compromise or is cancelled or struck out by the person who brings it and this is not later than the first pre-trial hearing.

Court fees are determined in accordance with the instance of the court. In proceedings before the High Court of Justice and when lodging an appeal (in whichever instance) court fees are fixed and range from a few hundred to a few thousand Israeli shekels. Fees for claims brought for compensation in respect of bodily damage are also fixed and vary between thousands and tens of thousands of shekels. The payment of such latter fee is made on a progressive basis in line with the progress of the trial. Court fees for monetary claims are 2.5 per cent of the value of the claim. On filing the claim 1.25 per cent of the value of such claim together with a fixed fee in respect of the court record shall be paid. The balance of such claim shall be paid on presentation of the evidence. Court fees for other proceedings including maintenance, succession and declaratory proceedings are fixed and are generally very low.

(b) Lawyers' fees

The Chamber of Advocates Law of 1961 makes provision for an advocate to receive his fee in money only, permitting it in certain circumstances to be a percentage of the subject matter concerned. A minimum tariff is laid down in terms of the Rules of the Chamber of Advocates (Minimum Tariff) with the district board of the Chamber of Advocates permitting a lower fee in certain circumstances and for a certain client. These rules furthermore provide for the conditioning and payment of a fee lower than the minimum fee in certain circumstances. The foregoing provisions are by way of recommendation only.

A maximum fee is laid down for certain claims being *inter alia* those handled in accordance with the Road Accident Victims Compensation Law of 1975 and also those entailing the registration of apartments. An advocate is entitled to accept a fee higher than the maximum fee only with the permission of the district board of the Chamber; his charging of a minimum fee though is peremptory and not obligatory.

Civil/commercial law practices in general charge on an hourly basis or in accordance with a global fee agreed to in advance. Those practices dealing in the main with damages and insurance claims generally work on a contingency basis.

(c) Recovery of costs from unsuccessful party

An order as to the payment of costs the amount of which was prescribed by the court may be executed in the manner of a court judgment in accordance with the provisions of the Execution Law 5727-1967.

(d) Security for costs

A plaintiff may be ordered to give security for payment of all the costs of the defendant. Where this security is not given timeously, the action shall be dismissed unless the plaintiff is permitted to discontinue. This is for example ordered by the court where the plaintiff is a non-resident and has no assets in the country, the plaintiff fails to stipulate an address in his statement of claim or where the plaintiff is a company and the court is of the opinion that it will have no resources to satisfy the claim.

5. INTERIM APPLICATIONS

(a) General

The following provisional measures are permitted in terms of Israeli law as security for proceedings, namely (i) interim arrest of the defendant and (ii) interim attachment of his assets.

(b) Criteria

(i) Interim arrest

Where an action is brought and it is proved to the satisfaction of the court that the defendant is about to leave the country permanently or for a protracted period and that his absence from the country may render consideration of the case or implementation of the judgment difficult, he may be prohibited from leaving the country or directed to deposit his passport or travel documents or may have conditions imposed on his leaving.

The person applying for an order inhibiting departure in (i) shall in his application specify the name and family name of the defendant and also in Latin characters, his address and identity number or, in lieu of the latter, such other particulars as are in the opinion of the court sufficient for his identification.

An order inhibiting departure shall be made only where the value of the claim exceeds 10,000 shekels unless the claim is one for maintenance.

An order inhibiting departure shall not remain in effect as against a foreign resident where no proof has been shown of his being in possession of any assets in the country; even in the instance where one can prove to the court that he is concealing such assets, the court will not lightly grant such an order.

An order inhibiting departure may be made immediately after judgment. In this event the provisions of security and those relating to value of claim shall not apply.

(ii) Interim attachment

Where an action for a sum of money is supported by documentary or ostensibly credible evidence, the court may order the interim attachment (until judgment is executed) of assets in the possession of the defendant or held by the plaintiff, as well as the assets of the defendant in the possession of another person, and this in the event of the court concluding that failure to make such an order is liable to make execution of a judgment difficult; in this same manner a court may order the attachment of a specific object where the claim is one for the recovery of the specific object. The granting of interim attachment orders has been severely restrained as a result of the implementation of the Basic Laws of the State of Israel and accordingly they will only be granted in situations where, for example, the defendant is in a dire financial state or where he is concealing assets.

Interim attachment orders are not granted as a matter of course and they will only be granted in instances where one can prove a real need for them.

The court may furthermore, when giving judgment or directly thereafter and in order to ensure implementation of the judgment, order attachment be imposed and in this instance there is no need to submit an application by way of motion or furnish security for this purpose.

(c) Is there a limit on jurisdictions whose proceedings are recognised for this purpose?

The various jurisdictional rules as elaborated in "Jurisdiction" above apply.

(d) Counter-security

In interim arrest proceedings as described in (i), the applicant is required to give security to indemnify both the defendant against harm caused by inhibiting his departure if the claim is dismissed, struck out or ceased and any other party for damage caused under the order where the applicant delivered incorrect or insufficient particulars to identify the defendant. In addition in claims other than those for maintenance, the grant of an *ex parte* order is made conditional on the deposit of a sum of money into court. The Rules do however provide for an exemption of the giving of the said security. The court may furthermore order a deposit by the defendant as security for the claim with the said deposit lapsing should the defendant return before the giving of judgment or after the order lapses, in which event the security shall be refunded to him. Where he does not return until judgment is given in favour of the plaintiff, the security shall serve in satisfaction of the claim.

In interim attachment proceedings as described in (ii) the plaintiff is required to furnish an undertaking and third party surety as compensation for any damage which may be caused by the attachment in the event that the claim is dismissed or the order expires for another reason. It is customary that a bank guaranty and a third party guarantee be furnished where the risk of damage is minimal or where the defendant is a foreign resident.

(e) Ex parte

Notice of the application as described in (i), shall be served upon the defendant and the application shall be heard in the parties' presence, but if to the satisfaction of the court facts are proved showing that delay of the hearing is likely to cause irreparable or serious damage to the applicant, the court may make an order *ex parte*. An *ex parte* order in this instance shall fix a date for hearing the application in the presence of both parties.

The application as described in (ii), is (as a matter of practice) heard *ex parte* but the court may direct that the opposite party be summoned. Where the attachment order is made *ex parte* the defendant and the holder may within a certain time after service of the order apply for it to be set aside and the parties may be summoned to the hearing of the application.

(f) How quickly can an order be made?

The speed with which an order may be made depends on the availability of dates for a hearing. An order granted *ex parte* may be granted on the same day as the filing of the application or within a few days.

(g) Third parties

The order inhibiting departure as described in (i), will affect third parties to the extent that a suit may be filed against them in the instance where it was incumbent upon them to prevent the departure of the defendant from the country and they neglected to do so, for example the Israel Border Police.

An attachment order as described in (ii) may be imposed by the court against the defendant's assets held by a possessor. In this instance it will notify the possessor that he is required to admit within a certain period by notice in writing whether the defendant's property is in his possession and whether he intends to contest the attachment. A possessor who admits same shall thereupon not be able to retract his admission unless granted leave by the court. The plaintiff may within a certain period thereafter submit to the court a reasoned application in writing for confirmation of the attachment should the possessor not admit it or for any other reason object to confirming it or not reply at all within the time period. Should the plaintiff not apply for confirmation of the attachment in this instance, the attachment shall be set aside as regards any property which the holder does not admit is in his possession. Where a plaintiff succeeds in his claim the court shall in the judgment confirm the interim attachment and charge the defendant with the costs thereof.

(h) Breach

The provisions of the Execution Law 5727-1967 has been made applicable to the execution of the interim attachment proceedings as described in (ii) and action under that law continues where the order is confirmed.

(i) Types of debts

The provisions relating to an order inhibiting departure as described in (i) shall apply even if an action is not brought, where it is proved to the court that the person against whom the order is sought owes the person submitting the application a debt which is due in the future, it appears that the debtor will be absent from Israel on the date of payment and that his absence from Israel is likely to make collection of the debt difficult.

An attachment order as described in (ii), may be imposed upon debts and rights whether or not the payment date has arrived. Furthermore an attachment order may be made against real estate and is done by way of giving notice to the officer in charge of the Land Registry who enters a note therein.

(j) What if third parties are affected, e.g. airliner?

The order for interim arrest will affect airlines to the extent that a suit may be filed against them in the instance where it was incumbent upon them to prevent the departure of the defendant from the country in accordance with an order of the court or the relevant authorities and they neglected to do so.

(k) Other provisional measures

Israeli case law makes provision for various interim procedures including interim injunctions to which the English common law indirectly applies, Mareva injunctions, Anton Piller orders, and interim declaratory orders, which may be given by civil courts as against the state, and which are similar in nature to interim injunctions.

The Anton Piller order which provides for civil search and discovery procedures on the part of the plaintiff is recognised in terms of Israeli law.

Israeli company law even makes provision for the appointment of an interim liquidator to a foreign company conducting business in Israel.

Appointment of receivers

The Rules further provide for the appointment of a receiver. The court, upon application for the appointment of a temporary receiver, may appoint a receiver for any property whether before or after judgment. There are in the main four types of receivers: namely in terms of the Companies Law for purposes of realisation of a debenture; and in terms of the Execution Law and Civil Procedure Regulations for purposes of attachment of an individual asset, and its interim management until the court's decision as to its status.

6. RECOGNITION OF JUDGMENTS/AWARDS

(a) Enforcements of foreign judgments

Enforcement of foreign judgments in Israel is governed by the Enforcement of Foreign Judgments Law 1958-5718. The existence of a convention or treaty by and between Israel and another country is not stated as a precondition for enforcement of foreign judgments; however a foreign judgment will not be declared enforceable if it was given in a state the laws of which do not provide for the enforcement of judgments of Israeli courts. The court may, however, on the application of the Attorney General enforce a foreign judgment even where reciprocity is not accorded. Furthermore a foreign judgment shall not be declared enforceable if its enforcement is likely to prejudice the sovereignty or security of Israel.

Recognition of judgments on a direct basis occurs as a consequence of a party addressing the court directly on this issue, by way of application. Such recognition is conditional however upon there being a treaty between Israel and the country of origin of the judgment. To date such a treaty exists only with Germany.

Recognition occurs on an incidental basis where the applicant, in the course of bringing an action in the Israeli courts, requests that the court recognise a judgment emanating from a foreign country.

A foreign judgment which has been declared enforceable has, for the purposes of execution, the effect of a judgment validly given in Israel.

(b) Procedure in respect of enforcement of foreign judgments

An application to declare a foreign judgment—including an interim foreign judgment and an interim order in matters of maintenance—an enforceable judgment, is brought by way of motion. "Foreign judgment" in terms of the Foreign Judgments Enforcement Law is defined as a judgment given by a court in a foreign state in a civil matter and includes a judgment for the payment of compensation or damages to an injured party even though it may not have been given in a civil matter.

A copy of the foreign judgment confirmed by a competent authority of the country in which it was given must be attached to the application together with a declaration confirming the facts proving compliance with conditions as laid down in the above Law.

Enforcement of a foreign judgment will occur where the judgment is *in personam* whereas the court will recognise judgments irrespective of whether they are *in rem* or *in personam*.

(c) Foreign arbitration awards

In terms of the Arbitration Law of 1968 an application for the confirmation or setting aside of a foreign arbitral award, i.e. one made outside Israel to which an international convention applies to which Israel is a party and which lays down provisions as to the matter in question, shall be filed and dealt with in accordance with and subject to those provisions.

Israel is party to the Geneva Protocol of 1923 and the New York Convention of 1958. Both the Protocol and the Convention provide for two non-residents to conduct arbitral proceedings in Israel. Israeli courts will in general not intervene in such proceedings.

(d) Proceeds of the judgment

Generally the proceeds of a foreign judgment are freely exportable to foreign residents or non-Israeli citizens, albeit that a specific permit from the Department of Foreign Currency Control may be required.

CHAPTER 13

ITALY

Pietro Palandri and Marco Lopez de Gonzalo
Studio Legale Mordiglia, via XX Settembre 14/17, 1612 Genova, Italy

1. JURISDICTION

What are the general grounds on which courts will accept jurisdiction?

The grounds on which Italian jurisdiction can be established are set out in Article 3 of law no. 218/1995, which refers to the rules provided by Article 5 of the EEC Convention on Civil Jurisdiction and Judgments. Thus the rules of the Convention are now the general law of Italy and apply even when the Convention by itself would not apply.

We would also mention that under Article 7 of law no. 218/1995 if proceedings on the same dispute have been previously instituted in another jurisdiction, the Italian court, if there is a reasonable expectation that the foreign judgment will be capable of being recognised in Italy, suspends the Italian proceedings. The Italian proceedings can then be resumed only if the foreign court eventually declines jurisdiction or if the recognition of the foreign judgment in Italy is denied. Within the scope of the EEC Convention, when the same proceedings are pending in a different jurisdiction the court later seized must suspend proceedings until the jurisdiction of the court first seized has been ascertained.

We now turn to consider the various specific grounds on which Italian jurisdiction can be established.

(a) Domicile

Defendants domiciled in Italy can always be sued before Italian courts.

(b) Place of business/residence/office

Foreign companies can be sued before Italian courts when they have in Italy an office or place of business, provided that the dispute refers to such office or place of business.

(c) Assets located within the jurisdiction

The presence of assets in Italy would establish Italian jurisdiction only for interim measures (arrest) of such assets, but would not in itself establish Italian jurisdiction on the merits of the dispute.

(d) Act complained of within the jurisdiction

For claims in contract, proceedings can be instituted in Italy when the obligation in dispute has been or should have been performed in Italy. There are however special rules for labour contracts, consumer contracts and insurance contracts.

For claims in tort, proceedings can be instituted in Italy when the negligent act/omission or the damage occurred in Italy.

(e) Contract governed by local law

This is not relevant in order to establish Italian jurisdiction.

(f) Conventions

Italy is a party to the EEC Convention on Civil Jurisdiction and Judgments (which, as we have said above, is now to a large extent Italian general law).

Italy is also a party to the 1952 Brussels Convention on Civil Jurisdiction on Collision Claims and to the 1952 Brussels Convention on Arrest of Ships.

(g) Clause attributing jurisdiction

Italian jurisdiction can be accepted by the defendant either explicitly (by means of a jurisdiction clause in the contract) or impliedly (by entering an appearance in the proceedings without objecting to Italian jurisdiction).

Italian jurisdiction can be excluded by means of choice of jurisdiction or arbitration clauses. Arbitration clauses are governed by the 1958 New York Convention, which requires them to be in writing. Jurisdiction clauses are governed by Article 4.2 of law no. 218/1995 which requires them to be evidenced in writing. Within the scope of the EEC Civil Jurisdiction Convention jurisdiction clauses are governed by Article 17 of the Convention, which requires them to be stipulated in writing or in a form which is acceptable under international trade usages.

(h) Other

Special rules relating to particular categories of disputes are contained in the Conventions mentioned at sub-paragraph (f) above.

(i) Counterclaim/third-party proceedings

When suit is brought against two or more defendants it is sufficient to establish Italian jurisdiction in respect of one of them and Italian jurisdiction would then apply to all of them. If Italian jurisdiction is established in respect of the main claim, it would then apply also to counterclaims arising out of the same contract or of the same facts and to indemnity or third-party claims.

2. MARITIME CLAIMS

(a) Is there special jurisdiction for maritime claims based on arrest of a vessel in the jurisdiction?

An order of arrest of a vessel can be obtained either when there is Italian jurisdiction on the merits of the claim (based on the criteria illustrated above) or when there is no Italian jurisdiction on the merits of the claim but the vessel to be arrested is at an Italian port.

The arrest of a vessel in Italy would not by itself establish Italian jurisdiction on the merits except when the 1952 Brussels Convention on the Arrest of Ships applies, in the cases provided by Article 7 of the Convention.

(b) Specific

Article 7 of the Convention provides for jurisdiction on the merits in the following cases:

- if the claimant has its principal place of business in Italy;
- if the claim arose in Italy;
- if the claim concerns the voyage of the ship during which the arrest was made;
- if the claim arose out of a collision;
- if the claim is for salvage;
- if the claim is based upon a mortgage.

(c) What are the grounds for arrest?

The grounds for arresting a ship are a *prima facie* claim and the likelihood of the debtor being or becoming insolvent (see section 5 below). This latter requisite is not necessary where the claim is assisted by a maritime lien.

Ships flying the flag of a Contracting State of the 1952 Arrest Convention, can be arrested only in connection with one of the maritime claims listed in Article 1 of the Convention.

(d) Need the arrested vessel be connected with the claim or can other vessels in the same legal (or beneficial) ownership also be arrested?

In addition to the ship to which the claim refers, a sister-ship can be arrested. Maritime liens however can be enforced only on the ship to which they refer.

(e) What procedural differences apply to special maritime jurisdiction?

Proceedings in maritime matters (both arrest proceedings and proceedings on the merits) are governed by the general rules of procedure provided by the Civil Procedure Code.

(f) What jurisdictional rules are there as to limitation of liability?

Italy did not ratify the 1976 London Limitation Convention and Article 11 of the Convention accordingly would not be applied.

According to Article 620 of the Italian Code of Navigation limitation proceedings in respect of an Italian flag vessel can always be instituted in Italy (more precisely in the court of the ship's port of registry). In addition to that, Article 6 *bis* of the EEC Convention on Civil Jurisdiction and Judgments (which is now the general law of Italy) provides that limitation proceedings can be instituted in Italy when Italian courts have jurisdiction on the claims subject to limitation.

When limitation proceedings are instituted in Italy in respect of non-Italian flag vessels, the Italian courts would apply the law of the flag to the substantive issues and Italian law to procedural matters.

3. SERVICE OF PROCEEDINGS

What rules apply to service of proceedings outside the jurisdiction?

In order to sue a foreign defendant before an Italian court a writ of summons must be served upon the defendant at his domicile or registered office.

Italy ratified the 1961 Hague Convention and therefore service to defendants located in a Contracting State is to be made in a manner prescribed by the Convention (i.e. through the designated Authority of the receiving state).

Service to defendants located in a non-Contracting State is to be made in compliance with Article 142 of the Civil Procedure Code, i.e. one copy by mail plus one copy through the Ministry of Foreign Affairs.

In cases of particular urgency the court may authorise service by telex or telefax.

4. COSTS

What are the costs implications of starting proceedings?

(a) Court fees

Deposit and exchange of pleadings are subject to stamp duties. Duties apply also to service of documents through court bailiff, to certify true copies, to notarised power of attorney.

(b) Lawyers' fees

Fees are calculated on the basis of a tariff set out by Italian law; such tariff takes into account the nature of the work carried out and the amount at stake and ranges between a minimum and a maximum. Alternatively, an hourly rate can be agreed upon.

Contingency fees are not allowed. In addition to fees, lawyers are entitled to a 10 per cent overhead for general costs plus actual disbursements.

(c) Recovery of costs from unsuccessful party

The general rule is that the unsuccessful party must reimburse costs to the successful party; such costs are taxed by the court and may not correspond to actual costs incurred. It is also in the discretion of the court to limit the recovery to part of the costs or even to order that each party bears its own costs.

(d) Security for costs

There is no provision in Italian procedural law in respect of security for costs. Italy is not a party to conventions providing for *cautio judicatum solvi*.

5. INTERIM ARREST

(a) Are interim arrest/freezing of assets/other provisional measures permitted to provide security for domestic proceedings and/or proceedings in another jurisdiction?

Under the heading "conservative measures", the Italian Code of Civil Procedure contemplates arrest proceedings which can be brought to provide security in respect of claims and/or actions referred or to be referred to the Italian jurisdiction or foreign jurisdictions.

There are two types of arrest proceeding, namely:

- the judicial seizure (*sequestro giudiziario*) aimed to seize/arrest movable or immovable assets the ownership of which is under dispute, or documentation constituting evidence which can be lost;
- conservative seizure (*sequestro conservativo*) aimed to arrest/attach/freeze assets of debtors in order to provide security in respect of a claim.

(b) What criteria apply to this?

Both the judicial and the conservative seizures can be granted by an Italian court on condition that the arrestor produces evidence satisfying the court of (a) the *prima facie* good grounds of the claim and (b) the risk of losing the possibility of enforcing the final judgment in the proceedings on the merits in case the arrest is not granted.

(c) Is there a limit on jurisdictions whose proceedings are recognised for this purpose?

There are no limits on jurisdictions whose proceedings are recognised for the purpose of bringing arrest proceedings before the Italian courts. However, an arrest order granted in view of a claim referred to ordinary or arbitration proceedings pending or to be instituted in another jurisdiction loses its effectiveness if proceedings on the merits are not instituted within the time limit fixed by the court with the order of arrest (which cannot exceed 30 days from the date of the order) or if, once the foreign judgment or award on the merits has been issued, proceedings for obtaining the recognition in Italy of such judgment or award are not instituted within 60 days from the date the judgment or award is issued.

(d) Is there a requirement for counter-security?

At the moment of the issue of the order of arrest or successively the court may, but is not bound to, order the arrestors to provide a counter-security covering the legal costs and the damages which the defendants may suffer as a consequence of a wrongful arrest. The amount of the counter-security is left to the discretion of the court, which also may determine the form (cash deposit or bank guarantee) in which the counter-security is to be given.

(e) Can applications be made ex parte?

The arrestors must lodge an application supported by pleadings, evidence and a Power of Attorney with the clerk of the competent court. The judge entrusted with the case (appointed by the President of the court immediately after the application is lodged) must urgently fix a hearing for the parties' appearance and cannot take any decision before such hearing is held. Nevertheless, in urgent cases (normally, for instance, in cases relating to the arrest of ships) the judge can issue an order of arrest on the basis of the application only, without first hearing the defendant. In such case, however, the judge must fix a hearing for the parties' attendance within the next 15 days, on which occasion the order of arrest can be confirmed, revoked or modified.

(f) How quickly can an order be made?

An order of arrest in an urgent case for which the judge decides to issue it without first hearing the defendant can be obtained in a few hours after the application is lodged.

In case the judge vested with the case decides to first hear the defendant before taking a decision, it may take a few days after the application is made to obtain an order.

(g) Will the order bind third parties?

An order of arrest has effect not only between the partes to the dispute but also as regards any other third parties. Sale and/or other transactions relating to assets seized by the arrest have no effect in relation to the arrestors, whilst third parties holding arrested assets belonging to debtors cannot dispose of them and are responsible as custodian.

On the other hand, the arrest of assets (formally or apparently) belonging to a party other than the debtor cannot be applied for unless proceedings for obtaining a declaration that such assets actually belong to the debtor are instituted.

(h) What are the consequences of breach of an order?

As a consequence of an order of arrest, assets seized by the arrest cannot be disposed of or sold or otherwise transferred to third parties. The breach of such provision does not however have any consequence for the arrestors, in relation to whom, as noted above, the sale of an asset seized by an arrest is ineffective. In case of arrest of assets in the hands of third parties, the third parties become responsible for the custody of the assets and a breach of the order of arrest by such third parties makes them responsible for damages towards the arrestors.

Breach of an order of arrest constitutes also a criminal offence.

(i) Is there a limit to types of asset, e.g. physical asset/account balances?

According to the Italian procedural law, arrestors may attach any type of assets, including physical assets, credits and account balances. There are indeed assets which according to the Code of Civil Procedure cannot be arrested, but in view of the nature of such assets (e.g. essential personal effects, etc.) the limitation is not relevant in practice.

(j) What if third parties are affected?

Third parties affected by an arrest order attaching their assets instead of those of debtors can take action for obtaining the release from arrest by entering an appearance in the arrest proceedings (if still pending) or in the proceedings regarding the merits of the dispute if such proceedings are pending before the Italian courts. If such proceedings are not pending, third parties have to bring separate proceedings to protect their interests and obtain the release from arrest of their assets.

(k) What other provisional measures may be ordered, e.g. appointment of surveyor or receiver, security?

Under the heading "conservative measures", the Italian Code of Civil Procedure contemplates the following additional measures.

(i) Preliminary investigation proceedings

These proceedings are aimed at the collection of evidence in respect of a dispute for which ordinary proceedings are not yet pending in cases in which such evidence can be lost before such ordinary proceedings are commenced. By means of such proceedings a party may obtain either the appointment of a Court Surveyor or of a judge tasked with taking oral testimony. It is however to be pointed out that, according to the most recent decisions of the Italian Court of Cassation, preliminary investigation proceedings cannot be brought in connection with disputes for which the Italian courts do not have jurisdiction.

(ii) Urgent orders

These are orders of conservative nature, other than arrest or similar orders, aimed to preserve for the applicant the possibility of the enforcement in the future of a judgment on the merits. The purpose of the proceedings for urgent orders is to grant a conservative measure in favour of the applicant in all cases in which the applicant has need of preserving a situation in view of the future enforcement of a judgment but the procedural law does not contemplate any specific remedy satisfying such need. For instance, a party damaged by the behaviour of another party may obtain an urgent order preventing such behaviour (which may cause unrepealable damages) pending the proceedings for obtaining a judgment in its favour.

6. RECOGNITION OF JUDGMENTS/AWARDS

(a) What treaties/conventions apply (i) to enable judgments to be enforced abroad and (ii) to enable enforcement of foreign judgments domestically?

(i) Italy is a party to the EEC Convention on Civil Jurisdiction and Judgments and to the Lugano Convention. Enforcement of judgments between Contracting States is therefore governed by such Conventions.

(ii) Enforcement in Italy of foreign judgments from non-Contracting States is governed by Articles. 64–67 of law no. 218/1995.

(b) What procedure is followed to enforce a foreign judgment (i) governed by a treaty/convention and (ii) not governed by a treaty/convention?

(i) Governed by a treaty/convention

When the EEC Convention or the Lugano Convention applies, applications for the enforcement in Italy of foreign judgments must be filed with the Court of Appeal of the place where enforcement is sought (i.e. the place where the defendant has his principal place of business or where the defendant's assets are located). The Court of Appeal considers the application *ex parte* (i.e. without the defendant being summonsed) and issues a decree. If the decree upholds the application, it is served upon the defendant who can file an opposition within 30 days; if the application is rejected, it is up to the plaintiff to file an opposition. If an opposition is filed (either by the defendant or by the plaintiff) ordinary proceedings will follow before the Court of Appeal.

The plaintiff must submit with his application the documents listed in Articles 46–47 of the Convention, namely:

- a certified copy of the judgment;
- if it is a default judgment, evidence that the writ of summons was properly served;
- evidence that the judgment is enforceable in the state where it was issued and has been served upon the defendant.

Enforcement can be denied only on the following grounds:

- if it is contrary to public policy;
- if the writ of summons was not properly served;
- if the judgment is in contrast to an Italian judgment on the same dispute;
- if the foreign court did not apply the proper law to some preliminary issues;

— if the foreign judgment is in contrast to a judgment previously issued in another state which could be recognised in Italy;
— if the provisions of Articles 7–16 of the Convention (regarding jurisdiction) were not properly applied by the foreign court.

(ii) Not governed by a treaty/convention

When the Conventions mentioned above do not apply, the enforcement of foreign judgments is governed by law no. 218/1995. Proceedings must be instituted before the competent Court of Appeal by means of a writ of summons. In order to obtain from the Court of Appeal a judgment allowing the enforcement of the foreign judgment the plaintiff must prove:

— that the foreign court had jurisdiction (on the basis of the Italian rules);
— that the writ of summons was properly served and the defendant was allowed to plead his case;
— that the defendant filed an appearance in the proceedings or that default proceedings were properly taken;
— that the judgment is final in the state where it was issued;
— that there are no proceedings on the same dispute pending in Italy which were instituted before the foreign proceedings;
— that the foreign judgment is not contrary to public policy.

(c) What about foreign arbitration awards?

The enforcement in Italy of foreign arbitration awards is governed by New York Convention 1958 (which was ratified by law no. 62/1968) and by law no. 25/1994.

The application must be filed with the Court of Appeal of the place where enforcement is sought, i.e. generally the place where the defendant has his principal place of business or where the defendant's assets are located. The Court of Appeal considers the application *ex parte* (i.e. without the defendant being summonsed) and issues a decree. If the decree upholds the application, it is served upon the defendant who can file an opposition within 30 days; if the application is rejected it is up to the plaintiff to file an opposition. If an opposition is filed (either by the defendant or by the plaintiff) ordinary proceedings will follow before the Court of Appeal.

The plaintiff must submit with his application the original or a certified copy of the contract including the arbitration clause and the original or a certified copy of the award.

Enforcement of the award can be denied only if the court finds that the arbitrators decided on a matter which under Italian law could not be referred to arbitration or that the award is contrary to public policy. Enforcement is also denied if the defendant proves:

- that the arbitration clause had not been validly stipulated;
- that the defendant had not been properly notified of proceedings;
- that the arbitrators exceeded their powers in issuing a decision on a matter which was not covered by the arbitration agreement;
- that the arbitral proceedings did not comply with the arbitration agreement or with the applicable law;
- that the award is not binding or has been set aside or suspended.

(d) Will proceeds of a judgment be freely exportable?

There are no restrictions on the transfer abroad of proceeds of a judgment in favour of a foreign plaintiff.

CHAPTER 14

LUXEMBOURG

Jean-Paul Kill (Doctor of Law)
Maritime & Commercial Consulting s.a.r.l., PO Box 1736, L-1017 Luxembourg

1. JURISDICTION

This summary will only focus on the principles governing territorial competence and will disregard the rules *ratione materiae* and *ratione personae*.

According to Luxembourg law the principles governing the conflict of laws and jurisdictions may be divided into two categories.

Brussels and Lugano Convention conflict

The provisions contained in the Convention on Jurisdiction and Enforcement of Judgments in Civil and Commercial Matters signed in Brussels and dated 27 September 1968 as amended by the Accession Conventions dated 6 October 1978 and 26 May 1989 as supplemented by the Interpretation Protocol dated 3 June 1971 (hereinafter "the Brussels Convention") are applicable in accordance with the interpretation thereof given by the European Court of Justice.

The Accession Convention dated 25 October 1982 only contains the necessary addenda for the new Contracting States.

The Lugano Convention dated 18 September 1988 contains similar provisions to those contained in the Brussels Convention and is applicable whenever EU and EFTA residents are parties to a litigation.

Non-convention conflict

The general provisions set out in the Civil Code and Code of Civil Procedure are applicable in all cases of non-convention conflict of laws and jurisdictions.

Such laws on conflict of jurisdiction apply to civil and commercial litigations where:

1. one party is a Luxembourg resident and the other party(ies) is/are non-EU and non-EFTA residents; or
2. all parties have their domicile in Luxembourg provided that the parties have not agreed upon a foreign law and jurisdiction clause in a contract with an international character.

In the absence of any specific law and jurisdiction clause the following rules on territorial competence are applicable.

(a) Domicile of the defendant

The provisions contained in Article 25 of the Code of Civil Procedure designate the jurisdiction of the domicile of the defendant, or failing that, of his residence for personal and *in personam* litigations. This principle is in accordance with Article 2(1) of the Brussels Convention. If the parties have elected a domicile for the execution of a contract the litigation may be brought before the court of such domicile. In the case of several defendant parties the litigation may be brought before the court of the domicile of any defendant.

(b) Branch and/or permanent establishment of a company defendant

With respect to companies Article 36 of the Commercial Code provides that a company may be summoned before the jurisdiction of its registered office as well as that of the branch and/or permanent establishment with the proviso that such branch and/or permanent establishment has an agent authorised to enter into negotiation with third parties and the claim is related to the activities of such branch. In the case of litigations relating to contractual insurance policies suit may also be brought before the court of the domicile of the general agent of the insurance company.

(c) Competence of the court where assets are located

For real estate litigants the claims may be brought before the court where such assets are located.

The general rules on territorial competence are not applicable where urgent and conservatory measures are to be taken. The jurisdictions may order an arrest (*saisie-arret*) of assets located in Luxembourg based on their legal competence to decide upon the execution of judgments and/or legal titles against third parties and/or assets within Luxembourg. The jurisprudence accepts authorisation of arrest of money deposited with a Luxembourg bank even in cases where the parties to a litigation are non-residents (Court of Justice, 26 September 1980). The validation demand for the arrest is brought before the jurisdiction of the domicile of the seized party.

In commercial litigation such competence is based on Article 417 *et seq.* of the Code of Civil Procedure which contain the rules for summary procedure.

(d) Act complained of within the jurisdiction

Article 25 of the Code of Civil Procedure provides further for competence of jurisdiction where contractual obligations have to be performed in that place.

This provision is interpreted in accordance with the rules contained in the

Convention on the law applicable to contractual obligations signed in Rome and dated June 1980 as supplemented by the two Protocols (hereinafter "the Rome Convention") and the Convention on the applicable law on international sales of goods signed in The Hague and dated 1 July 1964. Both conventions permit the determination of *forum conveniens* for a litigation in the absence of any specific jurisdiction and law clause.

Article 4 of the Rome Convention provides that the applicable law is that of the Contracting State with which the contract has the closest relation, where the closest relation means the place where the most characteristic obligation is deemed to be performed. In the absence of any jurisdiction clause the competent court is deemed to be that of the place where such characteristic obligations are performed.

Exceptional territorial competence of Articles 14 and 15 of the Civil Code

Article 14 of the Civil Code provides that a foreigner not resident in Luxembourg may be summoned before a Luxembourg court in regard to the execution of an obligation contracted with a Luxembourg citizen; the word "obligation" includes any kind of obligation, contractual, extracontractual or tortious, but excludes claims relating to real estate located outside Luxembourg.

Article 15 of the Civil Code provides that a Luxembourg citizen may be summoned before a Luxembourg jurisdiction for an obligation contracted outside Luxembourg with a foreigner. The definition of obligation is the same as the one set out in Article 14.

Such exceptional territorial competence may be waived by the parties in writing or tacitly.

The Brussels Convention has extended this privilege to any EU resident in Luxembourg and Luxembourg has waived such privileges in the Brussels Convention for EU residents pursuant to Article 3 thereof.

(e) Competence based on the applicable law

The Luxembourg courts are competent to decide on matters governed by Luxembourg law, whether such application derives from international private law convention or principle or from a governing law clause.

The Luxembourg jurisdiction will apply the rules governing their competence *ratione materiae*, *ratione personae* and *ratione loci*.

(f) Competence governed by international conventions

The most significant conventions entered into by Luxembourg for these purposes are the Brussels and Lugano Conventions. The present summary will only expand on the specific provisions regarding Luxembourg.

As mentioned above Luxembourg has waived the exceptional territorial competence contained in Articles 14 and 15 of the Civil Code pursuant to Article 3 of the Conventions. The most distinctive provisions regarding Luxembourg are contained in Article 1 of the Annex Protocol to the Conventions. Article 1(1) provides that any person domiciled in Luxembourg who has been summoned to a court of another Contracting State pursuant to Article 5(1) of the Conventions may decline such competence.

Article 5 of the Conventions provides: "A person domiciled in a Contracting State may in another Contracting State be sued in matters relating to contract in the courts of the place of performance of the obligation in question."

The second sentence of Article 1 of this Annex Protocol further provides that the foreign court declares itself not competent when the Luxembourg resident does not enter an appearance.

Although the refusal to accept competence has to be applied *ex officio* by the jurisdiction of the Contracting State, the presence or representation in court of the Luxembourg resident defendant is advisable in order to invoke this refusal of competence, since the Luxembourg court is not allowed to verify that such condition has been fulfilled when a judgment by default is presented for the *exequatur* and the execution of the judgment. The grounds for refusal of the *exequatur* are enumerated in a limited way in Article 27 of the Conventions.

Some authors express the opinion that such refusal of competence would be contrary to the provisions of Article 4(1) and (2) of the Rome Convention in which Luxembourg has not made a similar reservation.

Article 1(2) of the Annex to the Conventions provides that a foreign jurisdiction clause within the meaning of Article 17 thereof must be expressly and specially accepted by the Luxembourg party to an agreement as a condition for its validity. Such condition is interpreted as the necessity for a special provision exclusively dedicated to the attribution of jurisdiction duly signed by the Luxembourg resident which may be included in the same document. The signature of the Luxembourg resident on the agreement containing a jurisdiction clause does not fulfil this condition (ECJ, 6 May 1980, *Porta Leasing*).

(g) Competence based on a jurisdiction clause

A foreign jurisdiction clause is legal and binding provided such provision does not violate any public policy law (*ordre public*), for example where a final consumer is a party thereto.

(h) Lis pendens

The general rule is that the court first seised is competent to decide on the case where national jurisdictions are involved. Unlike the French doctrine the Luxembourg jurisdictions hesitate to declare the foreign court first seised competent even when there is non-exclusive competence and national public policy is not infringed.

(i) Counterclaims

The counterclaims based on the same contract or the same facts as the original claim are brought before the jurisdiction seised with the original claim whether the counterclaim gets a separate judgment or is based on a defence to the original claim. In this respect the national law differs from Article 6(3) of the Brussels Convention.

2. MARITIME CLAIMS

(a) Jurisdiction based on arrest

The International Convention for the Unification of Certain Rules relating to Arrest of Seagoing Ships signed in Brussels and dated 10 May 1952 (hereinafter "the Arrest Convention") and the Convention for the Unification of Certain Rules relating to Maritime Liens and Mortgages signed in Brussels and dated 10 April 1926 ("the Liens and Mortgages Convention") have been ratified and enacted into Luxembourg legislation.

The Luxembourg Maritime Act (hereinafter "LMA") does not provide for a special jurisdiction competent for maritime claims based on arrest of a vessel, so that the general rules set out in the Code of Civil Procedure and the Commercial Code apply.

Article 40 of the LMA enumerates in a limited way the liens which rank prior to other claims; the only reference to arrest of a vessel is contained in Article 54 of the LMA which laconically provides that such rights shall be extinguished by the forced sale of the vessel. According to the general applicable principles the privileges and mortgages are governed by the *lex rei sitae* rule, which in the specific case of a vessel designates the jurisdiction of the registration of the vessel as the competent one. Such law may be in competition with the law where the vessel is arrested (*lex fori arresti* and *lex concursus*) in the cases provided for in Articles 3 to 9 of the Arrest Convention each time the Convention applies.

In such absence the jurisdiction of the domicile and/or residence and/or the place of registration of the vessel will be competent, so the district court (*tribunal d'arondissement*) for that place able to deal with commercial matters will be competent.

The privileges and liens are limited in time and expire after a period of one year except in the case of claims relating to supplies necessary for the preservation of the vessel, for which the period is six months in accordance with Article 54 paragraph 2 of LMA.

The Law dated 14 July 1966 on the registration of waterway vessels provides for specific rules governing the arrest of such vessels but expressly excludes seagoing vessels.

Therefore in the absence of specific provisions and a judgment with *exequatur* the general rules set out in Articles 417 to 442 of the Code of Civil Procedure are applicable to conservatory proceedings (*saisie conservatoire commerciale*).

Article 417 of the Code of Civil Procedure enumerates the following conditions to be fulfilled for a conservatory arrest:

1. the circumstances request speed;
2. the claim has the appearance of certainty; and
3. the claim is due and payable or may be easily rendered so.

The demand is presented to the president of the district court (*tribunal d'arondissement*) and the period for summoning the defendant may be shortened to a few hours. Article 418 of the Code of Civil Procedure extends the same provisions to maritime claims.

The following international maritime conventions have been ratified and enacted into the national legislation by the LMA:

— International Convention for the Unification of certain Rules of Law with respect to Collision between Vessels signed in Brussels and dated 23 September 1910
— Convention for the Unification of certain Rules of Law relating to Assistance and Salvage at Sea signed in Brussels and dated 23 September 1910
— International Convention for the Unification of certain Rules of Law relating to Bills of Lading signed in Brussels and dated 25 August 1924 and Protocol of signature (Hague Rules)
— Protocol to amend the International Convention for the Unification of certain Rules of Law relating to Bills of Lading signed in Brussels and dated 23 February 1968 (Visby Rules)
— Protocol to amend the International Convention for the Unification of certain Rules of Law relating to Bills of Lading (25 August 1924 as amended by the Protocol of 23 February 1968) dated 21 December 1979
— International Convention for the Unification of certain Rules concerning the Immunity of State-owned Ships dated 10 April 1926
— International Convention on certain Rules concerning Civil Jurisdiction in Matters of Collision dated 10 May 1952
— International Convention relating to the Limitation of Owners of Seagoing Ships dated 10 October 1957 and the amendment Protocol dated 10 December 1979.

The following specific provisions have been enacted in the national law.

(b) Specific

(i) Collision

For the purposes of the application of Article 4 of the Collision Convention 1910, when the responsibility of one vessel *vis-à-vis* the victims and/or their heirs has been limited or cancelled by the law or by contract such victims may not claim more than the portion for which the other vessel is liable. The same provision shall also apply to Article 12–2 of the Convention.

(ii) Assistance at sea

In the case referred to in Article 15–2 of the Convention on Assistance and Salvage at Sea 1910 the provisions of the Convention shall apply.

(iii) Carriage under a bill of lading

The handling consignment and other operations involved in maritime transport which are not provided for by the conventions relating to carriage under a bill of lading referred to under Part 6 shall be subject to the law of the port where the company operates. The same provisions shall apply to deck cargo. The carriage under a bill of lading of livestock shall be subject to the risks and perils of the merchandise.

(iv) General average

General average shall be governed by the York-Antwerp Rules even if the contract does not specifically refer to the Rules. Any legal action involving general average will be time barred after five years from the date on which the voyage ended.

Any certain and payable claim may serve as ground for an arrest but the claim will rank below liens and privileges as set out in Article 40 LMA.

A claim giving rise to an arrest can be unconnected to the vessel subject to the arrest provided it is in the same ownership (sister ship); the liens which allow a right *in rem* are limited only to the specific vessel.

The LMA does not provide for a specific jurisdiction nor for a specific proceeding for maritime claims so that the general rules contained in the Commercial Code and the Code of Civil Procedure apply.

(c) Grounds for arrest

An order for an arrest may be presented for (i) any lien as mentioned in Article 40 of the LMA and (ii) any claim which fulfils the conditions mentioned in Article 417 of the Code of Civil Procedure (namely that the circumstances are of an urgent nature, the claim is due and payable and the claim has the appearance of certainty.

(d) Connection between the claim and the vessel

The liens ("*privilèges*") are confined to the vessel which gives rise to such lien whereas a general claim, on which an arrest may be based, allows the creditor to arrest any vessel belonging to the same beneficial owner.

(e) Procedural differences

Since the LMA does not provide for a special maritime jurisdiction the general rules contained the Code of Civil Procedure are applicable.

(f) Jurisdictional rules as to the limitation of liability

There are no specific jurisdictional rules regarding the limitation of liability.

3. SERVICE OF PROCEEDINGS

The Hague Convention

Luxembourg has enacted into national legislation the following conventions/ treaties on the service of proceedings and requests abroad in civil and commercial matters:

- the Convention signed in The Hague and dated 19 November 1965 amending the 1905 Convention and 1954 Convention;
- bilateral treaties with Germany (1 August 1909), Austria (12 March 1972), Belgium (11 and 19 March 1965), France (14 March 1884), the Netherlands (11 and 14 February 1974) and Switzerland (12 and 15 February 1979).

Luxembourg has designated the general prosecutor (*procureur générale*) of the Supreme Court of Justice as the central authority within the meaning of Article 2 of the 1965 Hague Convention.

The period during which an absent party may be relieved of the exemption resulting from the period of appeal has been fixed to one year.

4. COSTS

(a) Court fees

Court fees are moderate and cover the notification/summons costs and expenses; *ad valorem* registration tax on private agreements submitted to the court has been abolished except for real estate agreements.

(b) Lawyers' fees

There is no fee schedule of lawyers' fees incorporated in a law, therefore fees are subject to agreement. However, contingency fees are expressly prohibited.

(c) Recovery of costs from unsuccessful party

Article 131(1) of the Code of Civil Procedure provides that the court may order any party to pay an assessed amount of expenses incurred to the other party in connection with the lawsuit if such payment seems equitable.

(d) Security for costs

According to Article 166 of the Code of Civil Procedure a foreign party claimant must provide upon the defendant's request a security (*cautio judicatum solvi*) in order to provide security for the payment of expenses and damages which he may be ordered by the court to pay. However, in Article 17 of the 1954 Hague Convention the Contracting States have waived such provision.

5. INTERIM ARREST

(a) Are interim arrest/freezing of assets/other provisional measures permitted to provide security for domestic proceedings and/or proceedings in another jurisdiction?

In the absence of a judgment with *exequatur* the following legal proceedings apply:

- The president of the district court may in accordance with Article 806 of the Code of Civil Procedure relating to injunction/order (*référé-provision*) grant a provision to a claimant, when the claim subject to the request is not seriously contested. The urgency of the matter has been excluded as a condition to the granting of such injunction and/or order.
- Article 417 of the Code of Civil Procedure provides that assets may be arrested (*saisie-arret*) on a provisional basis without any title having the *exequatur* as security for domestic as well as foreign proceedings. The following conditions must be fulfilled in such cases in order to obtain an arrest-injunction:
  (a) urgency: the circumstances require urgent action
  (b) certainty: the claim appears to be justifiable
  (c) liquidity: the claim is due and payable.

(b) What criteria apply to this?

The arrest-injunction must be notified to the third party physically detaining the assets or owing an amount of money to the party subject to arrest in the case of a bank deposit. The third party and the arrestee party must be summoned, by means of a summons delivered to them, to appear before the court in order to have the arrest validated.

(c) Is there a limit on jurisdictions whose proceedings are recognised for this purpose?

Since no title vested with the *exequatur* is a condition precedent and the injunction is a provisional measure no limitation on jurisdiction exists.

(d) Is there a requirement for counter-security?

The provisions provided for in Article 166 of the Code of Civil Procedure (*cautio judicatum solvi*) are applicable to a foreign counterclaimant if the counterparty so requests. However, Luxembourg, as a Contracting State to the 1954 Hague Convention, has waived such provision pursuant to Article 17 thereto, with respect to signatory parties.

(e) Can applications be made ex parte?

A third party may exercise the rights of his debtor if such debtor is insolvent (*action oblique*) pursuant to Article 1166 of the Civil Code or if such debtor has acted in fraud of his creditor's rights and such creditor has suffered a prejudice (*action paulienne*).

(f) How quickly can an order be made?

The president of the district court may order the arrest without any time limit, and the parties may be summoned to appear within a short period of time as determined by the president.

(g) Will the order bind third parties?

A third party detaining assets or owing money to the party subject to arrest is bound by the arrest after being notified of the summons of arrest.

(h) What are the consequences of breach of an order?

If the third party fails to comply with the arrest he may be forced to pay a second time or to pay an amount corresponding to the actual value of the deposited and arrested assets according to the principle "he who pays badly pays twice".

(i) Is there a limit to types of assets?

Any kind of assets may be arrested; the legal definition may vary, i.e. *saisie-gagerie*, *saisie-arret*, etc.

6. RECOGNITION OF JUDGMENTS/AWARDS

(a) What treaties/conventions apply (i) to enable judgments to be enforced abroad and (ii) to enable enforcement of foreign judgments domestically?

The conditions for a foreign judgment to receive the *exequatur* in Luxembourg and to become enforceable vary, depending on whether the general provisions as set out in Articles 545–556 of the Code of Civil Procedure or the provisions of the Brussels Convention are applicable.

Luxembourg has up to now executed only one bilateral treaty with Austria for the recognition and enforcement of judgments.

(b) What procedure is followed to enforce a foreign judgment (i) governed by a treaty/convention and (ii) not governed by a treaty/convention?

The general provisions as set out in the Code of Civil Procedure

The following conditions for obtaining the *exequatur* in Luxembourg have to be fulfilled pursuant to Articles 2123–2128 of the Civil Code:

(a) the foreign judgment must have the *exequatur* in the country where it was rendered; and
(b) the foreign court was competent in accordance with Luxembourg law on conflict of jurisdiction;
(c) the foreign jurisdiction was competent in accordance with its proper law on conflict of jurisdiction;
(d) the law designated by the Luxembourg law was properly applied;
(e) the law regarding legal proceedings was properly applied; and finally
(f) the judgment does not violate national public policy (*ordre public*).

The demand for *exequatur* will be brought before the district court that decides civil matters.

The jurisdiction must verify that all the conditions are fulfilled, but is not entitled to restate the judgment.

The provisions of the Brussels and Lugano Conventions

The conditions to be fulfilled in order to enforce an EU/EFTA judgment are set out in Articles 26–45 of the Conventions. The request is brought before the president of the district court and an appeal may be brought before the Supreme Court dealing in civil appeal matters.

(c) What about foreign arbitration awards?

The Convention on the Recognition and Execution of Foreign Arbitral Awards signed in New York and dated 10 June 1958 ("the New York Convention") has been ratified and enacted into the national legislation. In order to qualify as a foreign arbitration award, the award must be rendered abroad according to Article 1028 paragraph 1 of the Code of Civil Procedure. Such foreign arbitration award must obtain the *exequatur* in order to become enforceable in Luxembourg. The demand of *exequatur* is presented to the president of the district court.

Such *exequatur* may be refused in the cases mentioned in the New York Convention if the state of the arbitration award is a Contracting State or failing this (i.e. non New York Convention state) under the following conditions:

- the award is still appealable in such state;
- the award and the execution thereof violate public policy; or
- it is not able to be submitted to arbitration; or
- any of the following cases of invalidation is determined:
  the arbitration agreement is not valid;
  the arbitrators have exceeded their competence;
  the arbitrators have omitted to decide on all the litigation issues;
  the arbitration court was irregularly composed;
  the right of defence has been infringed;
  the award is not set in motion unless agreed upon by the parties;
  the award contains contradictory provisions;
  the award is based on false evidence and declared so by a court decision;
  a decisive document is discovered after the award and was withheld by the defending party.

(d) Will proceeds of a judgment be freely exportable?

Luxembourg does not have any currency transfer restrictions.

CHAPTER 15

MALTA

Dr Louis Cassar-Pullicino
Prof. J.M. Ganado & Associates, 171 Old Bakery Street, Valletta VII 09, Malta

1. JURISDICTION

The various grounds on which courts will accept jurisdiction are contained in section 742 of the Code of Organisation and Civil Procedure. Such grounds of jurisdiction refer only to *in personam* jurisdiction. In admiralty matters the courts may exercise an *in rem* jurisdiction and this aspect is featured further later on in this chapter.

(a) Domicile

The concept of domicile has long served as a basis for jurisdiction although the courts have interpreted the concept in different ways. Traditionally "domicile" was equated with the concept of "residence", particularly as it was thought that the concept introduced into our legal system was in actual fact adopted from the Italian notion of "*domicilio*". More recently, however, our courts have applied the English notion of domicile, which in itself requires a more detailed investigation into the intention of the individual as well as other relevant circumstances concerning an individual's presence within our jurisdiction.

As a result of recent amendments to our Code of Organisation and Civil Procedure, domicile has now been put on an equal footing as "presence" and "residence" and essentially the courts will exercise jurisdiction in respect of any person so long as he is either domiciled, resident or present in Malta.

(b) Place of business/residence/office

A person's place of business does not feature directly as a basis of jurisdiction under Maltese law. However, it has been held by our courts that if it can be established that a foreign corporation has its principal place of business in Malta, then that corporation is to be deemed present in Malta and hence jurisdiction would be founded on the ground of "presence" in Malta (*Dr L. Cassar Pullicino noe* v. *Angelo Xuereb noe,* decided by the Court of Appeal on 7 October 1997).

The place of business would also become relevant in a case involving a person who has contracted an obligation in favour of a citizen or *resident* of Malta or of a body corporate incorporated or *operating* in Malta, provided that the judgment can be enforced in Malta.

(c) Assets located within the jurisdiction

The location of assets within the jurisdiction serves as a ground for the exercise of jurisdiction in those cases where the dispute brought before the courts concerns the assets situate or existing in Malta. The law does not qualify in any way the type of property in such cases and hence it is normally considered that any type of property, whether movable or immovable, corporeal or incorporeal, would create a basis of jurisdiction.

As has been referred to earlier, assets within the jurisdiction become an important consideration in those cases where the law requires that the judgment must be enforceable in Malta, such as in the case of any person who has contracted an obligation in favour of a Maltese citizen or ordinary resident, a company incorporated in Malta or merely operating in Malta.

(d) Act complained of within the jurisdiction

Section 742(d) of the Code of Organisation and Civil Procedure empowers a court to exercise its jurisdiction in cases involving "any person who has contracted an obligation in Malta, but only in regard to actions touching such obligation and provided such person is present in Malta". Our courts have interpreted the term "obligation" very widely and it is generally considered that even a tortuous obligation falls within the meaning of this provision. In this sense an act which is performed within our jurisdiction, whether falling within the law of contract, tort, quasi contract or quasi tort, would in all likelihood suffice for jurisdictional purposes.

(e) Contract governed by local law

The choice of Maltese law as the applicable law in a contract does not effect in any way the jurisdiction of the Maltese courts in any dispute arising from the same contract.

(f) Conventions

Malta is not a party to any international convention regulating jurisdiction.

(g) Clause attributing jurisdiction

In general, the parties to a contract are free to choose any forum for the resolution of disputes between them. Where proceedings are brought before the

Maltese courts notwithstanding a foreign jurisdiction clause in the contract, our courts have in many cases retained the discretionary power to determine whether in the particular circumstances of the case jurisdiction should be exercised all the same. In such cases the courts are guided by considerations such as whether any action in Malta is likely to be vexatious, oppressive or unjust or whether any party is likely to suffer undue prejudice. Where on the other hand the parties have agreed on an arbitration clause, the courts shall stay proceedings without prejudice to the right of the court to give any order or direction concerning the conduct of the arbitration proceedings.

(h) Other grounds of jurisdiction

The courts will exercise jurisdiction in matters concerning the following persons:

- (i) citizens of Malta, provided they have not established their domicile elsewhere;
- (ii) any person who has contracted an obligation in Malta in actions concerning such obligations and provided that he is present;
- (iii) any person who, expressly or tacitly, voluntarily submits or has agreed to submit to the jurisdiction of the courts.

(i) Counterclaim/third-party proceedings

(i) Counterclaim

The same rules would apply to a counterclaim brought forward by a defendant and in such circumstances a court would accept jurisdiction on the basis that such counterclaim would be construed as a submission to the local jurisdiction.

(ii) Third-party proceedings

The general rules of procedure would apply to such proceedings and one would have to determine whether the third party called in the suit falls within any of the categories of "persons" contemplated in section 742 of the Code of Organisation and Civil Procedure.

2. MARITIME CLAIMS

(a) Is there special jurisdiction for maritime claims based on arrest of a vessel in the jurisdiction?

The courts do exercise a special jurisdiction in respect of claims brought against a vessel *in rem*, which vessel must be present in the local jurisdiction.

Proceedings are in such case instituted against the ship itself as a defendant as represented by the master or failing this by the agent. *In rem* jurisdiction is exercised by virtue of English statutes adopted in our legal system. Malta adopts the Vice-Admiralty Court Act 1840 and the Admiralty Court Act 1861 and our admiralty jurisdiction is therefore determined in accordance with such laws.

(b) Specific

The specific heads of jurisdiction are the following:

(a) any mortgage of a ship;
(b) all claims relating to title to or ownership and possession of a ship arising in a cause of possession, salvage, damage, wages or bottomry;
(c) salvage claims;
(d) claims for damage received by a ship;
(e) claims for towage;
(f) claim for necessaries supplied;
(g) any claim for building, equipping or repairing any ship;
(h) any claim by the holder of a bill of lading of any goods imported into Malta for any damage done to the goods through negligence or breach of contract on the part of the owner or crew;
(i) any claims concerning ownership, possession, employment and earnings of a ship registered in Malta as between co-owners or any of them;
(j) any claim by a seaman for wages earned on a ship;
(k) claims by a master for disbursements made by him on account of the ship.

The above will serve to establish whether a court may exercise the *in rem* jurisdiction and it would not benefit a claimant to show that he enjoys a maritime lien as understood in English law or the Brussels Conventions 1926 and 1967 on maritime liens. Having said that, however, our courts have in one judgment hinted that where a claim is privileged in accordance with the provisions of the Merchant Shipping Act 1973 (which provisions essentially establish the priority of claims), then it would be possible for a claimant to arrest a ship notwithstanding that the particular privileged claim is not specifically contemplated in the law regulating admiralty jurisdiction.

(c) What are the grounds for arrest?

An arrest of a vessel can be obtained to secure a claim pending the outcome of proceedings on the merits, in which case the arrest is precautionary. Alternatively an arrest can be executive in order to enforce an executive title which the creditor has in his favour. An executive title can take the form of a judgment, a public deed, an arbitral award or a mortgage, local or foreign, provided that it is registered in respect of a sum of money which is certain, liquidated and due.

An arrest of a vessel can be obtained through the combined execution of a Warrant of Seizure and Warrant of Impediment of Departure against a vessel. This combined approach is normally resorted to by local lawyers, because whereas the Warrant of Seizure attaches the asset in the hands of the debtor, it does not serve the purpose of removing the asset from the control of the master or its owner. The Warrant of Impediment of Departure is effectively an order to the relevant authorities not to give clearance of the ship if it seeks to leave the island.

The claims envisaged in the various heads of jurisdiction mentioned above also serve as grounds for the arrest of vessels. A claimant intending to arrest a vessel *in rem* would have to show that his claim falls within the list contemplated in the Vice-Admiralty legislation applicable in Malta; if on the other hand a claimant wishes to proceed on an *in personam* basis, the claim need not fall within the list of claims envisaged in the admiralty legislation, although the courts must still have the ordinary jurisdiction as envisaged in the Code of Procedure.

The release of a ship from the effects of an arrest order can be obtained as a result of a deposit of security, which can take the form of either depositing the actual amount being claimed in the court registry pending the outcome of the dispute or alternatively a local bank guarantee. It would be necessary for the ship owner or master to appoint a local attorney in order that subsequent proceedings may continue against the appointed attorney. A ship owner is given the specific right of applying to the court for release of a vessel in cases where limitation of liability appears to be applicable. Section 357 of the Merchant Shipping Act allows the courts to order the release of a ship by ordering the creditor to accept a guarantee.

Where the ship owner feels that the arrest has been obtained maliciously or is oppressive, then he can apply to the court and request the removal of the arrest on such grounds. Alternatively, a ship owner may achieve the same result by requesting an order for counter-security in respect of damages which may be sustained as a result of an abusive or illegal arrest, which if not deposited by the plaintiff within the prescribed time will lead to the immediate revocation of the arrest.

(d) Need the arrested vessel be connected with the claim or can other vessels in the same legal (or beneficial) ownership also be arrested?

Arresting a sister ship is not contemplated in our law and it is generally accepted that it is not permissible for a creditor to arrest a vessel as security for debts created by another ship. In practice the problem arises in cases where various vessels are owned in the same beneficial ownership of the debtor. In the rare cases where fraud is alleged, the concept of lifting the corporate veil may be applied for in order to look beyond the owning company of a vessel and establish whether the sister vessel is owned by the same beneficial owner.

(e) What procedural differences apply to special maritime jurisdiction?

There are no procedural differences which are noteworthy in this regard. Admiralty actions are heard by the ordinary courts, i.e. the First Hall, Civil Court, like any other litigation and the procedural norms envisaged in the Code of Organisation and Civil Procedure apply equally to such maritime litigation. As a matter of fact by virtue of the Vice Admiralty (Transfer of Jurisdiction) Ordinance of 1892, it is expressly stated that the mode of procedure embodied in the Code of Organisation and Civil Procedure and as such our law excluded the procedural rules applicable to the Vice Admiralty Court in England.

(f) What jurisdictional rules are there as to limitation of liability?

Where an arrest of a ship has been ordered by the court in connection with a claim which appears to be founded on a liability to which a limit is set by virtue of the Merchant Shipping Act 1973, or security is given to prevent or obtain the release from such arrest, the court may in specific circumstances order the release of the ship where the security is satisfactory. In such cases the law states that the person upon whose application such an order is given shall be deemed to have submitted to the jurisdiction of the court to adjudicate on the claim and the court shall therefore have jurisdiction to determine the claim.

3. SERVICE OF PROCEEDINGS

Service of proceedings outside the jurisdiction is not specifically regulated and hence does not materialise in practice. When service of process is necessary with regard to a non-resident or absentee the law provides for the appointment of an official curator who is specifically appointed to receive service on behalf of the absentee and essentially inform him of the filing of the proceeding whilst protecting his interests until instructions are forthcoming. Prior to the appointment of an official curator, due notice of the pleadings must be served to a "friend" of the absentee in order to give him the opportunity to voluntarily accept the role of a curator and thus act in the interests of the defendant. Failing this the court will proceed and appoint a curator from a list of local lawyers.

4. COSTS

The commencement of judicial proceedings entails the payment of a court registry fee which is payable to the Registrar of Courts upon filing of proceedings. The costs are assessed in accordance with a court tariff and generally works out as a percentage of the value of the claim. Judicial fees payable to advocates and legal procurators are assessed similarly in accordance with an official tariff. In many cases it is also possible for such fees to be determined by agreement reached between the advocate and his client.

Liability for costs is decided by the court in the judgment and generally the judgment debtor would be held liable for the payment of costs. Security for costs is obligatory in appeal proceedings and a quantified amount has to be lodged in the court registry as security for the payment of registry fees and the opposing party's costs for an appeal to be heard and determined by the Court of Appeal.

5. INTERIM ARREST

(a) Are interim arrest/freezing of assets/other provisional measures permitted to provide security for domestic proceedings and/or proceedings in another jurisdiction?

Interim arrest is contemplated primarily in the context of domestic proceedings, although it is now also possible to obtain security in respect of a claim which is heard before arbitrators whether local or foreign. Pre-trial attachment is contemplated in the Code of Organisation and Civil Procedure and may assume different forms depending on the type of asset that the claimant seeks to attach. Bank accounts or any assets belonging to a debtor but which are held by third parties may be attached by means of a garnishee order. Assets in the control of the debtor may be subjected to a warrant of seizure, whereas real estate can be maintained in the ownership of the debtor by means of a warrant of prohibitory injunction, which is also served to the Director of Public Registry and Land Registrar who are statutorily bound to enter a note in a specially kept register. Such a warrant can also be availed of where it is necessary to issue a restraining order against a person.

(b) What criteria apply to this?

The criteria that generally apply to such interim measures is the need or justification of the claimant to obtain security prior to the final determination of the dispute. Such interim measures are issued and carried into effect on the sole responsibility of the person suing out the act. If it is shown to the court that the warrant was not necessary in view of the financial ability of the debtor to pay, or where it is clear that the claim is malicious, frivolous or vexatious, then the party issuing the precautionary warrant would be liable to the payment of a penalty of a sum ranging between LM 500 and LM 3000 as well as damages.

(c) Is there a limit on jurisdictions whose proceedings are recognised for this purpose?

Maltese law does not cater for the possibility of obtaining security locally in connection with a claim which is being heard before a foreign court. The only instance where such a remedy is available arises in claims against Maltese registered ships where a claimant has the possibility of applying to the Maltese courts for an order prohibiting any dealing in connection with a ship whilst proceeding on the merits before the appropriate foreign court or before arbitrators according to the circumstances of the case. In those cases where parties have agreed to submit a dispute to arbitration it is possible to obtain interim security and it is generally felt that such security can also be obtained where the arbitration is conducted overseas.

(d) Is there a requirement for counter-security?

Counter-security can be requested by the party against whom any interim measure has been ordered by the court on good cause being shown. If the court is satisfied that there are sufficient grounds for such counter-security to be ordered, the court will impose an obligation upon the applicant who obtained the precautionary warrant to deposit sufficient security within a fixed time frame in order to make good for the payment of any penalty that may be imposed as a result of a vexatious order, or alternatively to secure any damages that may be suffered as a result of the interim arrest. The failure to deposit such counter-security will lead to the revocation of the interim measures obtained by the claimant.

(e) Can applications be made ex parte?

With the exception of the warrant of prohibitory injunction, precautionary warrants are issued by the court upon an *ex parte* application containing an affidavit to the effect that the arrest is needed in order to secure the claim which is described in the application. An order can normally be obtained within hours of it being filed. Arrangements for service and execution of the arrest order are then necessary with the Court Marshals but generally such service is carried out expeditiously. Third parties would be bound by the order if they are particularly mentioned, such as in the cases of local banks when served with a garnishee order. The same would apply in the case of an arrest of a ship; service of such an order would be made to the relevant authorities, i.e. the Port Authority, Controller of Customs and Commissioner of Police. In the case of the warrant of prohibitory injunction the court serves the application on the respondent, who is granted a time limit within which to file a reply and the court may then either issue an order in camera or alternatively appoint the case for a further hearing prior to an order being made.

Pre-trial attachment has to be followed by proceedings on the merits within a specified time, which varies slightly according to the type of order obtained but generally speaking one may say that such proceedings have to follow within a period of between six and ten working days.

(f) How quickly can an order be made?

Precautionary attachment can be made and obtained within a day or two.

(g) Will the order bind third parties?

Third parties will be bound by such orders from the moment that they are formally served with the order and provided that the order actually requests that third party to comply with the order.

(h) What are the consequences of breach of an order?

Breach of an order may give rise to contempt of court proceedings.

(i) Is there a limit to types of asset, e.g. physical asset/account balances?

Not all assets or amounts held in bank accounts may be subjected to such interim measures. Thus in the case of the warrant of seizure, the law clearly excludes such assets as are necessary for the livelihood of a debtor or for the exercise of his profession or trade. Similarly, vessels chartered in the service of the Government of Malta are excluded. In the case of a garnishee order which affects salary or wages of the debtor in the account of his employer, it is only lawful to issue such order on a sum in excess of three hundred Liri (LM 300) per month. Any pension or social allowance is excluded by law. Similarly it is not lawful to issue a garnishee order upon any charitable grant made by the Government, any bequest which is expressly made for the purpose of maintenance, if the debtor has no other means of subsistence or upon any sum due by any civil or military department of the public service for the price of works or supplies. Finally it is also noteworthy to mention that a garnishee order will not affect any money which is payable by bank in execution of bank guarantee.

(j) What if third parties are affected, e.g. airliner?

Third parties affected as a result of such interim orders would not have a direct action against the party requesting the issue of an order, unless it can be shown that the order was obtained frivolously or maliciously or that it was unwarranted in the particular circumstances of the case. The mere fact alone that a creditor obtains security in order to protect or secure a right would not allow a third party the right to claim damages from him.

(k) What other provisional measures may be ordered, e.g. appointment of surveyor or receiver, security?

Other provisional measures that can be ordered by the court include the appointment of a consignatory at the provisional expense of the creditor in order to take charge of the asset seized, although where the debtor himself chooses or presents a suitable person who is willing to take charge of the property seized, the Marshal appoints such person as a consignatory. Moreover it is within the power of the court to order the sale *pendente lite* of particular assets in particular ships, aircraft, perishable goods and other deteriorating assets. For such an order to be obtained the court must be satisfied that the debtor is insolvent or otherwise unlikely to be able to continue trading and maintaining the asset.

6. RECOGNITION OF JUDGMENTS/AWARDS

(a) What treaties/conventions apply (i) to enable judgments to be enforced abroad and (ii) to enable enforcement of foreign judgments domestically?

The only treaty arrangement which exists for the reciprocal recognition and enforcement of judgments/awards was concluded with the United Kingdom. As a result the British Judgments (Reciprocal Enforcement) Act 1952 (Chapter 86 of the Revised Edition of the Laws of Malta) makes it possible for money judgments granted by a superior court in the United Kingdom or an arbitration award obtained in the United Kingdom to be recognised and enforced locally.

(b) What procedure is followed to enforce a foreign judgment (i) governed by a treaty/convention and (ii) not governed by a treaty/convention?

Under the British Judgments (Reciprocal Enforcement) Act, the procedure involves the filing of an application before the Court of Appeal and the law outlines the various grounds which must be satisfied, namely that:

(a) the original court acted with jurisdiction;

(b) the judgment debtor was a person who was either carrying on business or ordinarily resident in the jurisdiction of the court or alternatively voluntarily submitted to the jurisdiction of the court;
(c) the judgment debtor was duly served with the proceedings;
(d) the judgment was not obtained with fraud;
(e) the judgment is final;
(f) the judgment is compatible with Maltese public policy.

Where the judgment or award has not been obtained before a court in the United Kingdom, the procedure to follow is that established in the Code of Organisation and Civil Procedure. The procedure here is somewhat lengthier since it involves filing a writ before the Civil Court as a court of first instance and hence any judgment given by the Civil Court may be subject to appeal before the Court of Appeal. Again the law lays down various stringent conditions which must be satisfied for the courts to pronounce the enforcement of such foreign judgment. In the first place the plaintiff would have to bring evidence to show that the foreign judgment was obtained before a competent court and that the judgment is *res judicata*. The court, moreover, investigates whether

(a) the judgment sought to be enforced may be set aside on any grounds which would normally serve as a basis for a retrial under Maltese law;
(b) in the case of a judgment by default, the parties were not contumacious according to foreign law;
(c) the judgment contains any disposition which is contrary to public policy or to the internal public law of Malta.

(c) What about foreign arbitration awards?

In the sphere of arbitration, Malta at present adheres to the Geneva Protocol on Arbitration Clauses, 1923 and to the Convention on the Execution of Foreign Arbitral Awards, 1927. By means of the Arbitration (Foreign Awards) Ordinance of 1934 (Chapter 83 of the Revised Edition of the Laws of Malta) a foreign award can be enforced locally provided that it satisfies the specific criteria mentioned in the law, namely that the award is obtained—

(a) in pursuance of an agreement for arbitration to which the Protocol on Arbitration Clauses applies; and
(b) between persons of whom one is subject to the jurisdiction of a country which the Prime Minister may by order declare to be parties to the Convention on the Execution of Foreign Arbitral Awards, 1927; and
(c) in one of such territories as the Prime Minister may by order declare to be territories to which the said Convention applies.

It is to be noted, however, that to date no such order has ever been made by a serving Prime Minister, with the result that the machinery for the effective implementation of this legislation is sadly lacking. It remains an open question whether a court would decline the enforcement of a foreign award simply on the basis of this technicality and whether it will accept alternative evidence which would serve to establish the same criteria.

The above dilemma will be resolved when the Maltese Government brings into force the Arbitration Act 1996 (Act No. II of 1996), which provides for the establishment of the Malta Arbitration Centre as a centre for both domestic and international commercial arbitration as well as the recognition and enforcement of certain arbitral awards. This law will eventually replace the existing legislation regulating the recognition and enforcement of foreign arbitration awards and will incorporate in Maltese law the UNCITRAL Model law on International Commercial Arbitration adopted on 21 June 1985. In addition, the new law will provide for the enforcement of foreign arbitration awards to which the 1958 New York Convention on the Recognition and Enforcement of Foreign Arbitral Awards or the Convention on Investment Disputes between States and Nationals of other States (Washington 1965) applies.

(d) Will proceeds of a judgment be freely exportable?

Proceeds of a judgment or award obtained locally are freely remitted overseas with the authorisation of the Central Bank of Malta.

CHAPTER 16

MOROCCO

Abderrahman Frakech
398 Boulevard Mohammed V, Casablanca, Morocco

1. JURISDICTION

The grounds on which courts will accept jurisdiction

Under the 1974 reform of the Code of Civil Procedure (CCP), the Court of First Instance has jurisdiction in all contentious matters (civil, administrative and commercial).

However, this competence is now reduced by the creation of an Administrative Court and a Commercial Court. Maritime cases, as commercial matters, are from now on within the competence of the Commercial Courts (Law of 1995 which came into force on 7 May 1998).

(a) Domicile

Moroccan courts have jurisdiction where the defendant is based or has its office in Morocco. The domicile or residence of the plaintiff may also create jurisdiction.

(i) Defendant based in Morocco

This rule, laid down in Article 17 of the CCP is the basic rule of jurisdiction. The same rule is established by the legal provisions of the Commercial Courts Law (CCL) (Art. 10). Thus, the competence of the court *ratione loci* is based on the domicile or address for service of the defendant.

When he defendant has no domicile in Morocco, but an actual residence, the competence concerns the court of this residence.

Where there is more than one defendant, one of which is based in Morocco, the court of that defendant will hear the case against all defendants.

(ii) Plaintiff based in Morocco

Moroccan law attributes jurisdiction to the court of the plaintiff where the defendant has neither his domicile nor his residence in Morocco. Where there is more than one plaintiff the court of the domicile or residence of one of them will hear the case on behalf of all other plaintiffs.

(b) Place of business/residence/office

Under Moroccan law (Art. 522 of the CCP) the domicile of a person or a company is the place of its registered address or registered office. The office of a person or company is also regarded as a domicile or residence.

The above described rules for jurisdiction are laid down also in Article 11 of the Commercial Courts Law (CCL).

(c) Assets located within the jurisdiction

Moroccan courts have exclusive competence with respect to claims relating to real estate within the jurisdiction (Art. 27 of the CCP).

This rule is applicable for claims relating to a petitionary or to a possessory action.

With respect to a mixed action, the jurisdiction is the location of assets or the domicile or the residence of the defendant (Art. 27 of CCP).

With regard to a personal action the above described rules in (a) and (b) are applicable.

(d) Act complained of within the jurisdiction

Under Moroccan law the competence of a court *ratione materiae* is of law and order. In accordance with this rule the fact that the act complained of has been committed within Moroccan territory does attribute jurisdiction to the Moroccan courts.

However, there is an exception: parties can submit their dispute to an arbitrator (Art. 306 of CCP and Art. 5 of CCL). The arbitration procedure is the one applicable in comparative law.

(e) Contract governed by local law

It depends on many situations:

- Where supplies of goods, building work, renting and industry are concerned, the competence of Moroccan courts is the place where the contract has been concluded or the place of its performance.
- In the matter of civil engineering, the competence is within the jurisdiction of the place where the work has been performed.
- In the matter of contracts concluded by a state or a public service, the competence is based on the place where they have been signed (Art. 27 of the CCP).

(f) Conventions

It is admitted, under Moroccan law, that the competence of a court *ratione loci* is not of law and order. Actually, Article 16 of the CCP provides that incompetence in respect of the matter may be pronounced automatically by the judge. This means *a contrario* that the incompetence *ratione loci* cannot be raised *ex officio* by the judge. Thus parties are free to choose a territorial jurisdiction other than the one ordinarily competent.

(g) Clause attributing jurisdiction

This clause is valid under Moroccan law. Article 12 of the CCL provides that parties, in any case, may agree in writing a specific forum (court or arbitration). In maritime law, this clause is not valid where the carriage of goods by sea under a bill of lading is concerned. The Supreme Court has pronounced the absolute nullity of the clause when it is not in accordance with the national rules of competence.

This jurisprudence is not in contradiction to the provisions of Article 21(1)(c) of the Hamburg Rules, to which Morocco is a contracting party.

However, this jurisprudence is not applicable where charterparties are concerned. The clause attributing jurisdiction is valid between owners and charterers.

(h) Other (instruction)

Under Moroccan law (Art. 534 CCP) the address for service prevails over the residence or the domicile assigned by law in case of a conflict.

However, the domicile that is taken into account is the one which existed at the time of the registered claim.

(i) Counterclaim/third-party proceedings

Under Moroccan law (Art. 103 to Art. 118 of the CCP) a counterclaim is admitted when dealing with a claim. A court generally will accept jurisdiction for third-party proceedings.

2. MARITIME CLAIMS

(a) Jurisdiction through arrest of a ship

The court whose president has given leave for an arrest to be made or prevented through security is the one for the main claim. This principle is laid down in Article 110 of the Maritime Code of Commerce (MCC) and Article 148 of the CCP.

(b) Specific maritime jurisdiction

(i) Place of discharge in Morocco

(Art. 21 of the Hamburg Rules)

Moroccan courts are competent to hear a dispute between a carrier and a receiver, not being the shipper and concerning contracts of carriage by sea. The receiver is the plaintiff who institutes a claim for non-delivery.

(ii) Collision

The following Moroccan courts will assume jurisdiction:

- the court of the place of the defendant or one of them;
- the court within whose territory the collision took place;
- the court within whose territory the ship has been arrested;
- if none of these apply, before the court of the plaintiff.

(iii) Salvage

If there is a salvage agreement the forum can be chosen by the parties. In other cases assistance is based on the following Moroccan courts:

- the court of the place of the defendant or one of them;
- the court within whose territory the assistance took place;
- the court within whose territory an arrest has been made to secure the claim for assistance;
- if none of these apply, before the court of the plaintiff.

(c) The grounds for arrest

No specific grounds are required. The allegation of a claim suffices. An *ex parte* application can be presented by an attorney to the president of the local court, and signed within the hour.

Arrests can also be made after a judgment has obtained.

(d) Connection between arrested ship and claim

Under Moroccan law, all claims against an owner can be secured by an arrest upon all his ships. Arrests can be made for all claims.

Claim against a bareboat charterer can also be enforced against the ship to which the claim relates. But it is not possible to arrest a ship for claims against the time-charterer or voyage charterer. There is an exception: a seagoing ship can be arrested for claims against a carrier under a bill of lading. Such arrest may create jurisdiction within Morocco.

(e) Procedural differences applying to special maritime jurisdiction

Under Moroccan law there are few specific procedural differences which apply to maritime jurisdiction. There are special rules of procedure for the registration of ships, sale of cargo, appointment of court surveyors and general average. There is no specific procedure for the limitation of liability.

(f) Special rules as to limitation of liability

The limit of liability is based on the tonnage of the ship in Moroccan jurisdiction.

3. SERVICE OF PROCEEDINGS

(a) Rules applying to service of proceedings outside the jurisdiction

It is the bailiff who notifies the writ to the public prosecutor's office. The notification may be sent to a trustee. Where a defendant has no known place of establishment or office, it is required that an advertisement be placed in a local newspaper.

Where a convention applies, service is done in accordance with the rules of service in the defendant's jurisdiction.

4. COSTS IMPLICATIONS OF STARTING PROCEEDINGS

(a) Court fees

Court fees are payable upon inception of the proceedings at the first instance court. The amount of court fees depends on the amount claimed:

— from DH 1,000 to DH 5,000: 4 per cent with a minimum of DH 50;
— from DH 5,000 to DH 20,000: 5 per cent with a minimum of DH 200;
— if the amount claimed exceeds DH 20,000: 1 per cent plus DH 300.

In the case of proceedings before the Court of Appeal the amount of court fees is the same as those described above, but with a surcharge of 10 per cent.

In the case of proceedings before the Supreme Court there is a fixed fee of DH 1,500.

(b) Lawyers' fees

There is no standard scale for lawyers' fees. Lawyers' fees are generally fixed by agreement. Normally lawyers will charge on the basis of hours worked: an hourly tariff is between DH 800 and DH 1,200. Success fees are also allowed under Moroccan law.

(c) Recovery of costs from unsuccessful party

The fees to be paid by the unsuccessful party are the costs of procedural activities including court fees and a legal rate of interest of 6 per cent of the amount claimed. In addition to the amount of the claim, damages can also be fixed by the judge according to effective loss of the plaintiff and interest awarded by way of damages (Art. 89 of the Civil Code).

(d) Security for costs

Security for costs may be required by the court from the plaintiff before giving leave to arrest the ship. The release of the arrested ship is *ipso jure* when the defendant put up security (Art. 110 of the Maritime Code).

5. INTERIM ARREST

(a) For domestic proceedings or proceedings in another jurisdiction

As a general rule interim arrest/freezing of assets are possible, in the case of an unquestionable claim, unless there is a deposit of security.

(b) Criteria applying

The criteria are based on the urgency. In maritime law the urgency is always presumed. There is no distinction whether domestic proceedings or proceedings in another jurisdiction are involved.

(c) Limit on jurisdictions whose proceedings are recognised for the purpose of arrests

There is no such limit. The only requirement will be that substantive proceedings before the competent court must be started within the period fixed by the court upon the granting of leave for arrest.

(d) Counter-security

The providing of counter-security is at the discretion of the court (Art. 110 of the CCM).

(e) Can applications be made ex parte?

Applications are always made *ex parte.*

(f) How quickly can an order be made?

The order can be made in a few hours and even during feast days when the matter is urgent (Art. 150 of the CCP).

(g) Will the order bind third parties?

The order will bind all parties.

(h) The consequences of breach of an order

The breach of an order is punishable by imprisonment up to a maximum of one year. Where a third party arrest is concerned, this third party will be personally liable for the claim involved.

(i) Limit to types of asset

All assets can be arrested.

(j) What if third parties are affected?

Third parties may apply for an immediate court order setting aside the arrests. Where an airliner is ready for take off, no arrest is allowed.

(k) Other provisional measures to be ordered

Appointment of a surveyor by a conciliator or by judge's order (Art. 148 of CCP) or summary order injunction (Art. 149 of the CCP) can be done.

Also a trustee of sequestrated property may be appointed amicably or by an order.

6. RECOGNITION OF JUDGMENTS/AWARDS

(a) Treaty/convention—court judgments

Morocco is party to conventions with almost all European countries with respect to the reciprocal recognition and enforcement of judgments.

Judgments rendered in countries which are not covered by conventions are not recognised. New proceedings in Morocco will have to be held in this case.

Thus the *exequatur* will be given only to a judgment rendered in a country with which Morocco has a convention. For example with France, under the Convention of 6 October 1957.

(b) Procedures

The procedure is described in the various conventions. Generally, the original or certified copy of the judgment is required. This document is presented to the court with a written petition to have the judgment declared enforceable in Morocco.

(c) Foreign arbitral awards

Morocco is a party to the New York Convention of 9 June 1958 on the (reciprocal) recognition of arbitral awards (Law of 19 February 1960).

Arbitral award is enforceable by order of the President of the First Instance Court (Art. 320 of the CCP).

(d) Free exportability of proceeds

There are no limitations. The exportability of proceeds is possible in any currencies.

CHAPTER 17

THE NETHERLANDS

Carel J.H. baron van Lynden
Van Anken Knüppe Damstra, P.O. Box 25021, 3001 HA Rotterdam, Netherlands

1. JURISDICTION

The grounds on which courts will accept jurisdiction

A distinction can be made between the "relative" competency, the question of which local Dutch court has jurisdiction, and the "international" competency, the question whether there is a Dutch court which has jurisdiction at all. Under Dutch law the rules of relative competency also attribute international competency. This rule is only partly limited by the *forum non conveniens* rule (e.g. Article 429c, 15 Dutch Code of Civil Procedure, DCCP); where proceedings are involved which are initiated by a writ of summons, this rule does not apply.

(a) Domicile

Netherlands courts generally have or will assume jurisdiction where the defendant is based or has its office in The Netherlands. Also the domicile of the plaintiff may create jurisdiction.

(i) Defendant based in The Netherlands

This rule, laid down in Article 126, 1 DCCP is the most basic rule of jurisdiction; as is the case in most countries. The "own" courts of a person will accept jurisdiction.

The rule is laid down in many conventions (see for instance Article 2 of the EEX/EVEX Convention (hereinafter "EEX"), Article 7,1,a of the 1952 Arrest Convention, Article 1,1,a of the 1952 Convention on Civil Jurisdiction in Collisions, Article 21,1,a of the Hamburg Rules).

This rule will not apply where the parties have specifically agreed on a certain forum, as far as allowed by conventions and local law (see however below items 1(h) and 2(a)).

Where there is more than one defendant, one of which is based in The Netherlands, the court of that defendant will hear the case against all defendants (Article 126, 7 DCCP—see also Article 6 EEX).

Where carriage of goods by sea under a bill of lading is concerned, there may, under Dutch law, be more persons who are to be regarded carrier at the same time, and thus more defendants; the following persons are to be regarded as carriers (Article 8:461 Dutch Civil Code, DCC):

- he who signed the bill of lading or on whose behalf the bill of lading was signed;
- he on whose form the bill of lading was issued and in the case of a master's bill of lading (in addition thereto):
    - the last time or voyage charterer and (in addition thereto) in the case of a bareboat charter also the last bareboat charterer, or, where there is no bareboat charterer, the owner, unless the bill of lading explicitly appoints only the owner as carrier, or, as the case may be, the bareboat charterer, who then must be clearly identified in the bill of lading.

This article is of compelling law, which means that one cannot deviate from it by private contract. As, under Dutch law, the question who has to be regarded as carrier under a bill of lading, must be decided as per the law of the place of discharge, this article will always apply in the case of discharge from a seagoing ship in The Netherlands. There thus can be more than one carrier, and thus there may be more possibilities to seek Dutch jurisdiction.

This article also puts an end to the "identity of carrier" clause, where this clause does not in so many words name the owner or bareboat charterer.

It should be noted that this clause in fact is a species of representation: only when the charterer has the power to represent, can a valid representation be made.

(ii) Plaintiff based in The Netherlands

Dutch law attributes jurisdiction to the court of the plaintiff where the defendant has no own (other) place of business within The Netherlands, unless a convention stipulates otherwise (for instance Article 3 of the EEX Convention—see however other paragraphs of this Convention), or the parties have agreed on a specific (other) forum (see however below items 1(h) and 2(a)).

Where there is more than one plaintiff, and one of them is based in The Netherlands, the court will hear the case on behalf of all other plaintiffs as well (Article 126, 5 DCCP).

Future legislation will probably put an end to this possibility.

(b) Place of business/residence/office

Under Dutch law (Article 10 DCC) a person has its domicile at its registered address, whereas a corporation has its residence at the place of its incorporation. With respect to matters relating to an(other) office of a person or corporation, such office also is to be regarded as domicile or residence.

The above described rules for jurisdiction therefore also apply to offices, where the matter in issue relates to such office (Article 14 DCC). A person or corporation can also choose a domicile for a specific purpose (Article 15 DCC and Article 126, 16 DCCP). The above rules then also apply to such chosen domicile.

(c) Assets located within the jurisdiction

The fact that assets are located within the jurisdiction may give rise to courts accepting jurisdiction, but only in a limited number of cases, and in most cases not merely because of the location. In this respect it may be mentioned that, under certain circumstances (particularly where the EEX applies), the court of the place where a contract is to be carried out has jurisdiction.

(i) Real estate

Dutch courts will accept jurisdiction with respect to claims relating to real estate within the jurisdiction (Article 126, 8 DCCP—see also Article 16, 1 EEX).

(ii) Movables

The fact that a movable is within the jurisdiction does not *per se* give jurisdiction to Dutch courts. There must be international jurisdiction: jurisdiction must be based on one of the other factors creating jurisdiction (e.g. domicile of plaintiff or defendant, or arrest of the asset—see below under (h)(i)).

(iii) Claims against third parties in the jurisdiction

For claims against third parties the same rules apply as for movables.

(d) Act complained of within the jurisdiction

Under Dutch law the fact that the act complained of has been committed within Dutch territory, does not attribute jurisdiction to the Dutch courts. In international law this is different; see *inter alia*. Article 5(1), (2) and (3) of the EEX.

(e) Contract governed by local law

The fact that a contract is governed by Dutch law does not create jurisdiction of Dutch courts. Such jurisdiction must be decided by one of the other factors as described in this chapter.

(f) Conventions

Conventions are of a higher order than rules of local law. Thus, where a convention, to which The Netherlands is a party, attributes jurisdiction to a court in The Netherlands, this court has jurisdiction, also when this would not have been the case under local rules of law. Examples of conventions attributing jurisdiction to (Dutch) courts are the above-mentioned EEX Convention (e.g. Article 6*bis*, giving jurisdiction to the court, in which a claim is pending, to hear the matter of limitation of liability as well) and the 1952 Arrest Convention, under certain circumstances giving jurisdiction to the court granting leave to arrest.

(g) Clause attributing jurisdiction

Another general rule of Dutch law is the freedom of parties to choose a specific forum (court or arbitration). Therefore Dutch courts will generally uphold such clauses. However, as mentioned, specific rules of conventions override a choice of jurisdiction. Obviously the clause must be valid (see above under 1(a)(i), or Article 17 EEX). Where the clause forms part of general conditions these of course must validly have been agreed upon.

(h) Other

(i) Arrest

Article 767 DCCP, reads, freely translated:

> "Failing another way to obtain an enforceable title within The Netherlands, the claim . . . can be brought before the court whose president has given leave for an arrest to be made or prevented through security."

Article 767 DCCP thus determines that the court whose president has given leave to arrest, even when the arrest has not been made but prevented by security, may be addressed for the main claim when no other way is open for enforcement in The Netherlands. This article does not set aside jurisdiction clauses. Thus, a choice of forum supersedes this article. But in all cases where no (valid) jurisdiction clause has been agreed upon, an arrest (or the threat of an arrest, followed by security) creates jurisdiction. An arrest can be an arrest upon a ship, a movable or immovable, or an arrest under third parties upon claims or movables.

(ii) Instruction/transfer of the title to sue

As set out above under 1 (a) (ii) the court of the plaintiff may assume jurisdiction (where no convention or agreement on jurisdiction prevents it).

Under Dutch law one can transfer the title to sue. This is no material assignment of a claim, but merely the transfer of the right to bring proceedings in one's own name. Thus, by transferring a claim to a Dutch entity, jurisdiction in The Netherlands can be created. It should be noted that conventions override this principle. Thus, one cannot set aside a jurisdiction which applied as a consequence of the nationality of the original plaintiff, when such was based on a convention or agreement. In other cases this can however be an interesting possibility to avoid far away unattractive jurisdictions—as long as this possibility exists (see above under 1 (a) (ii)).

(i) Counterclaim/third-party proceedings

(i) Counterclaim

A court generally will accept jurisdiction for counter claims when dealing with a claim, provided that the claims have the same legal "origin". See also Article 6, 3 EEX.

(ii) Third-party proceedings

A court generally will accept jurisdiction for third-party proceedings (Article 126, 14 DCCP), unless a (valid) choice of forum clause is in force between the defendant and the third party (see also Article 6(3) versus Article 17 EEX).

2. MARITIME CLAIMS

(a) Jurisdiction through arrest on a ship

The fact that arrest can create jurisdiction has been described above. The principle is also laid down in a number of conventions (*inter alia* Article 7 of the 1952 Arrest Convention, Article 1,1,b of the 1952 Convention on Civil Jurisdiction in Collisions).

This principle does not override specific rules of jurisdiction in conventions.

The 1952 Arrest Convention states that ships can only be arrested for "maritime claims". This "limitation" only applies where an arrest is sought on a ship which flies the flag of a Contracting State. Ships not flying the flag of a Contracting State can be arrested for all other claims as well.

(b) Specific maritime jurisdiction

(i) Place of discharge in The Netherlands

Article 629 DCCP reads, freely translated:

> "1. The court competent to hear disputes between a carrier and a receiver, not being the shipper, concerning contracts of carriage wholly or partly by ship from a place outside of The Netherlands to a final destination within The Netherlands, is the court within whose district that place is situated. Receiver is [also] the person who institutes a claim for non-delivery.
> 2. Null and void is each stipulation, contrary hereto, unless such stipulation:
>   a. declares competent a court of a specifically named place in the territory of the state where either the carrier or the receiver is established, or
>   b. has been laid down in a separate document that does not revert to general conditions."

This paragraph can set aside the principal place of business clause. Usually such clause does not specifically mention a court, and is not laid down in a separate document that does not revert to general conditions. The paragraph, being part of Dutch procedural (and not material) law, must be applied by Dutch courts regardless of which law applies to the contract of carriage. Thus, the principal place of business choice of jurisdiction clause in a bill of lading can be set aside and proceedings can be brought before Dutch courts when the final destination is within The Netherlands.

(ii) Collision

Based on Article 635 DCCP, in cases of collision the following Dutch courts will assume jurisdiction:

- the court of the place of the defendant or one of them;
- the court within whose territory the collision took place;
- the court within whose territory the ship is registered;
- the court within whose territory the ship has been arrested;
- if none of these apply, before the court of the plaintiff.

(iii) Salvage

Based on Article 637 DCCP, in cases of assistance the following Dutch courts will assume jurisdiction:

- the court of the place of the defendant or one of them;
- the court within whose territory the assistance took place;
- the court within whose territory an arrest has been made to secure the claim for assistance;

— if none of these apply, before the court of the plaintiff.

(iv) Appointment of court surveyor

The court of the place where the goods to be examined are located, has jurisdiction to appoint a court surveyor.

(v) Tonnage limitation

The Rotterdam court has (relative) jurisdiction to hear requests for the tonnage limitation of foreign (i.e. non-Dutch) ships (Article 642a DCCP). But there must be "sufficient points of connection" with the Dutch sphere to have international jurisdiction as well, for instance an arrest of the ship. This jurisdiction may be limited by rules of conventions, such as the 1976 London Convention on limitation of liability (Article 11). See also Article 6*bis* EEX, based on where there is jurisdiction for limitation proceedings when main proceedings are already pending for that forum.

(c) The grounds for arrest

No specific grounds are required. The allegation of a claim suffices.

Arrest within The Netherlands is very easy, very quick and quite cheap. An *ex parte* application can be presented to and signed by the President of the local court within the hour. Arrest can be made immediately. No power of attorney is necessary. On the other hand, there is a kind of strict liability for damages due to wrongful arrest.

(d) Connection between arrested ship and claim

Under Dutch law one is liable for one's debts with all one's assets. Thus, all claims against an owner can be secured by an arrest upon all the owners' belongings, amongst which may be all his ships. Where the 1952 Arrest Convention applies (which is to say when the arrested ship flies the flag of a Contracting State), it should be noted that only for maritime claims in the sense of Article 1 can a conservatory arrest be made. This Convention does not apply to "executionary" arrests, arrests after a judgment has been obtained: in those cases and where the ship does not fly the flag of a Contracting State, arrests can be made for all claims. (Arrests under banks, agents or other people owing money to its debtor within The Netherlands are also possible, without restriction.) Apart from the security, obtained as a result, arrest creates jurisdiction for the substantive proceedings (see above under 1(h) and 2(a)).

Under Dutch law claims against a bareboat charterer can also be enforced against the ship to which the claims relate. Such ship can thus be arrested for claims against the bareboat charterer.

When Dutch law applies it is not permissible to arrest a seagoing ship for claims against any other person than the registered owner or bareboat charterer. In particular it is not possible to arrest a ship for claims against the time charterer or voyage charterer, whether the claims are maritime claims or not.

There are two exceptions.

— *(i) Claims under a bill of lading.* When Dutch law applies, a seagoing ship can be arrested for claims against a carrier under a bill of lading regardless of whether the bill of lading is a master's bill of lading, provided that Dutch law governs the contract of carriage or the contractual place of discharge is within The Netherlands. "Carrier(s)" (see also above under 1(a)(i)) can be the one who signed the bill of lading and the one whose bill of lading form has been used. When the bill of lading has been signed by or for the master, moreover the last voyage or time charterer will be regarded as carrier. For claims against all these parties security/enforcement against the relevant ship can be sought and an arrest can be made.

Such arrest may also create jurisdiction within The Netherlands: see above under 1(h) and 2(a).

For inland waterway ships this restriction does not apply: arrest/enforcement against the inland waterway ship is possible for all claims against the registered owner, or the bareboat charterer/lessee, and against any charterer of the ship, for claims incurred with respect to the ship, thus also against time and voyage charterers.

— *(ii) Applicable law to recovery.* In The Netherlands a ship can be arrested for all (maritime when the 1952 Arrest Convention applies) claims, when recovery against the vessel (by way of lien or right to arrest) is possible under the law of the relevant contract *and* under the law of the flag of the vessel. Such arrest creates jurisdiction as described above under 1(h) and 2(a).

(e) Procedural differences to special maritime jurisdiction

Under Dutch law there are only few specific procedural differences which apply to maritime jurisdiction. The law has special rules of procedure for specific maritime subjects such as registration of ships, sale of cargo, limitation of liability, appointment of court surveyors and general average.

Inland waterway law also contains some specific rules of procedure, where the Mannheim Convention applies.

(f) Special rules as to limitation of liability

The limiting of liability is not to be regarded as the resolving of a dispute. Therefore there are wide possibilities to limit liability based on the tonnage of the ship in Dutch jurisdiction. Clauses attributing jurisdiction to other courts will not hinder the possibility to limit in The Netherlands.

See also under 2(b)(v).

3. SERVICE OF PROCEEDINGS

Rules applying to service of proceedings outside the jurisdiction

(i) Where no convention is in force

Proceedings must be served to the office of the Public Prosecutor in the district where proceedings are to be held. Where a defendant has no known place of establishment or office, it is moreover required that an advertisement be placed in a local newspaper. In all cases the bailiff who notifies the writ to the Public Prosecutor's office, must also send a copy of the writ by registered mail to the defendant's address.

(ii) Where conventions apply

In particular the 1965 Hague Convention on the notification of judicial and extrajudicial documents abroad is of importance. The manner of service is as described above in item 1, but proceedings will only be heard by the court upon presentation to the court of confirmation by the local authorities in the defendant's jurisdiction of proper notification. The above-mentioned convention allows service to be done alternatively, i.e. in accordance with the rules of service in the defendant's jurisdiction, for instance by "simple acceptance" or through a local bailiff.

4. COSTS IMPLICATIONS OF STARTING PROCEEDINGS

(a) Court fees

Court fees are payable upon inscription of the proceedings at the first instance court. The amount of court fees is 1.9 per cent of the amount claimed in the case of proceedings before the first instance court (with a maximum of Dfl. 6,925), and 2.4 per cent in the case of proceedings before the Court of Appeal (with a maximum of Dfl. 8,700).

(b) Lawyers' fees

There is no standard scale for lawyers' fees. Lawyers generally calculate based on a (no longer applying) tariff scheme of the Dutch Bar Association. Generally speaking, Dutch lawyers normally will charge on the basis of hours worked, against an hourly tariff between Dfl. 300 and Dfl. 500.

It is not allowed under Dutch law to work on a "no cure no pay basis". (Additional) success fees are allowed under Dutch law. Dutch lawyers tend to invoice on a monthly or quarterly basis.

(c) Recovery of costs from unsuccessful party

The fees to be paid by the unsuccessful party are calculated through a tariff. The tariff takes into account the number of procedural activities on the one hand (such as statements, hearings of witnesses, pleadings), and the amount of the claim at stake (the "*Streitwert*") on the other hand. Court fees mentioned under 4(a) will be recoverable in full. The amount so repayable will generally be less than the costs actually incurred. Generally speaking therefore, the successful party will have to bear part of its own attorney's fees itself.

(d) Security for costs

Security for costs can only be required from claimants who are based in a country with which The Netherlands has not have entered into a convention excluding the *cautio judicatum solvi.*

5. INTERIM ARREST

(a) For domestic proceedings or proceedings in another jurisdiction

There is no distinction between domestic proceedings and proceedings (judicial or arbitral) in another jurisdiction. As a general rule interim arrest/freezing of assets are always possible.

(b) Criteria applying

Where arrest of assets of a person or company with domicile, seat or office in The Netherlands is concerned, the plaintiff must state in the application that he fears alienation of the assets to be arrested. Where a foreign defendant is concerned, or a third party arrest, no such requirement exists.

The Netherlands entered in 1965 into a convention with the USSR, which is now in force with the CIS and other sovereign states formerly belonging to the USSR. This convention does not permit arrest of state owned ships provided that such states agree to submit to the jurisdiction of The Netherlands.

(c) Limit on jurisdictions whose proceedings are recognised for the purpose of arrests

There is no such limit. Also where arbitration for main proceedings is concerned, the possibility to arrest exists. The only requirement will be that substantive proceedings before the competent forum (whichever that is) must be started within the period to be fixed by the court upon the granting of leave for arrest. Such period can be extended by the court (Article 700 DCCP).

(d) Counter-security

The court has discretion to set conditions, amongst which is the providing of counter-security (Article 701 DCCP). This discretion is seldom being exercised.

(e) Can applications be made ex parte?

Applications are made *ex parte*.

(f) How quickly can an order be made?

Where the matter is urgent, the order can be made immediately, also at night and weekends.

(g) Will the order bind third parties?

The order is a public order and will bind all parties.

(h) The consequences of breach of an order

The person breaching an order of arrest, i.e. removing an arrested asset from the jurisdiction, will commit a criminal offence punishable by imprisonment for up to two years.

Where a third-party arrest is concerned, the third party removing the asset from arrest will be personally liable for the claim involved.

(i) Limit to types of asset

All assets can be arrested. The formalities to be taken into account differ.

(j) What if third parties are affected?

Third parties may apply for an immediate court order setting aside the arrests. In some instances, such as where an airliner is ready for take off, no arrest is allowed.

(k) Other provisional measures to be ordered

The following provisional measures may be ordered:

— *Appointment of a surveyor.* The court where the goods are located will have jurisdiction.

— *Provisional hearing of witnesses.* The court which probably has jurisdiction to hear (future) substantive proceedings, or the court of the majority of the witnesses has jurisdiction (Article 215 DCCP).

— *Injunctions to do or abstain from doing something.* In principle this can be anything, such as an order to load or discharge a ship, (not) to shift a ship, to deliver cargo to a specific party or a specific place, or to allow persons on board to inspect a ship or cargo. The normal rules of jurisdiction will apply, with the following exception: where the jurisdiction would be based on the domicile of the plaintiff (only), then the measure requested must take effect within the territory of the court in order to attribute jurisdiction to that court.

— *Provisional orders for payment.* Where a claim is not seriously disputable, where there is an urgent interest, and where there is no serious risk of the impossibility of repaying in case of a different decision in later substantive proceedings, payment of a claim may be demanded in summary proceedings. This may for instance be done after an arrest has been made upon property within Dutch jurisdiction, followed by a claim by the opposing party for the release from arrest. Then a counterclaim could be instituted for payment. As such a claim is considered a provisional claim only (not a claim on the merits), the jurisdiction of the Dutch courts will not be blocked by a clause attributing (exclusive) jurisdiction to a forum outside The Netherlands or to arbitrators.

  Otherwise there must be jurisdiction as per the rules, set out above.

— *A request for security.* Without arrest the courts can be approached by way of injunction to order the defendant to put up security. The jurisdiction must be founded in the manners described above.

6. RECOGNITION OF JUDGMENTS/AWARDS

(a) Treaty/convention—court judgments

The Netherlands is a party to conventions with almost all Western European countries and a number of (former) overseas colonies of Western European countries with respect to the (reciprocal) recognition and enforcement of judgments.

Judgments rendered in countries or on subjects which are not covered by the aforementioned conventions, are not recognised. There is a system of relatively simple new ("recognition") proceedings (Article 431 DCCP). Equally, no *exequatur* will be given on a judgment rendered in a country with which The Netherlands does not have a convention, but which judgment has been declared enforceable in a country with which The Netherlands does have such convention (no "double" enforcement).

(b) Procedures

The procedure is described in the various conventions. Generally, the original or a certified copy of the judgment, and of a statement from the court which rendered the judgment that the judgment is (provisionally) enforceable, must be presented to the court, with a written petition to have the judgment declared enforceable in The Netherlands.

As set out above, for a judgment rendered in a non-Convention country, new proceedings must be held, whereby the above rules of jurisdiction apply.

(c) Foreign arbitral awards

The Netherlands is a party to the New York Convention on the (reciprocal) recognition of arbitral awards. No other conventions or treaties are in force. Arbitral awards rendered in countries with whom there are no conventions in force, are not recognised. New (court) proceedings in The Netherlands will have to be held (in as far as there would be jurisdiction) in order to try and enforce the claim within The Netherlands.

(d) Free exportability of proceeds

There are no limitations.

CHAPTER 18

NORWAY

Berit Stokke and Sigrid Surlien
Thommessen Krefting Greve Lind, Postboks 1484 Vika, 0116 Oslo, Norway

1. JURISDICTION

There are no general rules in Norwegian law which apply to the jurisdiction of Norwegian courts in international matters. The Civil Procedure Act of 13 August 1915 No. 6 §§ 17–36 ("CPA") deals primarily with the allocation of jurisdiction between Norwegian courts in a Norwegian dispute (so-called "relative competency") and not with the question of whether there is a Norwegian court which has jurisdiction at all (so-called "international competency"). However, the main rule is that the rules of relative competency also apply to international competency. This rule might be limited by principles of international law or by international conventions to which Norway is a signatory. The *forum non conveniens* doctrine does not exist in Norwegian law. If Norwegian forum for a case cannot be established, it will be dismissed.

(a) Domicile

(i) Residence

Any suit may be instituted in Norway where the defendant is domiciled, cf. CPA § 17. An individual is domiciled at the place where he is resident, cf. CPA § 18. The place of residence is the place of actual settlement combined with an intention to make that place a centre of his life for the long term. An individual may be domiciled in more than one place at a time, if he maintains a residence in several different locations at any given time. In this case the plaintiff can decide which court should take jurisdiction. Case law prescribes that it might be appropriate to undertake a broader evaluation of the parties' connections to Norway when dealing with the question of international competency.

(ii) Presence

A non-resident individual who is not domiciled, either in Norway or in a foreign country, is domiciled in the jurisdiction where he is present at the time the writ is served, cf. CPA § 19. This implies to a large extent that an individual temporarily located in Norway may be subject to legal action in Norway. This paragraph cannot be used against individuals who are domiciled in a Signatory State to the Lugano Convention.

(iii) Joint liability

If more than one individual or legal person is liable for a particular claim, e.g., as debtor(s) or guarantor(s), a legal action may normally be brought against all parties in the local court before which action may be brought against any one of them, cf. CPA § 33. However, it is not clear whether a non-resident individual or non-resident legal person can be brought before a Norwegian court pursuant to this paragraph solely on the fact that he has a jointly liable debtor in Norway. Legal authors are of the opinion that this paragraph itself might not suffice to give Norwegian courts international competency. It follows from the Lugano Act of 8 January 1993 No. 21 (the Lugano Act), which incorporates the Lugano Convention of 16 September 1988 into Norwegian law, that a person domiciled in a signatory State can be sued in Norway on the basis of a jointly liable debtor domiciled in Norway.

(b) Place of business/residence/office

Companies and other legal persons are domiciled at their business address as registered with the Norwegian Registry of Companies, cf. CPA § 21. A legal person who is not registered in the Registry of Companies will be domiciled where the Board of Directors has its seat or last had its seat. If no such domicile can be located, a legal person is deemed to have the same domicile as the individual on whom any petition or writ against the legal person in question is to be served, e.g. the Chairman of the Board.

(c) Assets located within the jurisdiction

The Civil Procedure Act lays down special jurisdictional rules which are applicable depending on the nature of the claim, and some rules are of mandatory application.

(i) Real estate

Norwegian courts will accept jurisdiction with respect to claims relating to real estate within the territory of Norway. Claims relating to the boundaries or servitudes of real estate or compensation for damage to real estate, shall be brought before the local court where the real estate is located, cf. CPA § 22. This rule has mandatory application. A local court may also exercise jurisdiction when the suit relates to real estate in its area for claims such as legal title or liability for a mortgage of real estate, cf. CPA § 23.

(ii) Movables

Norwegian courts can take jurisdiction over monetary claims even if the defendant is non-resident if the defendant has a capital asset of economic value within the jurisdiction at the time the writ is served, cf. CPA § 32. Claims related to non-negotiable documents can be brought before the court at the place where the debtor is resident, or, if the claim is secured by a mortgage, at the place where the mortgage is located. It is not a requirement that the property is in the defendant's possession. Norwegian courts are precluded from taking jurisdiction pursuant to CPA § 32 in cases which are governed by the Lugano Convention, cf. the Lugano Convention, Article 3.

(d) Act complained of within the jurisdiction

The fact that the act or the omission to act was committed or had effects within the territory of Norway gives rise to jurisdiction by Norwegian courts, cf. CPA § 29 (so-called "forum-damage"). The plaintiff can choose whether to initiate a legal action at the local court located where the act or the accident occurred or at the place where it had immediate effect. The claim can relate to physical or immaterial damage as well as to non-economic damage. There has to be a connection between the damage and the act or the omission to act. Suits related to contractual obligations can be brought at the place of performance or where performance can be requested, cf. CPA § 25.

(e) Contract governed by local law

The fact that the contract is governed by Norwegian law does not it itself suffice to create international competency of Norwegian courts. The Courts of Justice Act of 13 August 1915 No. 5 (CJA) § 39 might establish jurisdiction in this case. If the defendant objects to jurisdiction, the court will undertake an evaluation of the interests involved and the circumstances of the case generally.

(f) Conventions

The general and the special jurisdictional rules in the Norwegian Civil Procedure Act can be limited or deviated from by conventions to which Norway is a signatory or by the rule which states that Norwegian law is deemed to be in accordance with principles of international law. A convention which is of prime importance for the international competency of Norwegian courts is the 1988 Lugano Convention on Jurisdiction and the Enforcement of Judgments in Civil and Commercial Matters. The Lugano Convention was entered into between the EU Member States and the EFTA States and was incorporated into

Norwegian law by the Lugano Act. Its contents mirrors the 1968 Brussels Convention.

(g) Clause attributing jurisdiction

Norwegian courts will generally accept choice of forum clauses, cf. CPA § 36. Both derogation clauses, i.e. agreement that the dispute shall not come before a Norwegian court, and prorogation clauses, i.e. agreement that the dispute should be determined by a Norwegian court, even if Norwegian courts otherwise would not have international competency, will be accepted. However, the forum clause does not apply if it is contrary to mandatory jurisdictional rules or if it is invalid. Arbitration clauses will be accepted in so far as the parties have "free access" to the subject matter of the dispute, cf. CPA § 452. In all cases, such clauses have to be made in writing. A reference in a signed contract to standard terms with a forum clause will normally be accepted.

(h) Other

Appearance before the court/arbitration tribunal

If a person appears before the court without claiming that the court does not have jurisdiction (cf. CPA § 92) or the parties have started to negotiate a case before the arbitration tribunal (cf. CPA § 452), the court/arbitration tribunal will have jurisdiction.

(i) Counterclaim/third-party proceedings

A court will accept jurisdiction for counterclaims when it has assumed jurisdiction over the main claim, cf. CPA § 34 and § 56. Pursuant to CPA § 34, a court will generally accept jurisdiction for third party proceedings, such as for claims which derive from a court proceeding or interventions by non-resident individuals.

2. MARITIME CLAIMS

(a) Jurisdiction based on arrest of a vessel

An arrest of a vessel can provide jurisdiction in Norway. Pursuant to CPA § 31, if a vessel is arrested in Norway, or if security is posted to avoid or lift an arrest, a case can be brought in the forum where the arrest was made. The requirement is that it relates to the claim which triggered the arrest. Some specific jurisdictional provisions concerning maritime matters can be found in the Norwegian Maritime Code of 24 June 1994, No. 39 ("MC").

(b) Specific maritime jurisdiction

MC § 310 has provisions on jurisdiction and arbitration in matters relevant to international carriage of goods.

(i) Place of loading/discharge in Norway

Pursuant to MC § 310, the plaintiff can at his own discretion bring an action before the court at:

(a) the principal place of business/place of residence of the defendant;
(b) the place where the contract of carriage was concluded, provided that the defendant has a place of business or an agent there through whom the contract was concluded;
(c) the place of loading of carriage according to the contract of carriage; or
(d) the agreed or actual place of discharge of the goods according to the contract of carriage.

Any forum clause to the contrary which is agreed in advance of the dispute is invalid to the extent that the plaintiff's right to commence a suit at the places outlined above is limited. Further, the provisions outlined here do not prevent a plaintiff from commencing a suit at the court at the location stipulated in the contract for carriage.

(ii) Collision

MC Chapter 8 regulates collision, however there are no special jurisdictional rules governing collision claims. According to CPA § 31, an action can be brought at the court in the judicial circuit where the ship has its homeport, i.e. the homeport registered at the Shipping Registry, or when no registration is made, at the residence of the owner, or at the residence of the owner's representative if the owner is not resident in Norway. Following the other general jurisdictional rules, a case may be brought before the court at the place the accident occurred or had its effects, where an arrest was made or at the court of the place of the defendant or one of them.

(iii) Salvage

An action for the fixing or apportionment of salvage award or special compensation can be brought before the place where the salvage took place or where the salvaged items were brought ashore. An action for the apportionment of salvage reward between the shipowner and the crew must be brought in the jurisdiction where the salvage vessel has its homeport or, as the case may be, where the action for the fixing of a salvage reward or special compensation or for apportionment was brought between several salvors.

(iv) Appointment of court surveyor (maritime inquiry)

In Norway, maritime inquiry shall be held at the county or town court concerned, which shall be convened with two expert assessors.

(v) Tonnage limitation

Norwegian courts have jurisdiction to adjudicate actions against the owner of a ship or her insurer concerning liability for pollution damage, provided that the damage arose in the territory of Norway, including the economic zone, and also if steps were taken to prevent or limit pollution damage in Norway, cf. MC § 203. The competent court can then adjudicate all claims concerning the same occurrence, and thus also the question of tonnage limitation.

(c) The grounds for arrest

As a consequence of ratifying the Lugano Convention, Norway also ratified the 1952 Brussels Convention Relating to Arrest of Seagoing Ships. The provisions of the Convention are implemented into the Norwegian Maritime Code. As a general rule, the provisions governing arrest in the Enforcement Act of June 26 1992 (ECA) also govern the arrest of a ship; however, they are modified and supplemented by MC Chapter 4. Arrest that is limited to cargo, freight, fuel or parts of ships is not governed by the rules in the Maritime Code. Arrest based on such claims is solely governed by the ECA. As a main principle, a ship can only be arrested to secure a maritime claim. MC § 92 gives an exhaustive list of maritime claims and includes claims under ship mortgages. In broad terms, claims secured by maritime liens are included; however, also other claims can give rise to arrest of the ship (such as claims in connection with deliveries to the vessel). Pursuant to ECA § 14–2 subparagraph 2, a particular ship can be arrested "without a particular ground for arrest when the request is by a mortgagee with an overdue mortgage claim over the ship". This paragraph applies to contractual liens and mortgages. Maritime liens are governed by the MC § 92.

(d) Connection between arrested ship and claim

The right to arrest a ship does only apply to the ship the maritime claim relates to, cf. MC § 93. There are a few exemptions to this rule. If the owner of the ship to which the maritime claim relates is personally liable for the claim, arrest can be made on other ships owned by that person at the time the claim arose (the so-called "sister-ship exemption"). And further, if someone other than the owner of the ship to which the maritime claim relates is personally liable, arrest can be made on other ships owned by that person. These two provisions do not apply to arrests relevant to disputes over title to a ship or between co-owners relevant to title, possession, utilisation or income of a ship. Then only the ship to which the dispute relates can be arrested. The rules do not preclude that arrest in respect of maritime claims is made on other assets than the vessel.

(e) Procedural differences applying to special maritime jurisdiction

Norway does not have any general procedural rules governing maritime suits. However, the Maritime Code provides for some special procedural rules relating to, e.g. salvage rewards (joint suits), general average and maritime inquiries.

(f) Special rules as to limitation of liability

The Maritime Code provides for several specific rules governing limitation of liability, such as limitation of shipowner's liability for certain claims and the owner's right to global limitation; also limitation rules applying to contractual liability for carriage of goods and passengers, and limitation of liability for oil pollution.

3. SERVICE OF PROCEEDINGS

(a) Rules applying to service of proceedings outside the jurisdiction

(i) Where no convention applies

Where no bilateral or multilateral conventions apply, service of process is governed by the Court of Justice Act. Proceedings are commenced at the Conciliation Council (*forliksråd*) by means of a conciliation petition (*forliksklage*) or in the Court of First Instance by means of a writ of summons (*stevning*). After the Council/court have verified that the conciliation petition or the writ is in order, the Council/court will ensure that it is properly served on the defendant. Service of documents is generally undertaken by post to the defendant's address. Service may also be carried out personally at the domicile of the defendant. Letters rogatory from foreign courts or other foreign authorities are only complied with when they are sent through the Norwegian Ministry concerned, cf. the Courts of Justice Act, i.e. the Ministry of Justice, cf. the CJA § 46. The request will be sent to the local court and service of the action abroad will be effected in accordance with Norwegian law, i.e. by post or by personal service.

(ii) Where conventions apply

Norway is a signatory to the 1965 Hague Convention on the Notification of Judicial and Extrajudicial Documents Abroad. Under the Hague Convention, the foreign originating process may be submitted for service to the Norwegian Ministry of Justice as the designated central authority; alternatively, under the Convention, documents may also be sent directly to the relevant local court through the appropriate diplomatic channels. Service of the documents in question will then be implemented by the local court in the judicial circuit where the person on whom the documents are to be served is domiciled. Service will normally take place in accordance with the procedures applicable to the service of a petition or writ issued under Norwegian law. If the documents are not written in Norwegian, Swedish or Danish, they must be accompanied by a translation into such language.

Under the terms of separate multi-/bilateral agreements, documents originating in Sweden, Denmark, Finland, Iceland or Germany may be sent directly to the relevant local court by the competent authorities in the country of origin.

4. COST IMPLICATIONS OF STARTING PROCEEDINGS

(a) Court fees

The amount of court fees at the Conciliation Council is NOK 515, at the Court of First Instance NOK 3,090 and at the Appellate Court/Supreme Court NOK 12,875 (the amount is calculated on the basis of the standard court fee for 1998, which is NOK 515). Court fees are payable in advance; however, lawyers can pay in arrears.

(b) Lawyers' fees

There is no standard scale for lawyers' fees in Norway. The fee will be based on an overall assessment of the complexity of the case, the amount involved and the time spend on the matter. As a starting point, Norwegian lawyers will charge on the basis of hours worked, using an hourly rate between NOK 800 and NOK 2,000. Norwegian lawyers tend to invoice on a quarterly basis. Contingency fees are not recognised. Complaints over excessive lawyers' fees might be brought before the Lawyer's Dispute Council.

(c) Recovery of costs from unsuccessful party

The court can decide that the unsuccessful party in a lawsuit shall compensate the costs incurred by the other party, cf. CPA § 172. If the unsuccessful party loses the case on all issues, he shall compensate the other party for his legal costs. There are some exemptions to this rule. If the case if partly lost and partly won, each party shall cover his own legal costs. If the successful party has not won more through the judgment than what he would have obtained by accepting an offer made by the other party to settle the case, the successful party might be ordered to cover his own legal costs, cf. CPA § 174.

(d) Security for costs

The CPA § 182 grants a right for the defendant to demand that a non-resident plaintiff shall provide security for the defendant's legal costs. The level of security is fixed by the court, and should reflect the level of costs likely to be awarded to the defendant in the event that a judgment should be given in his favour. The Committee of the Appeal of the Norwegian Supreme Court has requested the EFTA Court to deliver an advisory opinion on this matter. The question raised is whether such national procedural rules are in accordance with the EEA Agreement, Article 4, where a company which is domiciled in another EEA country brings a legal action against a company domiciled in Norway (Case 5/97 *European Navigation Inc.* v. *Star Forsikring AS*). (The plaintiff has since withdrawn this case.) The right to demand security for costs has in many cases been abolished under conventions ratified by Norway.

5. INTERIM ARREST

(a) For domestic proceedings or proceedings in another jurisdiction

Provisional measures are governed by the Enforcement Act of 26 June 1992 No. 86 ("ECA"). The scope of the Enforcement Act might be limited by principles of international law or by conventions. It provides security for domestic proceedings as well as for proceedings (judicial and arbitral) in foreign jurisdictions.

(b) Criteria applying

An arrest order (*arrest*) is relevant for monetary claims, whether or not due. The application should take the form of a writ and be filed with the local Court of Execution and Enforcement (*namsrett*), either located in the judicial circuit where the defendant is domiciled, where the assets are located, or at the place where movables are expected to arrive in the near future. An attachment of the defendant's assets may be granted if the defendant's behaviour "gives reason to fear that enforcement or execution of the claim will be lost or made significantly more difficult or will have to take place abroad", cf. ECA § 14-2. The court will need to be satisfied that the underlying claim is reasonably justified, cf. ECA § 14-6. Further, the court can demand that the plaintiff provide security for possible liability for damages because of a wrongful arrest. The arrest order will not be implemented before such security is at hand.

(c) Limitation on jurisdictions whose proceedings are recognised for the purpose of arrest

There is no limitation on jurisdictions whose proceedings are recognised for the purpose of arrest. An arbitration tribunal does not have competency to deliver interim measures; however, an application can be made to the Court of Execution and Enforcement. The court will set a time limit within which the defendant must institute legal proceedings in respect of the claim, cf. ECA § 14-8. Upon request, the time limit may be extended by the court.

(d) Counter-security

The defendant can avoid implementation of the arrest order if he provides security for the plaintiff's claim, cf. ECA § 14-8. He can also place a security after the arrest order is implemented and make a request that the arrest order should be lifted, cf. ECA § 14-14.

(e) Can applications be made ex parte?

Application for an arrest order can be made *ex parte*, provided that it is necessary to take immediate action to secure the underlying claim. However, the general rule is that an oral hearing between all parties is held prior to the delivery of an arrest order.

(f) How quickly can an order be made?

The arrest order can be delivered the very same day or within a couple of days, depending on the urgency of the matter.

(g) Will the order bind third parties?

The effect of the arrest is that the defendant loses the right to physically or legally dispose of the arrested assets to the detriment of the plaintiff, cf. ECA § 14–11. Third parties will be bound by the arrest order and the order will obtain legal protection and priority pursuant to the Mortgage Act of 8 February 1980 No. 2.

(h) The consequences of breach of an order

Any person who breaches an arrest order commits a punishable offence and is liable for fines or imprisonment up to a maximum of four months, cf. the Criminal Act of 23 May 1902, No. 10, § 343. Criminal prosecution will only be initiated on a request from the aggrieved party.

(i) Limit to types of assets

The court will decide which assets should be attached by the order. Attachment can be made to all assets which the defendant owns at the time of the attachment and which can be converted into money.

(j) What if third parties are affected?

If the arrest order was given *ex parte*, third parties who are affected by it can request an oral hearing of the matter, cf. ECA § 14-13. In all other cases, third parties have to lodge an appeal within two weeks, cf. ECA § 2-12 and CPA § 398.

(k) Other provisional measures to be ordered

(i) Interlocutory order

An interlocutory order (*midlertidig forføyning*) may be granted for non-monetary claims, if the defendant's behaviour makes it necessary to secure enforcement or execution of the plaintiff's underlying claim. An interlocutory order can also be delivered if it is necessary to prevent substantial damage, inconvenience or violence, cf. ECA § 15-2.

(ii) Summary proceedings

Upon the consent of the parties, the court can decide the issue by summary proceedings, which is an expeditious way of legal proceedings and allows the court to decide to deliver a judgment solely on the basis of written documents. If the dispute does not exceed NOK 20,000, the matter is always decided by summary proceedings. In practice summary proceedings are not frequently used in Norway.

6. RECOGNITION OF JUDGMENTS/AWARDS

(a) Treaties/conventions applying (i) to enable Norwegian judgments to be enforced abroad; (ii) to enable enforcement of foreign judgments in Norway

Foreign judgments can provide a basis for enforcement in Norway, provided that there is a convention in force between the foreign country and Norway, cf. ECA § 4-1 (f)–(h). As a signatory of the Lugano Convention, Norway will recognise and enforce judgments rendered in another Signatory State, and other Signatory States will recognise and enforce judgments delivered in Norway. Enforcement of the judgment can only be refused on the specific grounds which are stated in the Convention. Norway can always refuse to recognise a judgment based on *ordre public* considerations, cf. CPA § 167 *i.f.* Norway has also entered into some bilateral conventions on the recognition and enforcement of judgments. It is worth noting that a judgment by a foreign court in accordance with a jurisdiction clause agreed by the parties, will provide a legal basis for enforcement in Norway, cf. ECA § 4-1 (g) and CPA § 168a.

(b) Procedures to be followed to enforce a foreign judgment

The various conventions set down procedural rules for enforcement. Under the Lugano Convention, an application for the enforcement of a judgment shall be made to the Local Court of Execution and Enforcement (*namsrett*) in the judicial circuit in which enforcement is to take place. The application has to be followed by a certified copy of the judgment documents which show that the judgment is enforceable in the country of origin and that it is properly served. The documents do not need to be legalised. If the judgment is rendered in a country with which Norway does not have a bilateral agreement, Norway will not recognise the judgment and new legal proceedings must be held. The foreign judgment will then only have evidentiary effect in the Norwegian proceedings.

(c) Foreign arbitral awards

Since Norway is a signatory to the 1958 New York Convention on the Recognition and Enforcement of Arbitral Awards, arbitration awards are easily enforced in Norway. Arbitration awards rendered in countries which are not signatories to the 1958 New York Convention will not be recognised.

(d) Free exportability of proceeds of a judgment

There are no regulatory limitations on the transfer of judgment proceeds abroad.

CHAPTER 19

PORTUGAL

Manuel P. Barrocas & Margarida Caldeira
Barrocas & Sarmento, Av. Fontes Pereira de Melo 15-7º, 1050 Lisbon, Portugal

1. JURISDICTION

A general framework of rules on the grounds on which Portuguese courts will accept jurisdiction are herein below described in items 1.1, 1.2, 1.3 and 1.4. A synopsis of certain grounds of acceptance of jurisdiction is afterwards provided in items (a) to (i) but the application of each of these items should be combined with the explanation on the general framework of rules set out in 1.1 to 1.4.

1.1 Exclusive jurisdiction

The Portuguese courts have exclusive jurisdiction, in relation to foreign courts, in the following cases:

(i) actions relating to rights over real estate located in Portugal;
(ii) actions of bankruptcy and companies' recovery relating to merchants or companies based in Portugal;
(iii) actions having as their object the validity of the incorporation or winding-up of associations or companies having a registered seat in Portugal, as well as actions on the validity of their resolutions;
(iv) actions whose cause is the validity of public registrations of any rights mandatorily registrable in Portugal.

1.2 International competence

The international competence of Portuguese courts without excluding foreign jurisdiction depends upon verification of the following factors:

(i) the defendant or one of the defendants is domiciled or has a registered seat or branch in Portugal, except where the action relates to rights over real estate located abroad;
(ii) the case is subject to domestic jurisdiction under the statutory rules of territorial competence of Portuguese courts, for instance:
    — actions relating to rights over immovable goods including termination of leases, mortgages, and the like;

— actions on the fulfilment of obligations or the indemnity or termination for non-fulfilment where the creditor may choose to file the claim either before the court of the place where the obligation should be fulfilled or before the court of domicile of the defendant;

— actions on civil liability based on tort where the competent court is that where the cause of action was committed;

(iii) actions relating to acts complained of within the jurisdiction;

(iv) actions where the plaintiff alleges that a Portugese court is the only one whose judgment may be effective in practical terms or where it would be unreasonable for the plaintiff to plead abroad, provided that there is a strong connection between the objects of the claim and the Portuguese territory.

1.3 Jurisdiction clause

The parties may enter into an agreement containing a clause attributing jurisdiction whether (a) designating a jurisdiction as exclusively competent or (b) designating a jurisdiction alternatively competent in relation to Portuguese courts, where the latter is verified under statute.

Such clause is only valid where it complies with the following prerequisites:

(i) the objects of the action are connected to more than one jurisdiction (the parties cannot designate a jurisdiction of a third country to which the situation has no relation whatsoever);

(ii) the matter will not concern personal or non-negotiable rights or matters upon which Portuguese courts have exclusive jurisdiction (see above item 1);

(iii) the recognition of competence is accepted by the law of the designated court;

(iv) the designation of such a jurisdiction must correspond to a real and serious advantage for the parties;

(v) the agreement should be written (e.g. it is sufficient to use a telecopier or telegram or the like) or later confirmed in writing, mentioning clearly the jurisdiction designated.

1.4 Extensions of competence

There are cases of extensions of competence:

(i) The court competent to hear the case is also competent to hear the incidents verified during court proceedings and all the matters alleged by the defendant. However, the decision adjudicated as to such incidents or matters is not definitive (i.e. it is not a *res judicata*) outside the main proceedings unless one of the parties asks for such effect of the decision and the court is internationally competent and has hierarchic and material jurisdiction to hear the case.

(ii) The court competent to hear the case is also competent to decide on any counterclaim if it has international, hierarchic and material jurisdiction.

(iii) When the hearing of the case depends on a decision on a matter for which a criminal or administrative court is competent, and if the said criminal or administrative proceedings instituted do not progress due to negligence of the parties, the judge may decide on such matter. This decision is not definitive outside such proceedings.

1.5 Summary

In synthesis, under the above conditions and sometimes with certain restrictions, the grounds for accepting jurisdiction can be:

(a) domicile
(b) place of business, residence or office
(c) assets located within jurisdiction
(d) an act complained of within jurisdiction
(e) contract governed by local law
(f) conventions
(g) clause attributing jurisdiction
(h) others: place of proceedings of bankruptcy of a company, incorporation of associations, public registries, immovable goods, civil liability, procedural incidents, subsidiary international competence of Portuguese courts
(i) counterclaim and third-party proceedings.

2. MARITIME CLAIMS

(a) Is there special jurisdiction for maritime claims based on arrest of a vessel in the jurisdiction?

There has been since 1987 a special jurisdiction for maritime claims regulated by the Maritime Courts Act (hereinafter "the Law"), located in Lisbon. Portugal has signed and ratified the following conventions (which prevail over Domestic Law) relating to maritime matters:

— the Convention for the Unification of Certain Rules Concerning the Immunity of State-Owned Ships, signed in Brussels on 10 April 1926 and amended on 29 May 1934, ratified by Portugal in 1957;
— the Convention for the Unification of Certain Rules Relating to

Maritime Liens and Mortgages, signed in Brussels on 10 April 1926, ratified by Portugal in 1931;

— the Convention on the Limitation of the Liability of Owners of Seagoing Ships, signed in Brussels on 10 October 1957, ratified by Portugal on 8 April 1968.

The jurisdiction of the maritime courts is regulated under strict criteria which does not provide for the application of *forum non conveniens*: in short, courts have no discretionary power to decline jurisdiction unless such discretion has been clearly conferred by statute.

(b) Specific

As referred to above in item 1—Jurisdiction, the Portuguese courts are competent under the criterion of internal territorial competence. This criterion has the following specific applications to maritime claims:

(i) the claims on regulation of gross repairs are heard at the court of the port where the cargo was or should have been discharged;
(ii) the claims for damage to a vessel done by another vessel may be litigated at the court (a) of the place of the accident or (b) of the domicile of the owner of the offending vessel or (c) of the nationality of the damaged vessel or where such vessel was found or (d) the first port where the damaged vessel arrives;
(iii) the claims for salaries due for the salvage or assistance of vessels may be litigated at (a) the place of occurrence of the salvage or assistance or (b) the domicile of the owner of the objects recovered or (c) the place of nationality or where the ship was found;
(iv) the claim for the lifting of privileges over a recently purchased vessel.

Besides the above factors that attribute jurisdiction to Portuguese courts, there are also applicable to maritime claims the general factors laid down in the Rules of the Portuguese Civil Procedural Code (see above item 1—Jurisdiction).

The Law applicable to maritime courts attributes jurisdiction over actions concerning the carriage of goods by sea where:

(i) the port of loading of discharge is in Portugal;
(ii) the contract of carriage has been performed in Portugal;
(iii) the relevant vessel is registered in Portugal;
(iv) the shipper, receiver, consignee or carrier has an office in Portugal.

(c) What are the grounds for arrest?

The powers of the Portuguese courts to arrest vessels in Portuguese waters are not affected by the question of whether the main action is to be settled by the

Portuguese courts. As to the type of claims for which an arrest may be requested: in cases where the owner of a vessel is the party liable *in personam*, any vessel belonging to that owner may be arrested in relation to any kind of civil claim; in cases where the shipowner is not personally liable for the claim, the regime applicable is the following:

— (1) If the 1952 Brussels Arrest Convention applies (i.e. if the vessel to be arrested flies the flag of another signatory jurisdiction), Article 2 of the Convention defines the claims that may ground an arrest.

— (2) If the Convention is not applicable, the relevant claims are set out in the Portuguese law as follows:

(a) any claim for damage done by or to a vessel;
(b) any claim related to the construction, repair, purchase or sale of a vessel;
(c) any claim arising out of any agreement as to the carriage of goods in a vessel by sea or river or canals;
(d) any claim arising out of any agreement as to the maritime use or hire of a vessel (e.g. charter and leasing contracts);
(e) any claim resulting from any insurance agreement as to a vessel or her cargo;
(f) any claim related to mortgages and maritime liens or other charges on a vessel or her cargo;
(g) any other maritime claim provided for elsewhere in Portuguese law, e.g. an action to compel judicial survey of a ship or cargo, or to appoint a trustee to take into custody cargoes not received by or rejected by a consignee;
(h) any claim which may lead to an arrest or other restraint of a vessel, her cargo, bunkers or appurtenances;
(i) any claim as to general or particular average;
(j) any claim relating to salvage;
(l) any claim relating to towage or pilot agreement;
(m) any claim regarding prosecution caused by a vessel;
(n) any claim regarding damage done by a vessel to state assets of maritime use (e.g. port and harbour installations);
(o) any claim of a general maritime nature, such as in respect of the possession or ownership or employment of a vessel, loss of or damage to goods carried in a ship, etc.

(d) Need the arrested vessel be connected with the claim or can other vessels in the same legal or beneficial ownership also be arrested?

The arrest may be maintained only in respect of a claim which has vested at the date of issue of the court proceedings but it is not necessary for the claim to have been exactly quantified.

(e) What procedural rules apply to special maritime jurisdiction?

As to the procedural rules, an arrest is always carried out as an adjunct to proceedings of the main action. Such proceedings are similar to the other preliminary injunctions (see below item 5—Interim Arrest).

The party requesting the arrest should demonstrate a need for security and must prove that he has reasonable grounds for believing that any subsequent monetary judgment in his favour may remain unsatisfied unless he is permitted to obtain security. In practice (and differently to other preliminary injunctions), the courts will invariably grant arrest applications since it is apparent that any seagoing vessel may leave Portuguese waters or have new maritime liens created over her at any time.

The plaintiff of an arrest should also demonstrate the nature of the credit and in many cases the arrest is not enforced if a bail (normally, a bank guarantee) is accepted by the creditor or if the judge considers (within two days) such bail acceptable taking into account the limit of liability relevant to the main action. However, the vessel cannot leave the port until the bail is provided.

(f) What jurisdictional rules are there as to limitation of liability?

There are no jurisdictional rules as to the limitation of liability.

3. SERVICE OF PROCEEDINGS

The Convention on the Service Abroad of Judicial and Extrajudicial Documents in Civil or Commercial Matters dated 15 November 1965 was ratified by Portugal on 18 May 1971 and entered into force on 25 February 1974 (hereinafter, "the Convention").

The Portuguese Civil Procedure Code (hereinafter, "CPC") provides for several rules regarding service of proceedings and communications to entities outside the jurisdiction, as set out below.

Any service of writ of summons or notifications that request the intervention of judicial entities (e.g. affidavits) may be made through a letter rogatory to the addressed foreign entity (courts or others), unless an international convention provides for differently.

In case the foreign state addressed only accepts the receiving of letters rogatory through diplomatic or consular channels, that method will be the manner of transmission to be followed. If the addressed state does not accept letters through an official channel, the letter rogatory will be sent directly to the intended entity.

The CPC provides for restrictions on the motives for the refusal of compliance of letters rogatory.

Where the service of writ of summons or other notification to persons abroad does not imply the intervention of foreign judicial entities, the communication is made in pursuance of international treaties or international agreements applicable. In the absence of treaties or agreements, the service of writ of summons is made by registered letter with acknowledgement of receipt, according to the local post regulations. In case it is not possible to serve the writ of summons by post it should be made either (a) through the nearest Portuguese consulate if the defendant is Portuguese or (b) if the defendant is foreign, through the respective consulate or, if that is not possible, through a letter rogatory.

4. COSTS

(a) Court fees

Court fees are assessed in relation to the size of the claim either concerning an injunction or the main action. Every action, including injunctions, has a value.

As an example, the regular court fees with regard to main action proceedings for a claim of US$100,000 would amount to about US$1,250. Injunction proceedings would cost between one quarter (if there is answer by the defendants) and one eighth of this amount (if there is no such answer).

(b) Lawyers' fees

Lawyers' fees are not subject to any fixed standard scale and are determined taking into account the following factors: time spent, complexity of the matter, final result, importance of the legal service provided by the lawyer, the usage in each specific area of practice.

The following practices are illegal:

(i) contingency fees;
(ii) sharing the fees with anyone, except with other lawyers who have co-operated in the case;
(iii) to agree on a "quota litis", i.e. to be remunerated sharing a part of the debt or the client's interest.

More recently, lawyers organised in law firms and specifically when representing corporate foreign clients have been charging their fees on an hourly basis, particularly when such system has been previously agreed with the client.

(c) Recovery of costs from unsuccessful party

The losing litigant pays for all costs and compensation for lawyers' fees. The law permits the successful litigant to recover the costs disbursed in advance to court from the losing litigant plus a certain pre-fixed amount of compensation of lawyers' fees.

This amount depends on the value of the action and does not relate to the exact amount of lawyers' fees, though it aims to be a contribution for such fees.

The parties of course are not prevented from agreeing in advance or in a latter stage that a party to a contract, arbitration or such like who has caused the lawyers' fees and expenses to be incurred must pay them. In this event, the lawyers' fees in whole are recoverable by the successful party from the party who has not contributed to the expenses incurred.

(d) Security for costs

The courts request advance retainers both from the plaintiff and from the defendant at several stages of the proceedings.

Beyond these advance payments of retainers there is no other security for costs.

5. INTERIM ARREST

(a) Are interim arrest/freezing of assets/other provisional measures permitted to provide security for domestic proceedings and/or proceedings in another jurisdiction?

Interim arrests and other provisional measures are permitted to provide security for domestic proceedings or proceedings in another jurisdiction.

(b) What criteria apply to this?

The criteria applicable are the following: Portuguese law provides for (a) seven provisional injunctions may may be granted where the specific conditions stated in the law (as detailed below) are met and (b) a so-called non-specified injunction, also subject to certain conditions which is claimed where no specific type of injunction is applicable.

The conditions to the grant of the non-specified injunction are, in short, the following:

(i) the plaintiff should demonstrate that he has a certain right and there is a reasonable fear that the defendant may cause serious injury to his right before the court determines a definitive remedy in the main action;

(ii) the prejudice that would result to the defendant by granting the injunction cannot be reasonably greater than the damage that the plaintiff intends to avoid by filing the injunction.

Each type of specific injunction has a specific object and thus if an application for one type of injunction is dismissed by the court because of unfounded factual or legal reasons, it is not permitted to use another one with the aim of obtaining, directly or indirectly, the typical effects of the first one.

However, the court is not obliged to decide on the grant of the specific injunction claimed and may consider that another kind of specific injunction is more appropriate. Moreover, the court may decide to order cumulatively more than one kind of injunction for the same situation.

In short, the injunction is drafted as a court order directing someone to refrain from doing an unlawful act or as an order imposing requirements in order to allow the plaintiff to do something; to arrest or seize assets in order to serve as guarantee for collecting a debt; and, in general, anything that can and/or must be done with a view to protecting a right or a legal situation which is in peril of being lost or disappearing. The injunction is therefore based on the *periculum in mora*, that is, it is based on the peril resulting from the delay and on the urgency of its necessity.

Main actions filed at a foreign jurisdiction may be taken into consideration before the grant of a preliminary injunction. As a matter of fact, in all cases that come under an international convention signed by the Portuguese State, the preliminary proceedings of injunction depend upon a main action that has been or should be heard in a foreign court; the plaintiff should produce evidence before the Portuguese court that the main action is pending in the foreign court, and should present for that purpose, a judicial certificate issued by the foreign court.

The counter-party's defence is heard by the court except where this hearing would seriously prejudice the purpose or the efficiency of the injunction.

(c) Is there a limit on jurisdictions whose proceedings are recognised for this purpose?

There is no limit on jurisdictions whose proceedings are recognised for this purpose.

(d) Is there a requirement for counter-security?

There is no compulsory counter-security. It is up to the judge to decide the imposition of bail or other security.

(e) Can applications be made ex parte?

The application should be made only by the plaintiff, who should be the plaintiff in the main action.

(f) How quickly can an order be made?

Any preliminary injunction depends on the main action and may precede the latter or be claimed simultaneously with the main action.

All preliminary injunctions have a character of urgency, and are processed during judicial vacation. The proceedings in which the defendant is not heard must be decided in the first instance within 15 days; if the defendant is heard, the decision must be adjudicated within two months.

(g) Will the order bind third parties?

As a general principle, the order binds only the defendant and is not addressed against third parties. However, in the case of arrest or seizure of goods, it implies that all third parties are automatically prohibited from prejudicing any physical act of the court's clerks or the police to enforce the order. Furthermore, the arrest may be claimed by the plaintiff against the purchaser of the assets of the debtor.

(h) What are the consequences of breach of an order?

The enforcement of the injunction order may be made, when necessary, with the co-operation of the police. The breach of the order implies, as a consequence, not only a civil liability for all damages caused (without restriction of kind or amount of liability) but also a criminal remedy. In fact, the breach of an injunction is considered a crime of qualified disobedience to public authorities.

(i) Is there a limit to types of assets?

There is no limitation to types of assets.

(j) What if third parties are affected, e.g. airliner?

As seen above, third parties may in certain cases, be affected and since there is no limitation to types of assets an airliner could be affected also.

(k) What other provisional measures may be ordered?

The specific kinds of injunctions provided for in the law are the following and the interim arrest, as seen below, is only a kind of injunction.

(i) Provisional restoration of possession

(ii) Suspension of resolutions of corporate bodies
(iii) Provisional alimonies
(iv) Provisional restoration of indemnity
(v) Arrest
(vi) Suspension of building
(vii) Enrolment.

The scope of the arrest is to obtain an order restraining the defendant from disposing of or otherwise dealing with his assets in order to frustrate the plaintiff's action for money; it thus facilitates the collection of the debt.

The seizure of assets to allow the exercise of another right, for instance a right to share certain assets (owned by a company as a consequence of winding-up) is a different injunction—the enrolment, above mentioned.

There is no legal restriction on the kind of assets to be arrested and these may be in the hands of third parties who have purchased the goods, should the plaintiff identify such third parties. The plaintiff should also identify the assets to be arrested. Also, the Public Prosecutor may request the arrest against any surveyor or state clerk or any association or company which detains such assets.

6. RECOGNITION OF JUDGMENTS AND AWARDS

(a) What treaties/conventions apply (i) to enable judgments to be enforced abroad and (ii) to enable enforcement of foreign judgments domestically?

For the recognition of judgments, enabling Portuguese court judgments to be enforced abroad and the enforcement of foreign judgments domestically, the following conventions are in force in Portugal:

- the Hague Convention on the Recognition and Enforcement of Foreign Judgments in Civil and Commercial Matters dated 1 February 1971 and the Protocol of the same date;
- the Convention on the Competence and Execution of Decisions on Civil and Commercial Matters, dated 27 September 1968 (hereinafter, "the Brussels Convention"). Portugal acceded to it through the Convention of San Sebastian which has been in force in Portugal since 1 July 1992;
- the Lugano Convention, which extended the application of the Brussels Convention to the EFTA countries, has been in force in Portugal since 1 July 1992;
- other bilateral conventions.

International conventions and treaties prevail over domestic law.

Within the EU, the recognition of judgments in civil or commercial matters, notwithstanding the exceptions of application provided for in the Brussels Convention, is also made under the procedure set forth in this Convention in relation to judgments of other Signatory States.

(b) What procedure is followed to enforce a foreign judgment (i) governed by a treaty/convention and (ii) not governed by a treaty/convention?

Where there is no Convention applicable or in relation to the matters excluded from the scope of the Conventions, the recognition and enforcement of foreign judgments or foreign arbitration awards is made under the CPC, as set out below.

Article 1094 of the CPC establishes that, without prejudice to treaties or special laws applicable, any foreign judgment or foreign arbitration award on private rights may be acknowledged and enforced in Portugal once they are granted the *exequatur* by a Portuguese court, irrespective of the nationality of the parties.

Nevertheless, attention should be drawn to the fact that the recognition is not necessary when the foreign judgment is used as a means of evidence in pending proceedings at a Portuguese court having a different object from the recognition of the foreign judgment. However, the judge of the proceedings will freely decide on the probatory value of such judgment.

The enforcement of such judgments and awards must abide by the following conditions:

- (i) that there is no doubt of the authenticity of the document in which the foreign judgment or award is set out;
- (ii) that the judgment or award has become *res judicata*—that is, that it admits no further ordinary appeal and is thus final and binding—in the country in which the decision has been adjudicated;
- (iii) that it has been adjudicated by a court or arbitration tribunal having jurisdiction to hear the case and that the Portuguese court was not the one exclusively entitled to hear the case, under Portuguese law;
- (iv) that there are no pending proceedings or *res judicata* (with the same plea, cause of plea and parties) relating to proceedings at a Portuguese court before being initiated at the foreign court;
- (v) that the defendant has been duly served with the writ of summons under the law of the foreign court that adjudicated the decision and that during proceedings at the foreign court the equal position of the parties has been safeguarded;
- (vi) that the acknowledgment of the decision is not clearly incompatible with Portuguese public policy.

(c) What about foreign arbitration awards?

As to foreign arbitration awards, Portugal has ratified both the 1958 New York Convention and the 1926 Geneva Convention on the Execution of Foreign Arbitral Awards as well as the 1923 Geneva Protocol on Arbitration Clauses in Commercial Matters, which are fully applicable.

(d) Will proceeds of a judgment be freely exportable?

A decision or award granted by a Portuguese court does not have effects outside Portuguese territory.

7. OTHER REMARKS

There is no limitation whatsoever on the right of foreigners to plead in Portuguese courts. Also the rights granted, e.g. of defence, are strictly the same as those granted to nationals under the Constitution of the Portuguese Republic.

Forum shopping: overall comment

Portuguese law, namely the Civil Code (in the part which regulates the conflicts of law of different countries) and the CPC, does not contain a specific provision on the restriction of forum shopping. Nevertheless, and as seen above, the statutory criteria for the attribution of competence of courts and other compulsory provisions—namely on the enforcement of judgments and awards not governed by an international treaty and of private agreements designating jurisdiction—provide for a restriction on forum shopping.

In conclusion Portuguese law does not admit a regime corresponding to the "*forum non conveniens*" of English law. As a matter of fact and as noted above, Portuguese courts must have jurisdiction to hear the case in pursuance of Portuguese law. Consequently, Portuguese courts cannot decide freely on the court in which the action may be more adequately instituted taking into account the best interests of the parties and the public.

In the event that there is no statutory jurisdiction the judge will only declare that he had no jurisdiction at law.

On the other hand, also as seen above, private agreements conferring jurisdiction cannot be freely drafted by the parties since they have to comply with the compulsory regime for their validity and certain matters are excluded from the scope of voluntary jurisdiction. Therefore, "forum shopping" is reasonably restricted.

CHAPTER 20

SCOTLAND

Gill Grassie
Maclay Murray & Spens, 3 Glenfinlay Street, Edinburgh, EH3 6AQ, Scotland

1. JURISDICTION

What are the general grounds on which the Scottish courts will accept jurisdiction

Scotland, although it forms part of the UK, has its own legal system and courts. In Scottish terminology, the plaintiff is called the "pursuer" and the defendant is called the "defender". As part of the UK Scotland is, by this means, a party to the 1968 Brussels Convention on Jurisdiction and Judgments entered into by the relevant EU member states and the later Lugano Convention (the "Jurisdiction Convention").

The Civil Jurisdiction and Judgments Act of 1982 as amended ("the 1982 Act"), as a UK Act, applies in Scotland. It requires UK courts to implement the Convention and to apply the relevant principles laid down by the European Court of Justice in so doing. The 1982 Act also makes provision for allocation of jurisdiction to the Scottish courts as against other courts elsewhere in the UK. It also introduced a new set of rules on jurisdiction for Scotland which are largely but not wholly derived from the rules of the Convention where the jurisdictional rules of the Convention or the scheme of allocation for the UK are not applicable. These rules, which will be outlined below, should be treated as the rules which will generally apply irrespective of whether the particular case has a connection with the UK/EU/EFTA states. There are additional grounds of jurisdiction which apply if there is no such connection and these are specifically identified. The rules below apply in Scotland generally to civil and commercial matters, although there are specific topics excluded which broadly speaking correlate with those listed as exclusions in the Jurisdiction Convention.

Exceptions

There are certain specified excluded subject matters, in which cases there are special jurisdictional rules, i.e. those in place before the 1982 Act was brought into force. The cases of most interest are perhaps as follows:

— proceedings in respect of sequestration or bankruptcy or the winding up of a company; or determining status or legal capacity of natural persons; or for regulating the custody of children. Furthermore, admiralty causes insofar as jurisdiction is based on arrestment *in rem* or *ad fundandam jursdictionem* to found jurisdiction of a ship, cargo or freight, are excluded from the general scheme. The latter will be commented upon further below.

(a) Domicile—primary ground of jurisdiction

Under the 1982 Act the fundamental principle is that the pursuer should follow the defender, whether an individual or a corporation, to the place or country of his "domicile" and sue him there. There are exceptions to this rule. These are where there is either concurrent grounds of jurisdiction or exclusive jurisdiction on some other ground (see below).

"Domicile" means place of "habitual residence". For an individual "domicile" in Scotland is established if the person is resident there and the nature and circumstances of his residence there indicate that he has a substantial connection with Scotland. The Scottish courts will apply a rebuttable presumption to the effect that, if the individual has been resident within Scotland for the last three years or more, he will be domiciled there.

Domicile is also the paramount ground of jurisdiction in relation to a corporation, partnership or unincorporated voluntary association, such as a club. Domicile for these purposes is defined as "the seat" of the body in question. The specific rules to decide whether a corporation has its seat in Scotland include whether it has its registered office or official address in Scotland, or its central management or control is exercised there or it has a place of business there.

(b) Place of business/residence/office

The Scottish courts will generally also assume jurisdiction where the defender has a place of business, residence or office within Scotland, because this will in most cases amount to an indication that they are domiciled there. Also where Scotland is the place where a branch, agency or other establishment is situated, out of whose operations the dispute has arisen, the Scottish courts will have jurisdiction.

(c) Assets located within the jurisdiction

Where the defender is not domiciled within the UK but is outwith the EU/EFTA he may be sued in Scotland where (a) he owns movable property which has been arrested within Scottish jurisdiction or (b) he owns or has a beneficial interest in any immovable property, i.e. land/buildings, which is situated in Scotland.

Where the defender is domiciled outwith EU/EFTA, or the matter is truly internal to Scotland where proceedings are brought concerning a debt secured over immovable property or to assert, declare or determine proprietary or possessory rights in movable property or rights in security over such property or to obtain authority to dispose of it, an action may be brought in the Scottish courts if the property is situated in Scotland.

(d) Act complained of within the jurisdiction

Where a tort, delict or quasi delict has occurred in Scotland the Scottish courts will assume jurisdiction. A "delict" is the Scottish term for "tort". Jurisdiction in Scotland may also be acquired if Scotland is the place where the wrong is threatened and likely to occur.

(e) Contract governed by local law

Where Scotland is the location for the place of performance of the obligation in question in matters relating to a contract the Scottish courts will assume jurisdiction.

(f) Conventions

The main conventions which regulate jurisdiction are the Brussels and Lugano Conventions, for which see above.

(g) Clause attributing jurisdiction

(i) Prorogation of jurisdiction

Where an agreement has been made between parties that the courts of Scotland are to have jurisdiction to settle any disputes which may arise in connection with their particular legal relationship, the Scottish courts have exclusive jurisdiction. If there is no external UK element, and the Scottish courts are selected, they do not have exclusive jurisdiction, but merely concurrent jurisdiction with any other courts which may otherwise have jurisdiction under the Act.

(h) Other

(i) Criminal proceedings

Where the Scottish courts are seised of criminal proceedings which result in a civil claim for damages or restitution, the Scottish courts will have jurisdiction to entertain civil proceedings in respect of that claim.

(ii) No fixed residence

Where a person has no fixed residence, he can be sued in any Scottish court within whose jurisdiction he is personally sited if he is domiciled outside the EU/EFTA or the matter is truly internal to Scotland. This is to give Scottish courts jurisdiction over itinerants who have no domicile.

(iii) Decision of corporate entity

Where proceedings have as their object a decision of an organ of a company or other legal person or of an association, the Scottish courts will have jurisdiction where that company or association has its seat within Scotland.

(iv) Arbitration

Where an arbitration is conducted in Scotland or where its procedure is governed by Scots law, Scottish courts will have jurisdiction and in particular the Court of Session.

(v) Intellectual property

Where proceedings are mainly concerned with the registration in the UK or the validity in the UK of patents, trade marks, designs and other similar IP rights which require to be deposited or registered, the Scottish Court of Session will have jurisdiction.

(vi) Compulsory grounds of jurisdiction

There are also compulsory grounds of jurisdiction which apply in Scotland under the 1982 Act:

- Where land and buildings in respect of which proceedings are to be brought which have as their object rights *in rem* or tenancies of that property are in Scotland.
- Where a company, legal person or association has its seat in Scotland and proceedings are to be brought to object to the validity of the constitution, the nullity of the dissolution of such companies, etc.
- Where Scotland is the place where the relevant public register is kept which contains an entry which is challenged as to validity.
- Where a judgment is being enforced in Scotland proceedings in connection with the enforcement of the judgment.

(i) Counterclaim/third-party proceedings/second defender

A defender may be sued in Scotland as a third party in any action on a warranty or guarantee or in any other third-party proceedings where the Scottish court is seised with the original proceedings, unless these were instituted solely with the object of removing him from the jurisdiction of the court which would be competent in his case.

Where there is an original claim pending before the Scottish court and a counterclaim is brought arising from the same contract or facts upon which the original claim is based, the counterclaim may be brought before the Scottish courts against the relevant pursuer.

Where the defender is one of a number of defenders, one of whom is domiciled in Scotland, the Scottish courts will assume jurisdiction over that other defender too.

2. MARITIME CLAIMS

(a) Is there special jurisdiction for maritime claims based on arrest of a vessel within the jurisdiction?

In Scottish maritime law there are, in principle, two types of arrestment. The first is effective to establish jurisdiction. It is known as an arrestment to found jurisdiction (or *ad fundandam jurisdictionem*). It can be used to found jurisdiction against the owner of a vessel in respect of a maritime claim or indeed in certain circumstances a non-maritime claim. It does not have effect to create a nexus or right in security over the vessel which can sail even though it is under such an arrest.

The second type is an arrest in security. Since the Administration of Justice Act 1956, it has only been possible to arrest a vessel in security of a claim if it falls into certain specific categories listed in section 47 of that Act. This Act was intended to incorporate into the law of Great Britain the Brussels Arrest Convention 1952. Part V of the Act applies in Scotland.

There are two types of arrestment in security or on the dependence of an action. The first is an arrestment *in rem*. This is only competent in Scotland where the claim is one for a maritime lien over the vessel in question. What constitutes a maritime lien in Scotland is similar to that in England, i.e. collision, salvage, crew's wages, master's disbursements and bonds of bottomry and respondentia. All other forms of admiralty action must be brought *in personam*. An action may be both *in rem* and *in personam* where there is a maritime lien and the proceeds of sale of the ship may not be enough to cover the claim. The pursuer may direct the action against the owner too *in personam* and attempt to enforce judgment against the owner's other personal assets as well as the ship.

(b) Special rules: collisions

Section 45 of the 1956 Act deals with this (see appendix). In terms of Section 45(1) and (3) the Scottish court has jurisdiction in respect of actions for payment for reparation arising out of any collision between ships; or the carrying out of or the omission to carry out a manoeuvre in the case of one or more or two or more ships; or the non-compliance on the part of one or more or two or more ships with the collision regulations in the following cases:

— where the defender has his habitual residence or place of business in Scotland; or where the cause of action arose in Scotland and either within inland waters or within the limits of a port; or the Scottish court has heard and determined an action arising out of the same incident or series of incidents; or the defender has prorogated the jurisdiction of the Scottish courts; or a ship in which the defender owns one or more shares has been arrested whether to found jurisdiction or on the dependence of the action within Scotland.

(c) What are the grounds for arrest?

These are set out in section 47 of the 1956 Act.

(d) Need the arrested vessel be connected with the claim or can other vessels in the same legal (or beneficial) ownership also be arrested?

Warrant to arrest a vessel *in personam* or *in rem* will only be granted if the claim falls within section 47 of the 1956 Act. All the shares in the ship must be owned by the defender, or if there is a maritime lien, or if the defender only owns some of the shares, the ship must be the one with which the action is concerned. Accordingly, if the defender owns more than one ship, it is possible to arrest the others which are not directly related to the claim *in personam*, provided the combined values do not exceed the appropriate level of security.

(e) What procedural differences apply to special maritime jurisdiction?

There are special rules for Admiralty actions in the Rules of Court of the Court of Session which is Scotland's highest civil court. These apply to claims which fall into the categories listed in section 47(2) of the Administration of Justice Act 1956, being claims in respect of which arrestments on the dependence either *in personam* or *in rem* may be laid. As to other types of maritime actions not included in section 47(2) these may proceed under the Commercial or ordinary Court Rules of the Court of Session. There are special rules of court applying to Admiralty actions in relation to ships and their cargo, the completion of arrestments by sale, ship collision cases, salvage and International Oil Pollution Compensation Fund matters. For example, the court may at its own instance or on the application of a party appoint an assessor to assist it. The assessor will take the place of the expert witness. Also, in collision cases, the parties must lodge sealed envelopes containing a preliminary act. This is a statement of fact, ranking as an admission of fact and is meant to prevent the defender from shaping his case to meet that of the pursuer.

Most forms of actions relating to shipping matters can be initiated in the sheriff court and heard there. An appeal from the decision of the Sheriff can be made either to the Sheriff Principal from whom in turn an appeal lies to the Inner House (the appeal court) of the Court of Session or it can be made direct from the Sheriff to the Inner House. Where arrestments on the dependence have been used, service of the summons (the initiating writ) must be executed within 20 days. Under Scottish law an action is deemed to start only when service has been effected. Arrestments may be used in order solely to get security for the claim and under Scottish proceedings may be sisted or stayed pending resolution of the dispute in another jurisdiction by arbitration, litigation or otherwise.

(f) What jurisdictional rules are there as to limitation of liability?

The rules in Scotland on this will be equivalent to those applying in England and Wales.

3. SERVICE OF PROCEEDINGS

(a) What rules apply to service of proceedings outside the jurisdiction?

No leave is required to serve out of the jurisdiction. Various methods can be employed. What is essential is that the service is effected in accordance with the relevant local law and certified as such. Usually local solicitors will be instructed to effect service and swear an affidavit accordingly. Different notice periods apply according to whether the defender is within the EU or outwith (21 and 42 days respectively).

4. COSTS

(a) Court fees

The Court of Session fee for a warrant on a summons to arrest is currently £95. The fees which will be payable to Messengers-at-Arms as officers of the court who must serve the writ and/or the arrestment on the vessel and its owners will vary depending on the location of it/them. If the vessel is readily accessible the fees are likely to be in the region of £150. If the vessel is, for example, located in one of Scotland's outer islands, the fees are likely to be substantially more than that since matters such as time and travelling costs must be taken into account.

(b) Lawyers' fees

The lawyers' fees for obtaining warrant to arrest and effecting the arrest will be in the region of £2,000 to £2,500. Lawyers' fees are usually negotiated with the clients by agreement. Contingency fees in the sense of no-win-no-fee are allowable in Scotland. However, the fee charged will be a set fee and will not vary in accordance with the level of success.

(c) Recovery of costs from unsuccessful party

Costs are usually awarded in favour of the successful party. In an action where an arrest has been served on the dependence *in personam* the costs of arrest will usually not be recoverable, even in the event of the pursuer succeeding, because they will be deemed not strictly necessary for the prosecution of the case. The costs of an arrestment *in rem* however will usually be recoverable since this form of arrest is required to give the ability to pursue the vessel itself in enforcement of a maritime lien. The costs of an arrestment to found jurisdiction should also be recoverable. Costs are taxed on a fixed judicial scale which usually results in around a 50 per cent to 60 per cent rate of recovery. An award of costs may be enforced against the party liable.

(d) Security for costs

If a vessel is arrested in security of a claim, clearly it will provide security for that claim and for the costs. The vessel will normally only be released when a sufficient equivalent security is offered. It is also possible to arrest on the dependence of an action any movable property or debts belonging to the defender held in the hands of third parties. This can be done immediately the action has started or at any point while it is current, to provide security for the claim and the costs. The defender may also seek security for his costs, which is known as caution, or may apply for a mandatory to be sisted. The formal application can be made at common law and is at the court's discretion. Normally caution is ordered at common law only in the case of bankruptcy or other exceptional circumstances such as where the pursuer does not reveal its address.

Caution may also be sought under section 726 of the Companies Act 1985 where the test is that a limited company pursuer may be required to find caution if it appears by credible testimony that there is reason to believe that the company will be unable to pay the defender's costs.

A pursuer resident abroad on the other hand is usually required to sist a mandatory rather than to provide security by caution. Caution cannot be required of foreigners seeking redress or in the enforcement of certain foreign judgments under certain international and European conventions such as the

Brussels and Lugano Conventions, the Geneva Convention on Contract for International Carriage of Goods by Road 1965 and the Geneva Convention on the Carriage of Passengers and Luggage by Road 1956. In those cases it may still be possible to force the pursuer to sist a mandatory. This involves the appointment of a responsible person within the jurisdiction responsible for the conduct of the cause and indeed for all the expenses of the cause including those incurred before his appointment.

5. INTERIM ARRESTS

(a) Are interim arrests/freezing of assets/other provisional measures permitted to provide security for domestic proceedings and/or proceedings in another jurisdiction?

Generally speaking it is possible to obtain interim arrests and other provisional measures to seek security for a claim in domestic proceedings. In respect of foreign proceedings it is only possible to do so in certain circumstances.

(b) What criteria apply to this?

It is possible to arrest any assets or debts due to a defender in this jurisdiction on the dependence of an action raised in Scotland for security for the claim interest and for costs. These can be physical or non-physical assets such as shares, cash in the bank, debts due, tax credits, etc. These assets must be in the hands of third parties at the time an arrest is served in order to be effective.

It is also possible to register what is called an inhibition on the dependence of an action. This involves placing a Notice of Inhibition on the Property Register in Scotland against the defender and prevents him from disposing of any heritable property within Scotland.

Where there are proceedings in another jurisdiction in an EU or EFTA member state which have been commenced, provisional and protective measures can be taken in Scotland in the absence of substantive proceedings here (section 27 of the 1982 Act). Where, for example, a similar warrant could have competently been granted in equivalent proceedings in Scottish courts it is possible to obtain a warrant for arrestment of any movable assets of the defender within Scotland, or to place an inhibition over the defender's property situated in Scotland. It may also be possible to obtain an interim interdict to prevent disposal of such assets in such circumstances even where a similar warrant could not have competently been granted in equivalent proceedings in the Scottish court. Thus an interim interdict might be sought to prevent the defender disposing of any assets situated within Scotland, on the dependence of an action raised elsewhere in one of those relevant member states.

(c) Is there a limit on jurisdictions whose proceedings are recognised for this purpose?

Where proceedings have been commenced in the courts of a country which is not an EU or EFTA member state and the defender has assets in Scotland, it is not usually possible to freeze them by seeking to arrest/inhibit them or apply for an interim interdict without also raising a further set of substantive proceedings before the Scottish courts which would be capable of challenge on *lis alibi pendens* grounds. The situation is different where the asset sought to be arrested is a ship belonging to the defender. If it is within the Scottish jurisdiction and the claim is one which falls within section 47 of the 1956 Act, it may be possible to arrest it on the dependence of an action *in rem* or *in personam* in security of the claim, even if there are proceedings pending elsewhere outwith EU and EFTA. The Scottish action could be sisted/stayed once security was obtained.

(d) Is there a requirement for counter-security?

There is no need for counter-security. It is very unusual for a Scottish court to order it. Applications can and indeed usually are made *ex parte*. Applications are made *periculo petentis*. If made maliciously or without legal cause, an action of damages may lie for wrongful use of diligence.

(e) Can applications be made ex parte?

Applications for arrests, institutions and interim interdicts may, and indeed usually are, made *ex parte*.

(f) How quickly can an order be made?

An order can be made very quickly—in some cases on the same day instructions are received. In interim interdict applications the time varies from a day to a week. An order is not required for an arrestment or an inhibition, which are given by warrant of the court on presentation of the summons. Once the summons is warranted, arrests and inhibitions can usually be placed that day if necessary.

(g) Will the order bind third parties?

Once the order is carried through and effected and an arrestment or inhibition or interim interdict is served and in place, third parties affected with notice of it are required to take notice of it and must not breach it or cause it to be breached.

(h) What are the consequences of breach of an order?

If the order is breached it will be contempt of court. This is treated as a quasi-criminal offence for which there can be a fine or period of imprisonment imposed. If the arrestment for example is ignored and the debt or asset is released to the defender, the arrestee will be liable for breach of arrest and can be sued.

(i) Is there a limit to types of asset?

Assets which may be arrested may be physical or non-physical. The main requisite is (except in the case of a ship) that they are in the possession of a third party with an obligation to account to the defender. There are limitations. The main categories of assets which may not be arrested are necessaries under section 16 of the Debtors (Scotland) Act 1987. There are special rules for arrestments of earnings. Contingent debts are usually not arrestable.

(j) What if third parties are affected, e.g. airliner?

If third parties are affected, they as interested parties can apply to have the arrest or inhibition or interim interdict recalled but they must show good cause and offer alternative security.

(k) What other provisional measures may be ordered—appointment of surveyor or receiver, security?

It is possible to appoint a provisional liquidator, or a receiver or administrator in certain circumstances.

6. RECOGNITION OF JUDGMENTS/AWARDS

(a) What treaties/conventions apply (i) to enable judgments to be enforced abroad and (ii) to enable enforcement of foreign judgments domestically?

The 1968 Jurisdiction Convention in Civil and Commercial Matters also applies to enable judgments to be enforced abroad and domestically where EU/EFTA states are involved. The Civil Jurisdiction and Judgments Act 1982 as amended regulates this. Under the 1982 Act, enforcement is generally by registration of judgment from other EU/EFTA states. The Scottish court will not generally look at the merits of the case or whether the foreign court had jurisdiction except in limited cases such as where it is contrary to public policy; where there has been lack of due and timely service of the originating process in default cases; where there is lack of jurisdiction in insurance or consumer cases;

where there is an exclusive jurisdiction clause to found jurisdiction elsewhere; or there is an incompatible prior judgment. The 1982 Act covers both interim and final judgments of the other EU countries.

There is another reciprocal enforcement regime under the Foreign Judgments (Reciprocal Enforcement) Act 1933 ("the 1933 Act") which provides for the enforcement in Scotland and indeed in the UK as a whole of judgments of recognised courts of certain foreign countries on the basis of reciprocity. The countries included are Australia, Austria, Canada (not Quebec), India, Israel, Netherlands, Antilles, Pakistan, Surinam, Tonga, Guernsey, Jersey and the Isle of Man.

Furthermore the Administration of Justice Act 1920 ("the 1920 Act") provides for the enforcement in the UK of the judgments of superior courts of most present and former colonies and commonwealth countries. It applies principally to Bermuda, Hong Kong, Ghana, Gibraltar, Nigeria, Kenya, New Zealand, Malaysia and Singapore.

(b) What procedure is followed to enforce a foreign judgment?

(i) Governed by treaty/convention

In the above cases, judgments are enforceable by a registration procedure. The following requirements must be met:

— The judgment must be final and conclusive (or interim) and for a definite sum of money, the judgment debtor must have received sufficient notice of the original proceedings; the judgment must not have been obtained by fraud; its enforcement must not be against public policy, the foreign court must have had jurisdiction over the judgment debtor on the basis of his consent or his presence/residence in the former country Foreign default judgments will not generally be enforceable against the defender who is not present in the former country.

(ii) Not governed by a treaty/convention

Where there is no Treaty or Convention and the above Acts do not apply, judgments may still be enforceable under common law.

At common law authority of the Scottish court must be obtained to enforce a foreign judgment in Scotland. This is obtained by raising an action for 'decree conform' in the Court of Session. The foreign judgment itself is founded upon as constituting the obligation and it must be produced and proved. Once granted the decree conform can be enforced in Scotland in the same manner as any other Scottish decree (judgment).

In an action for decree conform, the foreign judgment cannot be challenged on the grounds that the foreign court made an error in fact or in law. The grounds of challenge are not clearly defined but probably include:

1. foreign judgments obtained by fraud;
2. judgments contrary to public policy;
3. foreign judgments obtained contrary to the principles of natural justice.

If a person was not a party to the foreign action, the foreign judgment cannot be enforced against them by way of decree conform. It is incompetent to raise an action for decree conform where the decree can be recognised under the provisions of the 1933 Act or the 1982 Act.

(c) Foreign arbitration awards

These are governed by the "model law"—UNCITRAL model law on international commercial arbitration as adopted by the United Nations Commission on International Trade Law on 21 June 1985. The model law is enforceable in Scotland in the form set out in Schedule 7 of the Law Reform (Miscellaneous Provisions) (Scotland) Act 1990. An arbitral award, irrespective of the country in which it was made, shall be recognised as binding and, upon application in writing to the competent court, shall be enforced subject to the provisions of Articles 35 and 36. These Articles deal with recognition and enforcement based on provisions of the 1958 New York Convention ('the Convention').

(Model law is subject to Treaties, Conventions, etc, to which the UK is a party. Recognition or enforcement of an award in an international commercial arbitration made in the territory of the state which is party to the Convention, remains subject to the Arbitration Act 1975. In connection with awards made in international commercial arbitration, Convention awards are governed by the Arbitration Act 1975, "foreign" awards are governed by Part II of the Arbitration Act 1950, or in the case of all other awards made outwith Scotland (including elsewhere in the UK) and "domestic" awards, i.e. those made inside Scotland these are governed by Articles 35 and 36.)

If a party wishes the award to be recognised or enforced he must supply two things. First, the fully authenticated original award or a duly certified copy and secondly the original Arbitration Agreement or a duly certified copy. The Rules of Court make provision for the procedure to be adopted.

The general principle is that the enforceability of foreign awards in Scotland should be determined in the same way as for any other foreign personal contract. It is sufficient usually that it is made in accordance with the formal requirements of the law of the place where it is made.

A foreign decree arbitral may be enforced in Scotland at common law wherever it was pronounced by means of a decree conform. Now this is mostly governed by statutory provisions, for example the 1920 and the 1933 Acts mentioned above.

Where the award is made outside the UK and has become final in the country where it was made, enforcement may be obtained under the Arbitration Act 1950. The 1982 Act provides for the enforcement of UK judgements in other parts of the UK i.e. in Scotland.

(d) Will proceeds of a judgment be freely exportable?

Assuming the proceeds in most cases are financial as opposed to physical assets, we do not envisage any difficulty in transferring these to another jurisdiction.

In the event that the proceeds were to be the vessel or vessels themselves, or other movables, it is likely that the Scottish Court would be asked to grant an order transferring legal ownership to the claimant. Once so transferred the recipient of the proceeds would be free to export them outside the Scottish/UK jurisdiction.

CHAPTER 21

SPAIN

Dr Rodolfo A. Gonzalez-Lebrero
89 Serrano Street, 28006 Madrid, Spain

1. JURISDICTION

What are the general grounds on which courts will accept jurisdiction?

Spanish courts enjoy jurisdiction to take care of lawsuits brought in Spain involving Spanish nationals only, foreigners only, or Spaniards and foreigners, unless treaties or international conventions to which Spain is a contracting party determine otherwise or if certain rules of public international law establish situations of immunity of jurisdiction or of enforcement.

Failing the existence of a submission, the general rule for venue in actions *in personam*, namely those resulting from contractual obligations, is that the court of the place where the obligation is to be discharged is the one with jurisdiction to deal with the lawsuits arising thereof; if that place cannot be determined, the plaintiff has the option to lodge his claim either with the competent court in the defendants domicile or with that of the place where the contract was executed. If the complaint is brought simultaneously against two or more persons with domiciles in different towns, who are jointly and severally liable, the plaintiff may file his complaint with the court of the domicile of either defendant, at his sole option.

(a) Domicile

Persons with domicile in Spain can be sued before Spanish courts.

(b) Place of business/residence/office

A foreign company operating in Spain through a branch duly recorded with the Commercial Registry can be sued before Spanish courts in matters related to the activities of the branch in Spain.

(c) Assets located within the jurisdiction

Regarding actions *in rem*, the court of the place where the real estate is located has jurisdiction, but if personal property is involved the plaintiff has the option of lodging the lawsuit before the courts of the place where the property is located or those of the defendant's domicile.

Actions with both real and personal ingredients may also be filed before the courts of the place where the property is located or those of the defendant's domicile.

(d) Act complained of within the jurisdiction

Amongst other cases, Spanish courts have jurisdiction: (1) regarding contractual obligations created in Spain or to be discharged in Spain; (2) regarding claims in tort when the event took place in Spain or when both the wrongdoer and the damaged party have their residence in Spain, and (3) regarding actions involving chattels (ships are chattels) which at the time of the lodging of the claim are in Spanish territory.

(e) Contract governed by local law

Jurisdiction of Spanish courts is established as hereabove indicated; it is irrelevant that contracts are governed by local law or not.

(f) Conventions

Spain is a contracting party to several international conventions regarding jurisdiction, proceedings and arbitration, i.e. the 1961 Hague Convention abolishing the Requirement of Legalisation for Foreign Public Documents, the 1965 Hague Convention on the Service Abroad of Judicial and Extrajudicial Documents in Civil or Commercial Matters, the 1970 Hague Convention on the Taking of Evidence Abroad in Civil or Commercial Matters, the 1968 Brussels Convention on Jurisdiction and the Enforcement of Judgments in Civil and Commercial Matters, the 1988 Lugano Convention on Jurisdiction and the Enforcement of Judgments in Civil and Commercial Matters, the 1958 New York Convention on the Recognition and Enforcement of Foreign Arbitral Awards, the 1961 Geneva European Convention on International Commercial Arbitration.

(g) Clause attributing jurisdiction

The parties to a contract may submit, expressly or impliedly, to a particular court, which will therefore have venue to hear all lawsuits resulting from actions related to that contract. However, contractual clauses attributing jurisdiction to foreign courts when the matter falls within the jurisdiction of Spanish courts in accordance with the statutory rules of jurisdiction, are seldom admitted by Spanish courts.

Although currently there is not a firm position yet, an exception to be taken into account is the prorogation of jurisdiction as established by Article 17 of the 1968 Brussels Convention on Jurisdiction and the Enforcement of Judgments in Civil and Commercial Matters, as amended.

Express submission is to be made by both parties in a clear and absolute way, showing beyond any doubt the court to which they submit; implied submission is understood to take place by the plaintiff by merely lodging his complaint before a court and by the defendant by performing any procedural act after his appearance before a court, unless such performance is intended only to file a plea to the jurisdiction.

2. MARITIME CLAIMS

(a) Is there a special jurisdiction for maritime claims based on arrest of a vessel in the jurisdiction?

Presently, there is no special jurisdiction for maritime claims based on the arrest of a vessel in jurisdiction, or otherwise; there are no admiralty or maritime courts in Spain, all shipping and admiralty cases being handled by ordinary civil courts, with the exception of salvage claims which are still taken care of by navy maritime judges.

(b) Specific

Regarding salvage, the aforesaid navy maritime judges are officers of the Spanish Navy who, after collecting all relevant information, refer the matter to the Central Maritime Court, which is also under the control of the navy, for the latter to render the judgment; both these judges and the court are administrative in nature.

Regarding the arrest of ships, the 1952 Brussels Convention on the Arrest of Ships (1952 Arrest Convention), to which Spain is a contracting party, applies. Jurisdiction on the merits is granted when: (1) the claimant has his principal place of business in Spain; (2) the claim arose in Spain; (3) the claim is related to the voyage during which the vessel has been arrested in Spain; (4) the claim is the consequence of a collision or results from salvage operations; and (5) the claim is related to a mortgage on the ship.

(c) What are the grounds for arrest?

Regarding the matter of arrest of ships in Spain it must be said that the 1952 Arrest Convention is in force, and also Act 2/1967 which was passed on 8 April 1967, making it easier to arrest foreign flag ships in Spain. Spain is also a party to the 1926 Brussels Convention on Maritime Liens and Mortgages (1926 Maritime Liens Convention).

The procedure is basically the following. A petition is made before a court of first instance of the port or place where the ship is berthed or lies, or at which she is expected, just invoking a maritime claim; in other words, any one of those included in the 1952 Arrest Convention. A sister-ship can also be arrested.

Upon receipt of the application, the court will order the arrest of the vessel, subject to the production of a bank guarantee issued by a Spanish bank (usually the correspondent of the foreign bank through which the plaintiff carries on his business).

The amount of this guarantee is left to the absolute discretion of the court. The guarantee would be for an amount in the region of 20 per cent to 40 per cent of the claim, although it has become rather common that in some cases the acting judge has requested up to 100 per cent of such claim, which is completely out of proportion, but presently is a fact of life in this country.

The applicant has to act quickly to obtain the bank guarantee, because this is the matter which usually delays the carrying out of the arrest. In fact, the court will grant the cautionary arrest almost immediately after receiving the application, but the order to the Port Captain or Harbour Master will not go off until the bank guarantee is deposited with the court.

The arrest of a vessel is granted *ex parte*, in other words, without the actual participation of the debtor, and may be implemented quite quickly even though it must be emphasised that getting the bank guarantee is of paramount importance.

After the production of the guarantee before the court, and after acceptance of it by the court, the latter orders the Port Captain or Harbour Master not to allow the vessel to sail until further instructions.

Afterwards, within 20 days to be counted as from the date of the arrest (unless the court grants an extension of the period of time), the evidence that a lawsuit or, alternatively, arbitration proceedings, have been started, either in Spain or elsewhere, is to be produced before the court, failing which evidence the arrest will be lifted immediately upon application by the owners.

To apply for the arrest of a vessel in Spain the following information and documents are needed:

(1) Full name and address of the person or corporation seeking the arrest of the vessel.
(2) Short description of the facts and a copy of any document from which results the outstanding amount at stake.
(3) Copy of letters or faxes putting the debtor in default, and their respective replies.
(4) A Power of Attorney.

The power of attorney must be executed by an authorised official of the company, with sufficient powers to bind the company, before a notary; the notary's signature must be legalised by means of the apostille foreseen in the Hague Convention of 5 October 1961 relating to the cancellation of the legalisation of foreign public documents, or by the local Spanish Consul should the country in which the power of attorney is executed not be a party to the said Convention.

A ship which has been arrested may be released by a court order issued by the same court which decided on the arrest, provided the interested party (owners, charterers or operators, or their Protection and Indemnity Clubs) produces before the court a counterguarantee to obtain the lifting of the arrest, which security must be, in principle, for the amount for which the arrest was granted; alternatively, the party may challenge the arrest.

(d) Need the arrested vessel be connected with the claim or can other vessels in the same legal (or beneficial) ownership also be arrested?

As already stated, sister-ships can be arrested.

Regarding the matter of one-ship companies, it may be stated that nowadays Spanish courts admit more and more the "disregard of legal entity doctrine", which may prove to be useful in cases where said companies are involved, in order to arrest vessels belonging to companies with financial links as if they were sister-ships.

(e) What procedural differences apply to special maritime jurisdiction?

With the sole exception of salvage proceedings, all other maritime proceedings are subject to the general rules of procedure contained in the Civil Procedure Act.

(f) What procedural rules are there as to limitation of liability?

Regarding the limitation of liability, it must be said that Spain has adopted all the three international conventions regarding the limitation of liability of shipowners, namely, the 1924 Brussels Convention, the 1957 Brussels Convention, as amended by the 1979 Brussels Protocol and the 1976 London Convention. Since Spain has not notified its denunciation of either the first convention or the second one, currently all three conventions are simultaneously in force, which may create, and does create, confusing situations.

It is likely, though, that the last two conventions will be mostly applied, and more and more the 1976 London Convention which, in accordance with its Article 15, is applicable whenever any person entitled to limit liability as per Article 1, seeks to limit his liability before the courts of a state party.

Spanish courts have jurisdiction to hear petitions for limitation of liability in the following cases:

(1) when the occurrence takes place within Spanish territorial waters;
(2) when the ship is arrested at a Spanish port; and
(3) when the ship calls at a Spanish port as the first port of call after the occurrence.

It is very difficult to indicate how long it will take for the court to issue a decree of limitation, without knowing in advance the number of creditors involved and the attitude of these creditors towards the establishment of the fund; they may accept the limitation proceedings or they may fight against them. In the first case, the limitation decree would be obtained rather quickly, but in the second one the proceedings could last several years.

3. SERVICE OF PROCEEDINGS

What rules apply to service of proceedings outside the jurisdiction?

To carry out the service of proceedings on defendants domiciled in Spain, once the complaint has been filed the court summons the defendant, requesting him to appear before the court within a certain number of days, which number depends on the type of proceedings.

If the defendant's domicile is known, the service is personally performed by a process server, but should this officer fail to meet the defendant in person, he writes down a certificate which he delivers to the defendant's closest relative of at least 14 years old, or to the closest neighbour. In either case, a statement is made by the process server with the details and results of the service, which is attached to the court file later on.

If the defendant's domicile is unknown, the service is performed by publication; the certificate is posted at the courthouse and published in the Official Gazette of the corresponding province, in the court bulletin and, sometimes, in the national Official Gazette.

If the defendant's domicile is located outside the boundaries of the judicial district corresponding to the acting court, service may be performed by registered mail, but if the letter is not returned together with the signed acknowledgment of the defendant, or 15 days have elapsed without this acknowledgment having been received by the court, the latter is to issue a letter requisitorial addressed to the competent court at the defendant's domicile for the service to take place in the way hereabove indicated.

The service of proceedings of foreign defendants domiciled abroad is made in agreement with the applicable treaties or conventions in force, such as the 1965 Hague Convention on the Service Abroad of Judicial and Extrajudicial Documents in Civil and Commercial Matters, ratified by Spain in 1987. Should there be no treaty or convention applicable to the concrete case or situation, service of proceedings is made through diplomatic channels, in other words, via the Spanish Ministry of Foreign Affairs, which in turn conveys the file to the Ministry of Foreign Affairs of the country where the service is to take place, namely, that of the domicile of the defendant.

The foregoing applies also to corporate defendants.

4. COSTS

(a) Court fees

There are no court fees in Spain.

(b) Lawyers' fees (standard scale or by agreement or contingency fees)

Spanish lawyers usually charge their fees in accordance with the corresponding Bar Association Scale of Fees, which follows, with regard to practically all situations, the traditional approach where there is normally a graduated scale calculated on the value of the assets handled through probate; this procedure distorts reality in many cases.

The hourly rate system is seldom used, but it is not against the Code of Ethics of the Bar Association, and lawyers who are usually involved with foreign clients and colleagues charge their fees on a per hour basis, at least as far as these clients and colleagues are concerned.

However, time spent for a client has increasingly been the primary consideration in the setting of fees as far as out-of-court matters are concerned, i.e. legal opinions or any other action which does not need to be brought before courts or arbitrators.

It is also customary in intricate cases or cases which are likely to last a long time (as happens with cases to be dealt with in court) to request a retainer or an advance against costs or provision of funds to cover initial expenses, unless it is agreed to issue, monthly or quarterly, Notes of Expenses and Fees.

A client would be confronted with compulsory and fixed rates applied to "*Procuradores*", plus lawyer's fees, plus miscellaneous expenses (telephone, fax, photocopies, couriers, travel and sundries).

(c) Recovery of costs from unsuccessful party

Regarding the recovery of costs from the unsuccessful party, it must be said that in Spain, the party has usually to bear the costs of both parties, unless the court finds special and concrete reasons for deciding that each party is to bear its own costs.

(d) Security for costs

The security for costs is foreseen in ordinary proceedings, but in the case of enforcement of judgments or the arrest of ships, an amount covering costs may be added to the principal upon the lodging of the application.

5. INTERIM ARREST

(a) Are interim arrest/freezing of assets/other provisional measures permitted to provide security for domestic proceedings and/or proceedings in another jurisdiction?

Under Spanish law, there are remedies available to anybody who needs or wishes to secure an ordinary claim or to encourage the counterparty to fulfil its obligations under a contract.

It must be borne in mind that Spain is a civil law jurisdiction, where the pre-trial rights of arrest and attachment are contemplated in provisions made in the Civil Procedure Act, in the 1968 Brussels Convention on Jurisdiction and the Enforcement of Judgments in Civil and Commercial matters (Art. 24), in the Companies Act, and *inter alia* in some maritime international conventions (i.e. 1952 Arrest Convention, as has been seen already). In Spain, these rights (with the exception of the arrest of ships) involving the seizure of property (trial before a court of justice or an arbitral tribunal) are granted in very restricted circumstances.

The available remedies are the following ones:

(a) ordinary attachment (*embargo preventivo*);
(b) "unnamed" cautionary measures: Article 1428 of the Spanish Civil Proceedings Act opens the way to the most versatile of the remedies available, which is reminiscent of the Mareva injunction, although Spanish courts are very strict at the time of granting them. These measures cover the following situations:
    (i) the attachment of property belonging to the Defendant (debtor);
    (ii) whatever request or demand to the defendant that is necessary for the latter to abstain from doing something, or to continue doing something;
    (iii) the attachment of property (movable) belonging or not to the defendant, when there are reasons to believe that the latter is likely to damage or to remove it;
    (iv) the request for the exhibition (in the sense of production) and the subsequent deposit of property (movable only), by the person who is in the possession of said property, as a preliminary step before the filing of a lawsuit concerning such property; and

(v) other miscellaneous cases.

It must also be mentioned that Article 24 of the 1968 Brussels Convention on Jurisdiction and the Enforcement of Judgments in Civil and Commercial Matters permits application to Spanish courts for such provisional and protective measures as may be available under Spanish law, even if the courts of another Contracting State have jurisdiction as to the substance of the matter.

The results from this reference to the 1968 Brussels Convention are that whatever measure is decided by an arbitral tribunal, e.g. in London, may be enforced in Spain, provided it corresponds to a measure available within the framework of Spanish law; at the same time, Spanish courts will decide (once the *exequatur* proceedings are finished) on the basis of the *lex fori* on the relevant proceedings and on the enforceability of the measure, but they will always be guided by a restrictive attitude.

(b) What criteria apply to this?

Generally speaking, all precautionary measures are subject to several conditions precedent for them to be granted by Spanish courts; failure to fulfil any one of them would result in the rejection of the application.

The conditions or prerequisites are:

(a) the plaintiff must have a cause of action, his claim not being a derisory or frivolous one (*fumus boni iuris*);

(b) there must be a real danger that the defendant may (or will) remove assets from the jurisdiction, or dissipate them from the jurisdiction, before litigation in court or in arbitration is finished (*periculum in mora*);

(c) security is to be produced before the court by means of a bank guarantee issued by a Spanish bank, in the amount to be decided by the court, this amount being related to the amount claimed (something between 20 per cent and 40 per cent, even though some judges request 100 per cent);

(d) a formal and complete complaint is to be filed, either at the same time of the application for the interlocutory order, or immediately thereafter. The complaint must be produced before the courts or the arbitral tribunal not later than 20 days as from the date on which the attachment has been made, but this period could be 10 days upon the defendant's request, or even eight days as from the date on which the attachment has been granted or longer should the court so agree.

(c) Is there a limit on jurisdictions whose proceedings are recognised for this purpose?

There are no limits, but as stated above, after an arrest (e.g. of a ship) or an attachment has been made, a complaint on the substance of the claim is to be lodged either before a court of justice or an arbitration tribunal, failing which, the arrest or the attachment will be lifted.

(d) Is there a requirement for counter-security?

Yes, the arrest or the attachment is done once the applicant has lodged with the court a counterguarantee in the amount requested by the court.

(e) Can applications be made ex parte?

Yes, applications can be made without the court asking the potential defendant to appear before it. This is the case in the arrest of ships.

(f) How quickly can an order be made?

Spanish courts are very slow and usually not very co-operative; in attachment proceedings they are strict at the time of evaluating the conditions precedent to the grant; generally speaking, attachment proceedings would take easily one to three months. Arrest of ships can be made in one to three days.

(g) Will the order bind third parties?

Yes, an order of arrest binds third parties also.

(h) What are the consequences of breach of an order?

The breach of an order of arrest is a criminal offence and can make the custodian of the assets arrested or attached on the basis of such order, liable for the resulting damages.

(i) Is there a limit to types of asset, e.g. physical asset/account balances?

In principle, there are no limits regarding the types of asset to be subject to cautionary measures; however, the Civil Procedure Act establishes some limits on account of the nature of some assets: the debtor's bed and the beds of his family, his essential personal belongings, the debtor's salary up to a certain amount, etc.

(j) What if third parties are affected?

If an order of arrest is directed towards assets belonging to third parties, the latter can appear in the proceedings claiming ownership or making a third party intervention with a paramount right.

(k) What other provisional measures may be ordered, e.g. appointment of surveyor or receiver, security?

Several measures may be ordered by Spanish courts, some of them granted within jurisdictional proceedings (appointment of surveyors, collection of evidence, conservative measures, and amongst them those aimed at protecting a potential credit resulting from a future judgment, etc.). The Civil Procedure Act foresees also several measures which do not enjoy a jurisdictional nature, whose purpose is to put commodities or cargo under custody, to have said commodities or cargo examined by experts, to appoint general average adjusters, to unload cargo from a ship, etc.

6. RECOGNITION OF JUDGMENTS/AWARDS

(a) What treaties/conventions apply (i) to enable judgments to be enforced abroad and (ii) to enable enforcement of foreign judgments domestically?

Regarding Spanish judgments to be enforced abroad, it must be said that Spain is a party to the 1965 Hague Convention on the Service Abroad of Judicial and Extrajudicial Documents in Civil or Commercial Matters, of 15 November 1965.

With regard to foreign judgments able to be recognised and enforced in Spain, reference is to be made to the bilateral conventions in force in Spain, related to the enforcement of foreign decisions, such as the Convention made with Switzerland (19 November 1896), and the ones agreed with Czechoslovakia (26 November 1927), with France (28 May 1969) and with Italy (22 May 1973). The Spanish/Italian Convention permits the enforcement of "urgent and precautionary measures which are enforceable in the country of origin".

Spain is a party to the 1968 Brussels Convention on Jurisdiction and the Enforcement of Judgments in Civil and Commercial Matters and to the 1988 Lugano Convention on Jurisdiction and the Enforcement of Judgments in Civil and Commercial Matters.

(b) What procedure is followed to enforce a foreign judgment (i) governed by a treaty/convention and (ii) not governed by a treaty/convention?

Regarding the regulation in Spain on the recognition and enforcement of foreign judgments, other than those decisions covered by the 1968 Brussels or the 1988 Lugano Conventions, it can be stated that in Spain this matter is regulated by the Civil Procedure Act in its Articles 951 to 958. These articles refer to the *exequatur* which is a contentious procedure and, in principle, it may be considered that only those foreign judgments issued in a contentious procedure are able to obtain an *exequatur* in Spain, provided that such a judgment is final and binding on the parties.

The scope of the term "foreign judgment" is to be determined by a legal definition of the term "judgment", by the interpretation made by the Supreme Court in cases relating to the *exequatur* and by the provisions contained in international treaties.

The definition of "judgment" is given by the aforesaid Act in Article 369, which states that it is one which decides the questions submitted to litigation in one instance or in an extraordinary appeal. This qualification is to agree with the law of the country where the judicial decision has been rendered.

The requirements established by the above-mentioned Article 369 are:

(1) the decision has to be issued by a court of justice (arbitration awards are excluded);
(2) the decision is to be issued in contentious proceedings (voluntary procedures are excluded); and
(3) the decision has to put an end to the proceedings or the appeal.

There are three different regimes for obtaining an *exequatur* in Spain:

(1) that resulting from international conventions or treaties;
(2) that resulting from reciprocity; and
(3) that resulting from independent internal control.

The system of the international conventions or treaties has preference over the others; consequently, the provisions of the conventions or treaties enjoy a higher rank than the other regimes.

Failing the existence of an international convention or treaty with the state where the judgment has been rendered, the Civil Procedure Act establishes the principle of reciprocity, both positive and negative reciprocity.

Failing reciprocity, the Civil Procedure Act establishes as a last resort the regime of conditions, providing that foreign judgments will have force in Spain if they comply with the following conditions:

(a) the judgment has been issued as a result of a personal action (not an action *in rem*);
(b) the judgment has not been issued by default of the defendant;
(c) the obligation arising from the judgment is a lawful one in Spain;
(d) the judgment fulfils the requirements provided by the law of the country where it has been rendered for same to be considered authentic;
(e) the foreign judgment fulfils the requirements foreseen under Spanish law for the validity of public documents. In this respect, Articles 600 and 601 of the Civil Procedure Act require the necessary legalisation of the judgment and its translation into Spanish.

The first condition is that the judgment has to be the result of a personal action; it is considered that Spanish courts have exclusive jurisdiction to deal with actions *in rem* concerning assets located in Spanish territory. Therefore, in the first condition there is an effective control of jurisdiction.

An important condition is that the foreign judgment has not been rendered by default. This condition, the purpose of which is to protect Spanish defendants who did not have the opportunity to challenge the claim of the applicant, has been constantly used by the Supreme Court to reject the recognition and enforcement of foreign judgments. However, more recent decisions have made less use of this condition, rejecting it when it becomes evident that the defendant is making use of it for purely tactical purposes or to obtain some sort of profit.

(c) What about foreign arbitration awards?

Concerning foreign arbitral awards, it is to be stated that pursuant to Article 56, 1, of the 1988 Arbitration Act, they can be enforced on the basis of treaties or conventions, such as the 1958 New York Convention on the Recognition and Enforcement of Foreign Awards and the 1961 Geneva European Convention on International Commercial Arbitration, both of which conventions have been adopted by Spain.

(d) Will proceeds of a judgment be freely exportable?

Yes, a foreigner or a foreign company can receive abroad the proceeds of a judgment rendered in Spain, no restriction being presently in force in this regard.

CHAPTER 22

SWEDEN

Magnus Sjödin & Kristina Einarsson
Setterwalls, Arsenalsgatan 6, 111 47 Stockholm, Sweden

1. JURISDICTION

(a) Domicile

In domestic cases and in civil cases where the Lugano Convention does not apply, the general forum, i.e. the forum that is applicable in most cases, is the court for the defendant's domicile. However, there are supplementing rules allowing the plaintiff to choose a forum in certain cases.

(b) Place of business/residence/office

A person engaged in farming, mining, manufacturing, handicraft, commerce or similar business with a permanent establishment may for instance be sued in a dispute arising directly out of the activity carried on at the establishment at the place where the establishment is located.

(c) Assets located within the jurisdiction

In disputes concerning debt obligations, anyone without a known residence within the Swedish realm may be sued in the place where property belonging to him is located.

(d) Act complained of within the jurisdiction

Furthermore, anyone without known domicile within the Swedish realm, who has entered into a contract or otherwise has incurred a debt in the realm, may be sued in a dispute concerning the contract or debt at the place where the contract was formed or the debt incurred. Also an action for tort damages may be instituted at the court for the place where the tortious act occurred or had its impact.

(e) Clause attributing jurisdiction

Merely the fact that the contract is to be governed by Swedish law will not, however, give Swedish jurisdiction.

(f) Conventions

The Lugano Convention on Jurisdiction and Enforcement of Judgments in Civil and Commercial Matters (the Lugano Convention) has been ratified by Sweden and incorporated into Swedish law in accordance with the Act on account of Sweden's Accession to the Lugano Convention. It came into effect on 1 January 1993. The Lugano Convention stipulates that Contracting States' national courts have jurisdiction in cases of a civil and commercial nature involving more than one Contracting State in matters of a civil and commercial nature.

(g) Other

The parties may agree upon jurisdiction since the Swedish court will comply with a written contract stipulating that a dispute already in existence, or one that may arise in the future based upon a legal relationship detailed in the contract, may be instituted in a certain court or that a certain court exclusively shall be competent.

(h) Counterclaim/third-party proceedings

Counterclaims and third-party proceedings shall be instituted in the court at which the main action is pending.

2. MARITIME CLAIMS

(a) Is there special jurisdiction for maritime claims based on arrest of a vessel in the jurisdiction?

An arrest of a foreign vessel in Sweden automatically gives the relevant Swedish court competence to try the dispute giving rise to the arrest, unless the dispute arises out of a contract providing for arbitration or for foreign jurisdiction.

(b) Specific

Moreover, for two types of maritime claims there are mandatory rules regarding jurisdiction, although the proceedings may also be brought before the maritime court within whose geographical jurisdiction the vessel is located. The first is an action for damages on account of a contract or carriage of general cargo that shall be brought before a maritime court competent for the place where the defendant has its principal office or habitual residence; where the contract of carriage was made, provided the defendant there has a place of business, branch or agency through which the contract was made; where the agreed port of loading or the agreed or actual port of discharge is situated, or which is designated for this purpose in the contract of carriage.

The second is an action for damages on account of a contract of carriage of passengers or luggage that shall be brought before the maritime court competent for the place where the defendant has his habitual residence or his principal office; the maritime court competent for the contractual place of departure or destination; a court in the state where the plaintiff has his domicile or other permanent residence, provided the defendant has a place of business in that state and is subject to its jurisdiction; or a court in the state where the contract of carriage was made, provided the defendant has a place of business in that state and is subject to its jurisdiction.

All the rules on jurisdiction of the Maritime Code mentioned above are applicable subject to the Act on account of Sweden's Accession to the Lugano Convention. Nevertheless, even if the Lugano Convention is applicable an action may be brought at the maritime court competent for the place where the vessel is present.

(c) What are the grounds for arrest?

The International Convention relating to the arrest of seagoing ships ("the Arrest Convention") signed in Brussels on 10 May 1952 has been ratified by Sweden and incorporated into the Swedish Maritime Code with effect from 1 October 1994. The provisions in the Swedish Maritime Code in respect of arrest of vessels are, accordingly, based on the Arrest Convention, and they apply to vessels entered in the Swedish ship register or a corresponding foreign ship register. However, they do not apply to Swedish or non-registered vessels if the applicant has his residence or principal place of business in Sweden ("national claims"). Should the vessel be Swedish or non-registered and the applicant is Swedish, the general rules in the Code of Judicial Procedure will then be applicable. In the event the latter rules contain a different regulation in comparison to the rules of the Maritime Code, such difference will be specifically noted below.

Vessels may be arrested only for maritime claims, and the Maritime Code contains a complete enumeration of claims, which are to be regarded as maritime claims. This enumeration corresponds to Article 1 in the Arrest Convention. In respect of national claims vessels may be arrested for any type of pecuniary claim. The provisions do not apply to arrest for claims concerning taxes and charges levied by the State or a municipality.

In order to have an order for an arrest granted by a court, the claimant must show probable grounds for possession of a claim, which is or may be presumed to be subject to legal proceedings or adjudication in other similar form. Furthermore, if the claim is supported by a foreign judgment that is enforceable in Sweden by decision of a Swedish court, the claimant may be granted an order for an arrest until the court has rendered its final decision on enforceability.

The criteria for an arrest are the same as for other provisional measures that are discussed under section 5 below.

(d) Need the arrested vessel be connected with the claim or can other vessels in the same legal (or beneficial) ownership also be arrested?

Arrest may be made on the vessel to which the maritime claim relates. Arrest may also in most cases be made on another ship belonging to the person or legal entity that, at the time when the maritime claim arose, was owner of the vessel to which the maritime claim refers. If any other person than the owner of the vessel is liable for a maritime claim, arrest may instead be made either on the vessel to which the claim refers or on any other vessel belonging to the debtor.

(e) What procedural differences apply to special maritime jurisdiction?

The court of first instance in any civil litigation concerning any matter covered by the Swedish Maritime Code is the Maritime Court (being a division of an ordinary district court). There are at present seven maritime courts in Sweden located in different parts of the country. The general competence of a maritime court to try a case is determined by the provisions stated above in relation to the jurisdictional competence in general (see 1 above). However, an action before a maritime court may in addition to these rules always be brought before the maritime court within whose geographical jurisdiction the vessel is located, unless the parties are bound by a jurisdiction agreement. Furthermore, if security for a claim has been lodged with an enforcement authority (Sw. *Kronofogdemyndighet*) for release of a vessel from arrest or any other security measure, an action may also be brought at the maritime court competent for the place where the security is lodged.

There are no procedural differences to civil cases tried in a maritime court compared with civil cases tried in the ordinary courts. However, these are special procedural rules for Average matters.

(f) What jurisdictional rules are there as to limitation of liability?

There are specific provisions in the Maritime Code that entitle the operator of a vessel to limit his liability. The rules in the Swedish Maritime Code on limitation of liability are based on the provisions of the Convention on Liability for Maritime Claims, 1976.

3. SERVICE OF PROCEEDINGS

(a) What rules apply to service of proceedings outside the jurisdiction?

The defendant must be served the summons and other documents of legal proceedings. The principal obligation of serving the proceedings rests with the court. When the defendant is not resident in Sweden the proceedings are served by sending the relevant documents by post with a requirement that the defendant sign a receipt that is then returned to the court. If the defendant refuses to sign for the documents the court may ask for the assistance of the Swedish Ministry of Foreign Affairs to have the summons served. However, in civil cases where the defendant does not reside in Sweden, the plaintiff usually applies to the court to be given the opportunity to undertake the service of proceedings upon the defendant. Such an application by the plaintiff will be granted in most cases, and it implies that the court will stipulate a certain time limit within which the plaintiff must present sufficient documentation to the court indicating that the documents have been duly served.

Furthermore, Sweden has ratified the Hague Convention of 1965 and thus service of documents abroad in Member States may also be undertaken in accordance with the provisions of that convention.

If a foreign party to the proceeding has not named a legal counsel in Sweden or another European Community country, the court may order him to name such a counsel. If he does not do this, all following documents may be served upon him by ordinary post at his latest known address.

4. COSTS

(a) Court fees

The application fee for summons or arrest at the court is SEK 450, which will be recoverable in the event that the court's final judgment is in favour of the applicant.

(b) Lawyers' fees

Swedish lawyers usually invoice their clients for the actual time spent on the matter in question.

(c) Recovery of costs from unsuccessful party

Court costs are normally borne by the party that loses the contested case.

(d) Security for costs

A foreign plaintiff, who is not a resident of a European Community country, may be requested by the court to put up a security to cover the defendant's possible court costs if the plaintiff should be unsuccessful.

5. INTERIM ARREST

(a) Are interim arrest/freezing of assets/other provisional measures permitted to provide security for domestic proceedings and/or proceedings in another jurisdiction?

It is possible to obtain interim measures to provide security for legal proceedings, both domestic and international, or adjudication in other similar form. Such provisional measures may be arrest, freezing of assets or attachment of property.

(b) What criteria apply to this?

In order to obtain a provisional measure the applicant must show probable grounds for possession of a claim, which is or may be presumed to be subject to legal proceeding or adjudication in other similar form. Accordingly, it is not necessary to produce full proof of the claim. Swedish courts require only particulars of an incident or transaction which give rise to a claim against the opposing party. At this stage it is usually not necessary to have any documents notarised or otherwise authenticated. If the court finds that it can reasonably be expected that the opposing party by absconding, removal of property or by other means, will evade payment of the debt, it may order provisional attachment of so much of the adversary's property as the claim may be assumed to be covered in the event of distraint. Thus, in order to obtain a provisional measure it must be reasonably expected that the opposing party will take measures to evade payment. Consequently, it is not sufficient grounds for an arrest if the opposing party is merely insolvent and may be presumed unable to fulfil his obligations.

(c) Is there a limit on jurisdictions whose proceedings are recognised for this purpose?

In order to obtain a provisional measure the claim must ultimately be adjudicated in Sweden, a foreign jurisdiction or by arbitration. If the claim arises out of a contract referring to a foreign court whose decision can not be enforced in Sweden an order for a provisional measure will not be granted. When an interim measure has been granted, if an action has not already been brought, the claimant shall, within one month of the order, bring an action before a court, of, if the claim is to be entertained in another form, in accordance with the provisions pertaining thereto.

(d) Is there a requirement for counter-security?

An interim measure may only be granted if the claimant deposits with the court security to recompense the opposing party for the loss he may suffer due to the interim action. The court, in its discretion, will decide on the nature of the guarantee to be provided and also on the amount. A bank guarantee or a guarantee of equal security value will normally be accepted.

(e) Can an application be made ex parte?

A request for an interim measure may not according to the principal rule be granted unless an opportunity to respond has been given to the opposing party. When time is of the essence, however, the court may act immediately, by issuing an order which remains effective until it directs otherwise.

(f) How quickly can an order be made?

An immediate interim measure can usually be granted within a few days. However, it is almost impossible to achieve an arrest or attachment out of office hours.

(g) Will the order bind third parties?

The interim measure will not give priority to payment out of the proceeds from the sale of the property over other creditors unless another claimant, with a claim supported by a judgment, has received an attachment in the same property after the interim measure. The claimants will then have equal right and will have priority over claimants who have filed their claim at a later date.

(h) What are the consequences of breach of an order?

The breach of an order of security measures such as arrest or freezing of assets constitutes a criminal offence that will render a possible sentence up to one year's imprisonment.

(i) Is there a limit to types of assets?

The assets that may be subject to provisional measures may be any kind of property that will be possible to sell, account balances or ordinary third party claims of the debtor.

(j) What if third parties are affected?

The mere fact that third parties are affected by the attachment of a party's property does not affect the right to have an order from the court. However, the amount of security requested may be higher if the opposing party risks third party liability.

(k) What other provisional measures may be ordered?

In these matters no other provisional measures, such as appointment of surveyor or receiver, may be ordered by a court on the application of a claimant.

6. RECOGNITION OF JUDGMENTS/AWARDS

(a) What treaties/conventions apply (i) to enable judgments to be enforced abroad and (ii) to enable enforcement of foreign judgments domestically?

(i) Judgments to be enforced abroad

Whether a Swedish judgment will be recognised and/or enforceable in a foreign jurisdiction will depend on the applicable rules in that jurisdiction. Accordingly, no general rules in this respect can be outlined, and the position of Swedish judgments must be investigated in every specific case. However, it can be assumed that if the addressee state has ratified a convention (see further under (ii) below) which has been ratified by Sweden as well, a Swedish judgment will have the same status in that state as a judgment originating from that state would have in Sweden.

(ii) Enforcement of foreign judgments domestically

In addition to the Lugano Convention Sweden has ratified, *inter alia*, the following treaties/conventions which contain provisions regarding the enforcement of judgments:

the Paris Convention of 29 July 1960 on Nuclear Liability with amendments of 28 January 1964 and 16 November 1982;
Protocol of 31 January 1963 to Amend the Paris Convention on Nuclear Liability;
the International Convention of 1969 on Civil Liability for Oil Pollution Damage;
the International Convention of 1971 on the Establishment of an International Fund for Compensation for Oil Pollution Damage;

Protocols of 1992 to Amend the International Convention on Civil Liability for Oil Pollution Damage and the International Convention on the Establishment of an International Fund for Compensation for Oil Pollution Damage;
Convention of 1980 on International Railway Traffic (COTIF); and
the Hague Convention of 25 October 1980 on international access to justice.

(b) What procedure is followed to enforce a foreign judgment (i) governed by a treaty/convention and (ii) not governed by a treaty/convention?

(i) Governed by a treaty/convention

A foreign judgment, which is recognised by statute (see further in subsection (b) (ii) below), gains generally *res judicata* effect in Sweden without the undertaking of any particular formalities. However, in the event a party seeks enforcement of the foreign judgment, the initiating of a separate enforcement proceeding (*exequatur*) in the Svea Court of Appeal (Sw. *Svea hovrätt*) in Stockholm is normally required. The court shall give the other party opportunity to file a statement in respect of the application for enforcement before rendering its decision. The original or a certified copy of the foreign judgment shall be attached to the application, accompanied with a declaration from the relevant authority in the state where the judgment was rendered stating that the judgment refers to compensation in accordance with the convention in question, that the judgment has gained legal force and that the judgment is enforceable in the state of origin. However, some foreign judgments rendered in another Nordic country are directly enforceable upon application to the Swedish Enforcement Authority (Sw. *Kronofogdemyndighet*).

The Lugano Convention: in respect of judgments rendered in another Contracting State of the Lugano Convention such judgments will generally be recognised in Sweden from the moment it was rendered, provided none of the rules contained in Articles 27 and 28 concerning the non-recognition of judgments are applicable. However, judgments given *ex parte* will not be recognised. In contrast to recognition, the enforcement of judgments under the Lugano Convention requires a formal decision from a competent authority, which in Sweden is the Svea Court of Appeal. The Svea Court of Appeal shall give its decision without delay, and an application for enforcement is an *ex parte* procedure. The party against whom enforcement is sought, or the applicant if his application is denied, may appeal against the decision for enforcement to the Svea Court of Appeal, i.e. the same court which gave the decision. The judgment then rendered may be contested by an appeal to the Swedish Supreme Court.

(ii) Not governed by a treaty/convention

Sweden does not have any uniform regulation of the question of recognition and enforcement of foreign judgments. The prospects of recognition and enforcement vary greatly, depending on the subject matter of the judgment and in which country the judgment was rendered. With few exceptions, foreign judgments will neither be recognised nor enforced in the absence of statutory support (generally based on a treaty/convention) therefor. However, in the event that a foreign judgment is not recognised or enforced as such, it may still be used by the parties as proof of certain facts or of the contents of foreign law in the Swedish proceedings.

Statutory support for recognition and/or enforcement has been instituted in respect of the conventions referred to in subsection (a)(ii) above.

(c) What about arbitration awards?

Sweden has ratified both the Geneva Convention of 1927 and the New York Convention of 1958 on the Execution of Foreign Arbitral Awards. The provisions have been laid down in the Act on Foreign Arbitration Agreements and Awards (1929:147). Foreign arbitral awards may be enforced in Sweden to the full extent. It should be noted that when Sweden ratified the New York Convention Sweden did not make the reservations open to the Contracting States. Thus, recognition is not limited to awards rendered in the territories of Contracting States nor to awards in disputes of a commercial character.

A foreign arbitral award shall be recognised in Sweden, unless the party against whom the award is invoked establishes, *inter alia*, any of the following:

- (i) invalidity of arbitration agreement;
- (ii) the party was not given proper notice of the arbitration proceedings;
- (iii) terms of submission in the arbitration agreement were exceeded;
- (iv) improper composition of the tribunal or improper arbitral procedure; or
- (v) the award is not binding on the parties.

Moreover, a foreign arbitration award will not be considered as valid in Sweden if the award includes a decision of any question which under Swedish law is not arbitrable or the implementation of the award would be patently incompatible with the basic principles of Swedish law.

Application for recognition and enforcement shall be submitted to the Svea Court of Appeal. The original document or a certified copy of the award and a certified translation into the Swedish language shall be attached to the application. The court will notify the party against whom enforcement is sought, who then is given the opportunity to raise any objection he may have. If necessary, the court may request further exchanges of written statements and also arrange a hearing. The decision of the Svea Court of Appeal may be appealed to the Supreme Court.

If the Svea Court of Appeal grants an application for enforcement of a foreign judgment/arbitral award as described in this section the prevailing party has to apply for execution to the enforcement authority (Sw. *Kronofogdemyndighet*) in the area where the defendant is domiciled. The execution may take place even if the decision of the Svea Court of Appeal has been appealed to the Supreme Court. However, until the decision to grant enforcement has gained legal force, the enforcement authority will only take provisional security measures in order to secure the future sale or transfer of the property. If the Supreme Court reverses the decision the execution will be revoked and any property transferred by virtue thereof shall be returned.

(d) Will proceeds of a judgment be freely exportable?

Proceeds of a judgment/arbitral award are generally freely exportable from Sweden.

CHAPTER 23

SWITZERLAND

Dr Christian Benz
Benz & Partners law firm, P.O. Box 1910, CH–8032 Zürich, Switzerland

1. JURISDICTION

Generalities

The issue of jurisdiction in international cases is governed either by the Convention on Jurisdiction and the Enforcement of Judgments in Civil and Commercial Matters 1988 (Lugano Convention) or by the Swiss Federal Law on Private International Law of 1987 (hereafter PIL). For Switzerland the Lugano Convention (hereafter LC) entered into force on 1 January 1992. In Switzerland international conventions are applicable without transformation into domestic federal law; stipulations of such conventions can be invoked directly before all courts and take precedence over domestic federal law including the PIL.

The LC deals with the jurisdiction of the courts of the Contracting States in "international matters" which are "civil and commercial".

As a rule the LC shall always be applicable in place of the PIL provided the defendant is domiciled in a Contracting State. Consequently, in all cases where the defendant is domiciled in a Contracting State the LC must be applied.

The PIL provides the following.

(a)(i) Domicile of defendant

The general principle stipulated by the PIL is that in international cases the Swiss courts have jurisdiction provided the defendant is domiciled in Switzerland (Art. 2 PIL). However, this general jurisdiction is only subsidiary. The jurisdictions provided by the special part of the PIL generally apply as additional possibilities.

Such additional jurisdictions depend on the subject of the dispute. The most important cases are the following.

(a)(ii) Domicile of plaintiff

Jurisdiction at the domicile of the claimant (Art. 59 PIL: divorce or separation).

(b) Residence/place of business

(i) General

Jurisdiction at the place of business establishment (Art. 112 II PIL: claims arising out of the activities of a business establishment).

(ii) Residence of defendant

Jurisdiction at the ordinary residence of the defendant (e.g. Arts. 33, 98, 112 I PIL: civil status, rights *in rem* to movables, contractual claims).

(c) Assets located within the jurisdiction

Jurisdiction at the situs (Arts. 97, 98 II PIL: rights *in rem* to real property and movables).

(d) Act complained of within the jurisdiction

Jurisdiction at the place where the act was committed or had its effects (Art. 129 II PIL: tort).

(e) Contract governed by local law

See (g) below.

(f) Conventions

Where appropriate the subsequent text refers to the subparagraphs of the main heading (Jurisdiction).

The provisions on jurisdiction of Swiss courts according to the LC differ partly from those of the PIL.

The general provision is identical to that of the PIL: subject of the provisions of the LC persons domiciled in a Contracting State shall, whatever their nationality, be sued in the courts of that state (1(a), Art. 2 LC).

A person domiciled in a Contracting State may be sued in another Contracting State in matters for which the LC provides a particular jurisdiction.

The LC provides such particular jurisdiction in matters relating to a contract (1(h), Art. 5 para 1 LC), in matters relating to tort (1(d), Art. 5 para 3 LC), regarding disputes arising out of the operations of a branch, agency or other establishment (1(b), Art. 5 para 5 LC) or for counterclaims arising from the same contract or facts on which the original claim was based (1(i), Art. 3 para 3 LC).

For certain proceedings an exclusive jurisdiction is provided (1(c), Art. 16 LC). The meaning of exclusive is that prorogation is not possible.

Instances of such exclusive jurisdiction are for instance in proceedings having as their object rights *in rem* in immovable property in the courts of the

Contracting State in which the property is situated (1(c), Art. 16 para 1 LC) or in proceedings concerned with the enforcement of judgments in the courts of the Contracting State in which the judgment has been or is to be enforced (Art. 16 para 5 LC).

An additional exclusive jurisdiction may be established by prorogation or by entering an appearance without reservation respectively joining issue (Arts. 17 and 18 LC). In such instance exclusive jurisdiction means that no other jurisdiction than that established as per Articles 17 and 18 LC is available. The formal requirements of the prorogation clause are less stringent that those set by the PIL. An agreement conferring jurisdiction may be either in writing or evidenced in writing; it may also be in a form which accords with practices which the parties have established between themselves; in addition such agreement may also be in a form which accords with a usage of which the parties are or ought to have been aware and which in such trade or commerce is widely known to and regularly observed by the parties (Art. 17 para 1 subpara a, b and c).

The LC provides in its Article 7 a particular jurisdiction in matters relating to insurance. Certain restrictions are made with respect to the admissibility of prorogation clauses.

(g) Clause attributing jurisdiction

As to pecuniary claims, the parties are free to choose a Swiss forum (Art. 5 PIL). The prorogation clause must be in writing or by any other means of communication evidencing the terms of the agreement by text. The court agreed upon is bound to accept its own jurisdiction, provided one of the parties has his ordinary residence or place of business in the canton in which the court is situated, or provided Swiss law is applicable to the case by virtue of the stipulations on conflict of law of the PIL, or by virtue of a choice of Swiss law by the parties.

In pecuniary disputes, moreover, an appearance without reservation does establish the jurisdiction of the Swiss court seized, provided this court would also have to accept jurisdiction based on agreement (Art. 6 PIL). As to prorogation according to LC, see above, paragraph 1 in fine.

(h) Other

Jurisdiction at the place of performance (Art. 113 PIL: contracts).

The general part of the PIL provides in addition two subsidiary fora on condition that the PIL does not provide jurisdiction in Switzerland:

- According to Article 3 PIL the Swiss at the place having a sufficient connection with the factual situation of the case shall have jurisdiction provided proceedings abroad are not possible or would be unreasonable.

— According to Article 4 PIL an action in validation of an attachment may be brought at the place in Switzerland where the attachment has been obtained.

(i) Counterclaim

The court before which the main action is pending will also adjudge any counterclaim, provided a factual connection exists between the main action and the counterclaim (Art. 8 PIL).

2. MARITIME CLAIMS

Generalities

The basic source of law is the Federal Law on Maritime Navigation under the Swiss Flag of 1953 (hereafter Swiss Shipping Act, SSA) and its executive regulations of 1956. Switzerland has ratified the Visby Protocol of 1968 as well as the SDR Protocol of 1979. At the occasion of the last revision of the Swiss Shipping Act both protocols have been transformed into domestic federal law. Consequently, there is basically one source of Swiss maritime law, namely the SSA.

Claims against a Swiss owner of a vessel flying the Swiss flag may be brought before the competent Swiss court at his Swiss domicile (Art. 14 para 1 SSA, Art. 2 PIL).

Particular jurisdictions in maritime matters are provided in Article 14 SSA. Regardless of the domicile of the defendant all actions *in rem* relating to vessels registered in the Swiss Federal Shipping Registry in Basel, Switzerland, may be brought before the competent court in Basel, Switzerland (Art. 14 para 1 SSA).

All actions for tort committed on board a Swiss vessel as well as "all other civil actions based on the Swiss Shipping Act" may be brought before the competent court in Basel, Switzerland, provided, however, no other Swiss court can be seized (Art. 14 para 2 SSA). Article 14 para 2 SSA is of particular interest. According to prevailing doctrine and two decisions of the Swiss Federal Court (1968, 1989) the SSA (although primarily conceived for seagoing vessels flying the Swiss flag) shall be applicable to carriages performed by vessels flying a foreign flag; if based on the rules of conflict of law Swiss law shall be applicable. It is therefore debatable what the scope of "all other civil actions based on the SSA" may be. Case law on the subject is not available.

(a) Is there special jurisdiction for maritime claims based on arrest of a vessel in the jurisdiction?

Switzerland has ratified the International Convention for the Unification of Certain Rules relating to the Arrest of Seagoing Ships of 10 May 1952.

It is rather unlikely that Swiss courts shall ever be involved in proceedings aimed at arresting a foreign seagoing vessel or for a decision on the merits. Should that ever be the case federal law and the law of the respective canton applicable to such proceedings would be restricted by the stipulations of the Convention. In principle the Swiss court at the Swiss domicile of a Swiss carrier can be seized by the claimant (Art. 14 para 1 SSA, Art. 2 PIL) to decide on the merits as a consequence of an arrest made in any seaport. However, assets of a defendant owner of a foreign seagoing vessel which are located in Switzerland may be arrested according to the general rules as set out below (see para 5).

(b) Specific

Switzerland has also ratified the International Convention on Certain Rules relating to Civil Jurisdiction in Matters of Collision of 10 May 1952. Theoretically, in application of that Convention a Swiss court, being the court where the defendant has his habitual residence or a place of business, could be seized. (Art. 1 para a of the Collision Convention 1952).

Actions in connection with the approval of an average adjustment may be brought before the competent court at Basel city (Art. 14 para 3 SSA).

(c) What are the grounds for arrest?

See para (a) above.

(d) Need the arrested vessel be connected with the claim or can other vessels in the same legal (or beneficial) ownership also be arrested?

See Arrest Convention Article 3 paragraph 1.

Under national law the arrested vessel does not need to be connected with the claim; other vessels or assets in the same ownership can be arrested.

(e) What procedural differences apply to special maritime jurisdiction?

The Swiss Shipping Act, respectively its Executive Regulation, does provide certain procedural differences applying to special maritime jurisdiction as opposed to normal jurisdiction (see Executive Regulation 1953, Articles 45–72). They mainly relate to cases of limitation of liability and general average. The regulation refers to the Debt Enforcement and Bankruptcy Law for all cases where the SSA and its Executive Regulation is silent. Where cases are brought before the courts of Basel in application of Article 14 SSA the Code of

Civil Procedure of the canton of Basel and other pertinent procedural rules of that canton will subsidiarily apply (see also below paragraph (f)).

(f) What jurisdictional rules are there as to limitation of liability?

Switzerland has ratified the Convention on Limitation of Liability for Maritime Claims of 19 November 1976 which has been incorporated into national law by reference in Article 49 SSA. As to damages due to oil pollution SSA Article 49 refers to the International Convention on Civil Liability for Oil Pollution Damage of 25 November 1969 and the respective Protocol of 19 November 1976.

Actions in connection with the limitation of the liability of owners of seagoing vessels may be brought before the competent court at Basel, Switzerland, as well (Art. 14 para 3 SSA).

According to the Executive Regulation of the SSA, Article 71, the legislation of the State of Basel city must designate the authority before which matters relating to limitation of liability can be brought and must establish the necessary procedure. Local law on the organisation of the judiciary provides jurisdiction to the Civil Court of Basel city composed of three professional judges.

The SSA further contains a stipulation on the burden of proof relating to conduct barring limitation of the liability of the owner, charterer, manager and operator. The party pleading such conduct bears the respective burden of proof (Art. 49 para 3 SSA). See also paragraph (e) above.

3. SERVICE OF PROCEEDINGS

(a) The basic source of law relating to international legal assistance in matters of civil procedure is the Hague Convention on the Law of Civil Procedure of 1 March 1954; it has been in force in Switzerland since 5 July 1957. The Convention basically governs international service of proceedings and legal assistance relating to the taking of evidence amongst the Contracting States.

The Hague Convention of 1954 is complemented by various bilateral treaties providing direct communication and contact amongst the judiciary of the respective Contracting States.

Outside the scope of the Hague Convention Article 11 PIL is applicable. The rule is that acts of legal assistance will be performed in Switzerland according to the law of the canton in which they are made.

(b) For the service of proceedings and legal assistance relating to the taking of evidence the Hague Convention provides the intervention of the consular representations of the Contracting States.

The Contracting States however are at liberty, by means of bilateral treaties, to provide the direct communication of their mutual indiciary bodies (Art. 1 para 4 Hague Convention). A few such bilateral treaties between Switzerland and certain European states do exist.

(c) Outside the scope of the Hague Convention and in the absence of a bilateral treaty, in principle diplomatic channels must be used. In Switzerland respective incoming and outgoing requests must be channelled through the Federal Office for Police Matters in Bern.

(d) According to Article 11 II paragraph 3 of the Hague Convention international legal assistance may be denied if the request violates rights of sovereignty or jeopardises the security of the requested state. The same applies by analogy to international legal assistance outside the scope of multi- and/or bilateral treaties based on the procedural law of the cantons. According to the procedural law of the canton of Zurich, for instance, international legal assistance may be denied in cases of lack of reciprocity.

(e) Swiss federal law reserves the right to take evidence for the competent Swiss courts, respectively the competent Swiss authorities. Generally an interrogatory mission must be made by the foreign court through the diplomatic channels to the competent Swiss court. Individuals, for instance attorneys, carrying out such taking of evidence in Switzerland without permission of the competent Swiss authorities are acting in violation of the Swiss federal criminal law (Art. 271 para 1 Federal Criminal Code).

4. COSTS

(a) Court fees

In all cantons of the federation local legal tariffs for court fees exist. The Federal Tribunal in Lausanne applies its own legal tariffs.

(b) Lawyers' fees (standard scale or by agreement or contingency fees)

In practically all cantons of the federation tariffs for lawyers' fees exist. As a rule (but with some exceptions) separate tariffs for litigation and legal counselling exist. Tariffs for litigation are regularly based on cantonal law, whereas scales for legal counselling are established by the bar of the respective canton. Fee agreements relating to legal counselling are permitted. In certain cantons fee agreements between client and attorney deviating from the legal cantonal litigation tariff are permitted. The courts, however, apply the official tariffs regardless of the existence of such fee agreement.

Contingency fees are not allowed in Switzerland.

Official litigation tariffs of a canton and individual fee arrangements between client and attorney may lead to totally different amounts assessed or calculated for the same kind of services. That quite often and particularly depending on the value in litigation means that the victorious party may not get full compensation for its lawyers' fees.

(c) Recovery of costs from unsuccessful party

As a general rule the Swiss courts in the final award automatically assess the lawyers' fees as well as the court fees payable by either party based on a legal tariff.

The court will further automatically decide what proportion the (wholly or partly) losing party must reimburse to the (wholly or partly) winning party. The rule is that a party wholly losing the case must fully reimburse the wholly winning party for his lawyers' fees and must in addition bear all court fees. Free legal aid is provided by both the Codes of Civil Procedure of the cantons and the Federal Constitution (Article 4 section 1 of the Swiss Federal Constitution). Free legal aid is available in principle for parties residing abroad but not for legal entities regardless of their domicile. The party requesting free legal aid has the burden of proof of the respective need and the court will preliminarily examine the merits of the case before granting a request for free legal aid.

(d) Security for costs

Court fees and opponents' attorneys' fees normally must be guaranteed and/or advanced to the court by plaintiffs not residing in Switzerland nor in a Contracting State of the Hague Convention 1954; the same applies as a general rule to insolvent plaintiffs. The same system basically is applied to parties bringing an appeal. Outside the scope of multi- and/or bilateral treaties governing court fees, bonds etc., the law of civil procedure of the respective canton will apply. Any one of the 26 Swiss cantons has its own code of civil procedure and its own organisation of the judiciary. There is no uniform federal law of civil procedure governing the procedure of the judiciary of the various cantons. To check the applicable procedural law of the respective canton is essential.

5. INTERIM ARREST

(a) Are interim arrest/freezing of assests/other provisional measures permitted to provide security for domestic proceedings and/or proceedings in another jurisdiction?

Interim arrest or freezing of assets is permitted to provide security for domestic proceedings as well as for proceedings in another jurisdiction as far as claims for money are concerned.

For claims other than claims for money the law provides a number of provisional conservatory measures.

The Codes of Civil Procedure or other procedural laws of some cantons provide the possibility to obtain the taking of evidence by a court prior to commencing litigation.

Where a Swiss court has international jurisdiction for the main issue (be it according to the PIL or the LC) it is also competent to grant temporary measures.

As a general rule interim arrest as well as provisional temporary measures are permitted regardless of whether or not the Swiss courts have jurisdiction in the main issue of not (Art. 10 PIL, Art. 24 LC).

(b) What criteria apply to this?

The court at the place where the assets to be arrested are located has jurisdiction to decide on the request (Swiss Federal Law on Debt Enforcement and Bankruptcy, DEBL, Art. 272). That applies to cases within the scope of the LC as well. Article 24 LC is applicable to arrests.

The requirements for the granting of an arrest are as follows (Art. 272 DEBL):

- The claim for which security is sought must be a claim for money or for security.
- The assets to be arrested must be realisable, meaning convertible into money. The law lists those assets which can neither be seized nor arrested (Arts. 92–94 DEBL).
- The law lists the grounds for distraint. The list is final and exhaustive. The most important and most frequently used ground for distraint is that a plaintiff is seeking to freeze assets located in Switzerland belonging to a debtor residing outside Switzerland. Requirements are amongst others that the debtor is not domiciled in Switzerland and that the claim has a sufficient connection to Switzerland.

All legal requirements of motion for distraint must be sufficiently established but not literally proven.

In order to maintain the effect of a distraint order (arrest) granted by the court the plaintiff must within a relatively short time limit (10 days from receipt of the so-called arrest record) initiate ordinary legal proceedings before the competent court. Where the plaintiff fails to do so in time the interim arrest will be automatically lifted. In international cases the court granting the interim arrest order has jurisdiction only for the ordinary proceedings by which the temporary measure is maintained provided the LC is not applicable (Art. 4 PIL, Art. 3 LC, see paragraph 1 above).

Temporary measures for claims other than for money are decided upon by the courts in summary proceedings.

In cases where the Swiss courts have no jurisdiction for the main issue the question what local Swiss court shall have jurisdiction for temporary measures is governed by Swiss federal and cantonal law and can only be decided on a case by case basis. Neither Article 24 of the LC nor the PIL (Art. 10) regulate the local jurisdiction within Switzerland.

There are basically three categories of temporary measures (as opposed to distraint order or arrest):

— Conservatory, regulatory and executorial measures depending on the purpose to be achieved by such temporary measures.

Conditions under which such temporary measures will be granted by the courts are stipulated in the respective federal laws. Besides, particular requirements and the procedure are regulated by the legislation of the respective canton.

As a rule the following requirements must be met:

— Imminent not easily repairable prejudice of the applicant;
— Probability that the main issue is well founded.

(c) Is there a limit on jurisdictions whose proceedings are recognised for this purpose?

No such limit exists. However, arrest and/or provisional measures can be taken in Switzerland even prior to initiating the proceedings on the merits.

(d) Is there a requirement for counter-security?

In cases of arrest as well as of temporary measures of another nature the debtor may put up a sufficient security or bond to prevent lifting the arrest or the temporary measure. As to arrests such possibility is foreseen in Article 277 DEBL. As to temporary measures of another kind the procedural law of the respective canton is applicable.

In arrest cases the judge may order that the applicant must give security for possible financial damages incurred by the debtor as a consequence of an unjustified arrest (Art. 273 DEBL).

The same applies for temporary measures. The court is at liberty to grant such measures subject to a sufficient security to be put up by the applicant for imminent damages caused by such measure. The procedural law of most cantons provides for such securities. In certain areas there are respective stipulations of federal law.

(e) Can an application be made ex parte?

The courts decide on requests for an interim arrest in a summary *ex parte* proceeding.

In cases of emergency provisional measures may be granted in *ex parte* proceedings; subsequently the court will summon both parties to appear and then decide whether or not to confirm the temporary measure.

(f) How quickly can the order be made?

An application for an arrest will normally be decided upon the courts within a week from the date of application. Temporary measures decided upon in *ex parte* proceedings can be obtained within one business day. In cases of temporary measures where both parties must be heard the courts may take several months before a decision is handed down. The time needed depends on the complexity of the claim and the procedural law applicable.

(g) Will the order bind third parties?

As a rule temporary measures can have the effect of binding third parties. According to Swiss law an arrest, for instance, does bind also the party holding the goods arrested.

(h) What are the consequences of breach of an order?

The consequences of a breach of distraint orders and orders on temporary measures of all kinds are governed by Article 292 of the Swiss Federal Criminal Code; the punishment may be a fine or even imprisonment.

(i) Is there a limit to types of asset, e.g. physical asset/account balances?

See paragraph (b) above.

(j) What if third parties are affected?

Any person whose rights are affected by a freezing order (arrest) may file an objection with the judge who made the order within 10 days of learning of it (Art. 278 para 1 DEBL). Such objection, however, does not prevent the freezing order from deploying its effects. Any such person may also appeal against the execution of the order by the enforcement agency to the supervising body.

The law also provides so-called third party claims (Art. 106 ff DEBL).

If it is claimed that a third party is owner of a seized asset or has a security interest or another right thereto which frustrates the seizure or which should be taken into account during the further proceedings, the enforcement office records the third-party claim in the deed of seizure or, if the latter has already been served on the parties, informs the parties separately.

Third parties may file such claims as long as the proceeds from the realisation of the seized asset have not yet been distributed.

After realisation of the assets the third party may pursue the rights conferred by private law in cases of theft, loss or other form of deprivation of a chattel (Arts. 934 and 935 Civil Code) or in the event of bad faith of the acquiring party (Arts. 936 and 974 para 3 Civil Code) outside the enforcement proceedings.

Both debtor and creditor may file a contestation of the third party claim with the enforcement office if the claim relates, for instance, to:

1. a chattel which is in the sole possession of the debtor;
2. a claim or other rights, if the entitlement of the debtor is more probable than that of the creditor.

If the claim is contested, the enforcement office sets the third party a deadline of 20 days to bring an action for confirmation of his right before the court granting the arrest. If no action is brought, the alleged right is disregarded for the purposes of the current enforcement proceedings.

Debtor and creditor may bring an action against the third party for confirmation that the latter has no right, if the right relates, for instance, to:

1. a chattel which is in the sole or joint possession of the third party;
2. a claim or other right, if the entitlement of the third party appears more probable than that of the debtor.

(k) What other provisional measures may be ordered, e.g. appointment of surveyor or receiver, security?

Many of the 26 cantons have procedural stipulations allowing for conservatory measures in relation to the taking of evidence prior to initiating ordinary proceedings; the court may order the hearing of witnesses, a survey or expertise, etc. in cases of particular need.

6. RECOGNITION OF JUDGMENTS

Generalities

Foreign distraint orders or other court orders on temporary measures are not enforceable nor recognised in Switzerland as they are not final for the purposes of Article 25 lit. b PIL. The PIL, however, makes some particular exceptions relating to the law of decedents' estates.

Within the scope of the LC, however, foreign decisions granting temporary measures are enforceable in Switzerland like awards rendered on the main issue. An exception to that rule are orders granted in *ex parte* proceedings. Consequently, even where the LC is applicable foreign distraint orders may not be enforceable in Switzerland if granted in an *ex parte* proceeding.

(a) What treaties/conventions apply (i) to enable judgments to be enforced abroad and (ii) to enable enforcement of foreign judgments domestically?

Recognition and enforcement of foreign awards in international cases are mainly governed by the LC or the PIL. In addition Switzerland has entered into various bilateral treaties on recognition and enforcement of judgments, such as for example the bilateral treaty between Switzerland and Austria.

(b) What procedure is followed to enforce a foreign judgment (i) governed by a treaty/convention and (ii) not governed by a treaty/convention?

The PIL defines the jurisdiction of foreign courts and authorities. The general provisions state under what circumstances a foreign judgment must be recognised in Switzerland in cases where the defendant is resident in the state in which the judgment was rendered or where the defendant has submitted to the jurisdiction of this state either by a prorogation agreement or tacitly (Art. 26 PIL).

As a rule, recognition does not depend upon reciprocity except for the recognition of foreign bankruptcy decrees. Recognition may be denied if a party establishes that he was not duly notified of the proceeding or that the decision was rendered in violation of fundamental principles of Swiss procedural law, especially in violation of due process of law, or if in a general way, recognition would be manifestly incompatible with material Swiss public policy (Art. 27 PIL).

The LC deals with recognition and enforcement of judgments in its title III. The overall aim is to break down legal barriers and to achieve a system of "free circulation of judgments".

Judgments are generally capable of recognition and enforcement pursuant to the LC provided that they are rendered in a Contracting State.

The most prominent feature of the LC is that the court before which a judgment is sought to be recognised or enforced is not entitled to deny enforcement on the ground that the foreign court lacked jurisdiction (Art. 28 IV LC).

Jurisdiction of the foreign court may only be reviewed in the limited category of cases set out by Art. 28 I and II LC.

The definition of the categories of judgments capable of recognition and enforcement is very broad (Art. 25 LC) and includes also interim measures.

Enforcement of any kind of foreign judgment is made by means of a request to the competent judge and is decided upon in a summary proceeding. That applies to Lugano Convention governed decisions and others. The cantons have transformed the respective provisions of the LC into local procedural law in various and differing ways. The question whether or not the arrest may be used as a means of security enforcement is not yet resolved.

As a principle it is essential to clearly distinguish the three procedures of recognition of the LC, namely the concrete, the abstract and the incidental one. For details relating to non-treaty governed judgments the reader is referred to the 26 different cantonal procedural laws.

(c) What about foreign arbitration awards?

Arbitral awards are not within the scope of the LC (Art. 1 subpara 4 LC).

Arbitral awards rendered outside the scope of the New York Convention are enforced in accordance with the rules of the PIL applicable to awards of foreign state courts (Art. 31 PIL, see above para (b)).

For the recognition and enforcement of foreign arbitral awards the New York Convention of 1958 on Recognition and Enforcement of Foreign Arbitral Awards (ratified by Switzerland) is applicable (Art. 194 PIL). By virtue of Article 194 PIL the New York Convention applies regardless of whether the foreign state where the award was rendered is a contracting party to the New York Convention or not.

(d) Will proceeds of a judgment be freely exportable?

Proceeds of judgments will be freely exportable. Money transfer is not restricted. Export of goods is subject to customs and excise law.

INDEX